The Friedman System

Economic Analysis of Time Series

WILLIAM FRAZER

Westport, Connecticut
London

Library of Congress Cataloging-in-Publication Data

Frazer, William Johnson, 1924–
    The Friedman system : economic analysis of time series / by
William Frazer.
        p.   cm.
    Includes bibliographical references and index.
    ISBN 0–275–95843–4 (alk. paper)
    1. Economics—Statistical methods.   2. Time-series analysis.
3. Neoclassical school of economics.   4. Friedman, Milton, 1912–
I. Title.
HB137.F73   1997
330′.01′5195—DC21   96–37117

British Library Cataloguing in Publication Data is available.

Library of Congress Catalog Card Number: 96–37117
ISBN: 0–275–95843–4

First published in 1997

Praeger Publishers, 88 Post Road West, Westport, CT 06881
An imprint of Greenwood Publishing Group, Inc.

Printed in the United States of America

The paper used in this book complies with the
Permanent Paper Standard issued by the National
Information Standards Organization (Z39.48–1984).

10 9 8 7 6 5 4 3 2 1

Copyright Acknowledgments

The author and publisher gratefully acknowledge permission to use the following previously published materials:

Excerpts from Milton Friedman, *Essays in Positive Economics*, copyright © 1953 by the University of Chicago Press.

Excerpts from William Frazer, *The Legacy of Keynes and Friedman: Economic Analysis, Money, and Ideology*, published in 1994 by Praeger Publishers, an imprint of Greenwood Publishing Group, Inc., Westport, CT.

Excerpts from James Wible, "Institutional Economics, Positive Economics, Pragmatism, and Recent Philosophy of Science: Reply to Liebhafsky and Liebhafsky," *Journal of Economic Issues*, 19, 4 (December 1985), pp. 984–995); and from James Webb, "Is Friedman's Methodological Instrumentalism a Special Case of Dewey's Instrumental Philosophy? A Comment on Wible," *Journal of Economic Issues*, 21, 1 (March 1987), pp. 393–429. Reprinted from the *Journal of Economic Issues* by special permission of the copyright holder, the Association for Evolutionary Economics.

An adaptation of William Frazer, "Review of *Milton Friedman: Economics in Theory and Practice*," *History of Political Economy*, 23, 4 (Winter 1992), pp. 767–769, with the permission of Duke University Press.

Excerpts from Milton Friedman and Anna J. Schwartz, "Alternative Approaches to Analyzing Economic Data," *American Economic Review*, 81 (March 1991), pp. 39–49. Reprinted with permission of the American Economic Association.

To

Will

Galton [Sir Francis] examined the heights of fathers and sons, and found that the sons of tall fathers tended to be shorter than their fathers, i.e., regressed toward the mean; similarly, the fathers of tall sons tended to be shorter than their sons, i.e., regressed toward the mean.

Milton Friedman

Contents

Preface

This book extends the delineation of what I presented as the "Friedman system" in *The Legacy of Keynes and Friedman* (Frazer 1994a). I state it not so much as Friedman's economics (as to what he actually said and wrote), but rather as a more rounded, more full-blown system which takes its clues from a combination of Friedman's ideas and an awareness of the unique breadth of his educational experiences as they connect to statistical matters and the National Bureau of Economic Research (NBER) during the era from Wesley C. Mitchell through the Friedman and Anna J. Schwartz period. In doing this, I bring in some experiences and work of my own that date back to the 1950s, do some reconstructions of the theory, and otherwise bring in some topics Friedman did not consider. In all instances the goal has been one that grew out of Wesley C. Mitchell's work and Friedman's assignments at Mitchell's National Bureau of Economic Research—namely, to move economics along theory-, fact-, and policy-oriented lines.

Quite early in my work experiences, as I was researching sources and uses of funds for manufacturing corporations, I also reported on the calendar of new bond issues coming to the New York capital markets. This combination of experience and research led me to question the acclaimed link between interest rates and J. M. Keynes's marginal efficiency of capital, as it was linked to industrial corporations, later presented in textbooks and taught at Columbia University.

This acclaimed link also held the prospects for direct control over spending via discount rates, bank reserves, and bank borrowing. Although I reach back and recast some of my prior research and experiences in the matters at hand, I do not mean to convey the idea that I am dealing with old or currently irrelevant subjects. Indeed, what amazes me as I look back is that we have learned so little from the past—that in general we still think of central banks (or the U.S. Federal

Reserve) in terms of fairly direct controls, such as directly raising and lowering interest rates and exchange rates, and that the simplicity of this precludes us from potentially more fruitful psychological analyses that appear relevant at almost every turn. To be sure, some among us embraced the New Classical School's (NCS's) rational expectations (RE) simply because they appeared to open a route to the study of expectations regarding economic change and events, even when it did almost just the opposite, as I indicate in Chapter 10. The idea along that line was so impressive to some as to alter the writing of textbooks and to lead the Nobel awards committee to bestow the 1995 Nobel Prize in economics upon Chicago's Robert Lucas for his NCS/RE impact on macroeconomics. Even though the "Friedman system" I write about has its own connections via Friedman's 1946–1976 tenure at the University of Chicago, and even though it too does not reject in total the mechanical apparatus of received economics, the Friedman system gives more attention to policy, facts, and Friedman's statistical orientation than to economic modeling and the mathematical elegance associated with such modeling.

Even though my early Columbia/National Bureau contacts led me to a heightened awareness of Milton Friedman and clumsy, unguided efforts at reading his 1953 collection *Essays in Positive Economics*, I rather systematically did the following, which underlie the construction I call "the Friedman system": I analyzed abundant amounts of cross-sectional data bearing on the liquidity of firms at different times and over time; engaged in research on the management of the U.S.'s federal debt; compiled in some instances and surveyed and reinterpreted in others massive amounts of empirical data on the demand for money, before and after the rise of Lawrence Klein's big-models methods; participated in studies of interest rates and uncertainty; analyzed varieties of data on the crucial years spanning the 1970s and the 1980s for the United States, the United Kingdom, and the Federal Republic of Germany; and brought broad interpretations and experiences to the writing (with John Guthrie) of *The Florida Land Boom: Money, Speculation and the Banks* (1995).

In these instances the focus on the theoretic topics—interest rates and credit, plus money and bond markets—never changed, even as I sought a consistent overall view and read massive amounts of work by other economists. In the first instance, I was working on what I saw as economic behavior and J. M. Keynes's banking views about monetary policy (perhaps better called "credit" policy in its day). This orientation led me to what I see as a break in the nexus between interest rates in the credit markets and the financing of expenditures on additions to real capital by industrial concerns. As I further studied interest rates, I was unable to embrace the views encountered in economics about direct central-bank controls over the long-bond rates as they appeared in J. M. Keynes's *General Theory* (1936), and numerous other theoretic works, hence H_{TW}, page 46 of the present text. Moreover—following the impacts of Friedman's monetarist studies (often with Anna Schwartz)—I returned to the study of the Federal Reserve and Bank of England and extended it to the Bundesbank (Frazer 1994b). I came to see their traditions and practices as influencing the theories they embraced in the process of implementing policy (hence, H_{CB}, page 46).

Along the way, in all of the above, Friedman and Schwartz (hereafter FS) captured my attention. On the one hand, they searched for a stable statistical relationship, and on the other, they reported changes in the structure underlying the formation of inflationary expectations (FS 1982, 478, 558–573). My orientation, consequently, centered on the rounded, fuller-blown system of analysis, which I presently call "the Friedman system." It encompasses the prospects for the rapid processing of information bearing on bond prices by the group I call "the bond traders." Furthermore, as some others have realized, I come to see the financial resources available to the bond and foreign exchange dealers as giving them the power to move interest rates, as well as exchange rates, in ways that are at odds with any central bank efforts to impose rates that are deemed inappropriate to the circumstances. At this point, I note the phenomena I label "New York's revenge" and "the Bundesbank effect."

The main clues taken from Friedman in my construction of "the Friedman system" include the permanent and transitory components of time series (Friedman and Kuznets 1945, 331; Friedman 1992, 2131) and such closely related/principal building blocks as Friedman's Marshallian demand view (Frazer 1994a, 13–16), the liquidity preference demand for money with transitory and time rates of change (Frazer 1994a, 40–42), and the consumption function work (Frazer 1994a, 165–181). In retaining these concepts and in extending the delineation of "the Friedman system," I especially deal with conflicts regarding theoretic economics and data analyses and present what I call "economic analysis with undertones of George Katona."

Regarding the controversy spawned by Friedman's 1953 essay, a key passage from it states:

I venture the judgment . . . that currently in the Western world, and especially in the United States, differences about economic policy among disinterested citizens derive predominantly from different predictions about the economic consequences of taking action . . . rather than from fundamental differences in basic values, differences about which men can ultimately only fight. (Friedman 1953a, 5)

The way I view it, the 1953 essay itself remains controversial among many economists to this day and, at least among economists, Friedman's economics and uses of statistical methods brought out differences in basic values rather than agreements about "different predictions about the consequences of taking action." Indeed, in introducing such conflict in *The Legacy of Keynes and Friedman*, I was reminded of Rose Friedman's challenge, which I partly paraphrased:

Economists' empirical, data-analysis views are readily predicted from knowledge of their political orientation and, she says, "I have never been able to persuade myself that their political orientation was a consequence of the positive [empirical-economic] views." To be sure, I recognize that political and social orientations on the part of economists and others may be significant (and indeed overriding in many cases) in the selection of one or the other approaches of policy oriented economics. (Frazer 1994a, 203)

In further depicting "the Friedman system," I deal with several interrelated matters that go beyond my 1983 essay on Friedman (with Lawrence Boland) and my books that followed (Frazer 1988; 1994a; 1994b). First, I take a new look at Friedman's 1953 essay. I view it as a discourse on the uses of statistical methods in relation to economic theory and the philosophy implied by the uses of statistical methods.

Second, I deal with matters regarding the generality of "the Friedman system," when further emphasis is placed on Friedman's statistical criteria (Frazer 1994a, 46, 73, 240–241) and the Friedman/Schwartz position that the structure underlying the formation of inflationary expectations by economic agents changed in the 60s (FS 1982, 478, 558–573).

Third, I confront a selected portion of Friedman's critics, namely: those who had pieces published in volume 4 of the collection of critical assessments edited by Wood and Woods (1990); and those who reacted to my 1983 essay with Boland.

Fourth, an emphasis on "psychological economics" comes forward, to use a label applied to George Katona's work (Morgan 1987a). The foregoing matters, taken as a whole, point to "the Friedman system" as a behavioral analytical system.

Acknowledgments

C hapter 9, "Tenets of Monetarism," was initially written as a basis for my article in *The Encyclopedia of Keynesian Economics* (1997). In preparing it, I made inquiries of Allan Meltzer, David Laidler, and Richard Selden regarding their current works. For their responses, I am most appreciative.

For Chapter 13, I consulted Kevin Polin and Will Frazer, my favorite bond trader. I also turned to Bruce Greenstein, of Florida's Agency for Health Care Administration.

Chapter 14, "An Analytical System with Emphasis on Behavior," was initially drafted for meetings in Athens, Greece, and Orlando, Florida. In Athens I discussed my work with Richard Selden and Waclawa Starzynska, who kindly shared their insights on this matter. I am appreciative of their comments, as well as those of my former student Kevin Polin.

Also, along more general lines, I am grateful to John Guthrie for comments on the overall manuscript, to Professor Shogo Doi of Shikoku Gakuin University for his questions and suggestions (including the use of the term "open-ended closeness" with reference to *The Friedman System*), to John Wegenka for reading proofs, to Susan Thornton for copy editing, to Katie Chase for production editing, to Janet Fletcher for typesetting, and to Milton Friedman for the openness he showed over the years in discussing his work and in dealing with inquiries. However, as I indicate in the Preface to *The Friedman System,* the reconstruction, interpretations, and modifications I make in deriving "the system" are my own, as Friedman would recognize. So Friedman is absolved of responsibility for nuances, extensions, and interpretations I add to produce *The Friedman System.*

Part I

Introduction

In Chapter 1, of the three-chapter introduction to *The Friedman System*, I reintroduce a system of analysis with strong emphasis on "expectations" in the fullest psychological sense as they bear on households, firms, financial market participants, and logical/empirical economics. The presence of expectations, and formations and changes regarding them, concerns especially inflation rates, interest rates, incomes, monetary policy (as specifically treated in *The Central Banks* [1994]), and business conditions generally. In fact, in Chapter 14, I end as I did in *The Legacy* with claims about an open-ended analytical system. In the analytical system information is always being processed and outside (or episodic) events constantly appear to bombard the system of time series and thereby give rise to effects that have more to do with "psychological time" (as restated later) and phases of business conditions than with fixed time, distributed lag effects on the time series.

Chapter 2 takes up economics as a way of thinking, after reviewing a very wide swath from the history of economics since Adam Smith's 1776 publication. In particular, as we come to the post–World War II years, we note the presence of the computer, the high hopes for mathematically formulated structures, and widespread analyses of empirical data. Contrary to the hopes, however, such prospects fall short. The failures of strictly mathematically formulated constructions, econometrics, and even Friedman's economics in some respects to deliver what they promised leads us to view the alternatives simply as different ways of thinking in terms of economics. There are choices whereby the Friedman system is described as a way of thinking in economics.

More is introduced as regards the delineation of the Friedman system in Chapter 3. There I take up the false claim that Friedman is a neoclassical economist, and note the vested interest some economists have in retaining this position. I also take advantage of the opportunity provided by Abraham Hirsch and Neil de Marchi's book *Milton Friedman* to introduce additional issues and to reintroduce Friedman's famous 1953 essay with the prepublication title "The Relevance of Economic Analysis to Prediction and Policy." A central issue concerns the prospect and false claim that Friedman's economics is somehow directly tied to the American philosopher John Dewey.

Chapter 1

An Overview

*T*he Friedman System is about economic analysis broadly viewed in ways that are connected to Milton Friedman's reorientation of the main Keynesian building blocks and to Friedman the monetary/statistical-methods revolutionary of the second half of the twentieth century. This breadth and the generality I consider later are achieved by using the uniqueness of Friedman's educational experiences and his compatible ideas as a vehicle for even more extended analysis. Early in his career Friedman gained an unusual regard for both facts and theory. The theory, as it emerged, was cast to combine facts, uses of statistical methods, and economic analysis, and, at the same time, to shun the more common search for mathematical elegance with ceteris paribus overtones.

Friedman's early career was broadened considerably when he did several things in less than a decade: First, he gained prominence for his statistical work at the Columbia University war-related Statistical Research Group (Frazer 1988, 155–159). He then undertook the teaching of the graduate price theory course at the University of Chicago (Frazer 1988, 180). Finally, he extended his research at the Wesley Mitchell-founded National Bureau of Economic Research (NBER) when he took over a part of Wesley Mitchell's grand design for research on money matters, business conditions, and what may be seen by conventionalists as macroeconomics (Frazer 1988, 181–182). This combination of experiences—again over a short period of time—led Friedman to stake out a very special view of Alfred Marshall's demand curve (Frazer 1994a, 13–17); to change the Marshallian view and otherwise common orientation toward the utility of income (Frazer 1988, 160; 1994a, 155–165); to set in motion a rather dynamic line of monetary research (Frazer 1988, 153–155, 181); and to introduce a variant of instrumentalism as it would regard facts, uses of methods, and economic theory/analysis (Frazer 1988, 107–136; 1984a).

In Friedman's variant, the reoriented mechanical constructions are simply instruments for prediction (mainly, for predicting the effects of policy). The most basic of the reoriented mechanical constructions concern the Marshallian demand curve and the Keynes/Keynesian building blocks.

Friedman achieved his extensions of the basic economics without engaging in an outright rejection of it. Said differently, there remained something of a cumulative nature in the work of the first and second revolutionaries. The Keynes building blocks in question include the theory of the consumption function, the liquidity preference demand for money (Frazer 1994a, 31-52, 176-177), and, by implication, closely related investment spending by industrial corporations (Frazer 1994a, 135-143).

What must be amazing about every element of this grand research design is the harmony cutting across the research and writing on the parts. Uses of the statistical methods were consistent across otherwise disparate topics. The harmonious elements found in the parts as a whole extend from Friedman's piece on the Marshallian demand curve to the equation of exchange as it appeared at Cambridge University in J. M. Keynes's hands.

Before Friedman embarked on the Wesley Mitchell inspired part of his research at the NBER, Tjalling Koopmans (1947) charged the Bureau of engaging in "facts without theory." With the end of Friedman's career there I credited Friedman as the Bureau's theorist for the era running from Mitchell through Friedman (Frazer 1988, 153-155). Recognizing Koopman's 1947 piece and Friedman's research on policy-connected money matters, I concluded that there were "no facts without theory, no economic policy without theory, and no theory without facts."

Having an audacious mind, Friedman embraced expectations regarding the utility of a good and the utility of income. It is at this juncture that we first find his introduction of probability—the prospects for the probability weighting of expected returns (text pages 6-7, 14) and the utility, the risky prospect of the prize or income (Frazer 1994a, 155-165). Even so, the weighting prospects may be extended to the interest rate, and indeed even consumption comes to depend on expected income.[1] This emphasis comes about at a time when too many economists wanted to avoid the treatment of expectations, although J. M. Keynes had introduced dramatic roles for expectations as they relate to the demand for money, the motives for holding money (Frazer 1994a, 47-49), and the future stream of returns for long-term capital outlays. Indeed, later, when we turn to the tenets of monetarism, Karl Brunner (a proclaimed monetarist of Friedman's era) attempted to suppress the treatment of expectations on the grounds that it would play into the hands of policymakers and thereby provide them with an excuse for avoiding rigorously derived conclusions about monetary policy. But here again, the artificial, ceteris paribus-based conclusions have such appeal as to linger on and on in the minds of analysts confronting monetary matters. Even while applauding the success of Alan Greenspan during his tenure as the Federal Reserve's chairman, such analysts may lament that funds become available outside the Fed's direct control via reserve requirements, that other financial institutions have gained importance as sources of funds relative to the commercial and central banking sectors, that firms are not directly dependent on bank borrowing, that money substitutes arise when the central bank pursues restrictive policy (meaning, actually, the prevalence of high interest rates), and that the Fed cannot be counted on to ease future shocks (meaning, perhaps, an oil crisis).

The fact is that those who harbor these lamentations are looking in the wrong place to find the power and the influence of the central bank, as Alan Greenspan would concede (Frazer 1994b, xiv, 8-9, 57-58 n.2, 75-76, 79, 94).

An analytical problem with Keynes's imaginative treatment of expectations regarding the stream of returns and the rate of interest in particular was that what he gave with one hand, he took away with the other. He held the anticipations constant, for example, while the interest rate (namely, the long-bond rate, i_L) could be manipulated by the central bank. This central position is critically disputed in terms of both fact and analysis (Frazer 1994a, 135-143).

The nexus between interest rates and direct borrowing by industrial concerns is broken via treatment of the liquidity structure of firms, the planning of capital expenditures, and the roles of anticipations generally (Frazer 1994a, 150-153 n.5 through n.13). In fact, I come to use the long-bond rate (i_L) as a surrogate for monetary accommodation and discipline (Frazer 1994b, 35-50), to introduce phenomena such as "the Bundesbank effect" (Frazer 1994b, 7, 8, 98, 199). With that, I have low (high) interest rates as reflecting monetary discipline (accommodation) with a use of time frames growing out of the great works of Keynes and Friedman.

Extending this overview, we turn to the schema shown as Figures 1.1, 1.2, and 1.3, and to a subsequent introduction to expectations and the generality of the theory at hand.

PROBABILITY

Figure 1.1 illustrates personalistic probability, while Figure 1.2 sketches the most relevant links and alternatives regarding Friedman's uses of statistical methods and probability. Probability at Friedman's hands is personalistic (or Bayesian), as distinct from classical. Figure 1.3 takes up the deductive/theoretic part of the analysis. The essentially Friedman cell in Figure 1.3 brings forward the Friedman data analysis views from the Friedman data analysis cell at the bottom of Figure 1.2.

The illustration in Figure 1.1 indicates, in other words, that the probability judgment of an outcome after gathering new information is proportional to ($\propto$) some combination of prior and new information. The present relevance of the illustration lies in the personalistic or judgmental aspect of a probability where old information enters and the agent may also learn from new information of an episodic sort. In this context, on the one hand, we have

Figure 1.1
An Illustration of Personalistic Probability

| Posterior probability of a parameter θ (*i.e., judgment of probability subsequent to acquiring experience or new data*) | $\propto$ | Subjective probability of event, prior to acquiring new information or experience | Probability of observing a sample of data, given the variable parameter θ |

episodes of price controls, oil shocks, military intervention, budget balancing, and the like, that provide shocks to the agents and markets with regards to the formation of expectations, and, on the other, we have a credible central banker, who may impose and intervene with counter or reinforcing shocks of his/her own, which themselves are designed to impact the outlook of markets and economic agents generally. To be sure, there is also the prospect of agent learning from the new information. Indeed, impacts on data arranged as series over time contain a sizable and often predominant component in time series of a nonrepetitive nature. We are dealing with uncertainty about outcomes where probability theory is the language of uncertainty.

Probabilistically weighted outcomes [e.g., Pb[E], for probability of the event (E)] such as introduced earlier may be denoted as follows: Pb[U]U, for the utility, Pb[S]S, for the probability of a success with the lottery ticket, Pb[P^e] for an expected inflation rate, and Pb[R_1] for the probability of the expected return during the first year of holding the bond (or after an outlay on a planned expenditure). Making the probability factor explicit, as in these instances, is superior to just having agents fudge the expected outcome up or down to allow for less or more uncertainty. Most notably this is because in many instances, the expected outcome from a lottery, from a coupon in a bond contract, and from an interest rate is either known or readily estimated.

Setting aside the easy case of the lottery, we have the nominal value of a long-term bond rate (i), approximately as may be found in Irving Fisher's 1896 case (Fisher 1896, 8–11, 66–67), $i_L = i(\text{real}) + P^e$. Adding the uncertainty in the forecast eight or so months hence, we have what I call on some occasions the bond-market equation,

$$i_L = i(\text{real}) + Pb[\dot{P}^e]\dot{P}^e$$

here the probability of realizing the expectation is most likely the mean value of a number of separate but interdependent forecasts for inflation rates (say, eight months hence).

This distinction between an expected inflation rate (as a mean in a forecasted rate) and the use of a standard deviation (s) in an inflation rate forecast as uncertainty forecasting agents is exactly what we find in the Federal Reserve Bank of Philadelphia's Livingston data series (Frazer 1994a, 244-245). More importantly, while the probability may be personalistic, we still separate the uncertainty regarding the return itself. For example, in a bond contract with the Confederate States of America (1861-1865) the government issued bond contracts with coupons denominating annual payment (say, of five Confederate dollars) with no backing except the military successes in the field and belief in the Confederate government. Since this waxed and waned and eventually ended, the expected monetary value of the next year's coupon was nil (0.0), say, Pb[$5.00] $5.00 = 0.0 ($5.00). Probabilities of this sort may also be expressed in terms of confidence, and evidence may be gathered through surveys of confidence, such as confidence in the economic outlook. A contemporary example of survey information is the Conference Board's confidence index regarding business conditions. Confidence (say, a number x, $1 \geq x \geq 0$, with 1 times 100 as total confidence and 0 times 100 as zero confidence) herein is analogous to what we have called certainty, when x = 1, and complete uncertainty when x = 0.[2]

By contrast to the personalistic view of probability, there is classical probability. According to it, the universe (or sampling environment) underlying the probability is unchanging as we move through time. We are gathering information from the same universe. Learning and shocks afrfecting the outcomes are secondary, controlled, or otherwise of no relevance. The probability of an outcome is actuarial, as in insurance and coin tossing experiments. After flipping the coin a large number of times under controlled conditions, the probability of heads (or success) is one half. The University of Chicago's Frank H. Knight considered this kind of probability as risk only. What one may know or not know beyond that is relegated to uncertainty, meaning incomplete information and not probability.

Further linkages and antecedents regarding these probabilities and the classical statistics where probability enters appear in Figure 1.2. From the classical statistics cell at the top we move to the Ronald Fisher cell toward the left to a line of thought and to the right to what Friedman would call "fashionable econometrics." Its highest development appears at the hands of Lawrence Klein (Frazer 1984b, 210-214), for which he received the 1980 Nobel Prize in economics. As current representatives of the fashionable econometric method, we turn to David Hendry and Neil Ericson in Chapter 7.

The Ronald Fisher connection is embodied in Harold Hotelling, who in turn was a principal figure leading to the Statistical Research Group. Friedman connects to that and encounters Leonard Savage, who himself had taken up a personalistic/probabilistic orientation. Friedman also ties to Mitchell, as via the latter's business cycles course at Columbia and the Mitchell-founded NBER. The Savage and Mitchell influences on Friedman are primary as he emerges as an "empirical scientist" and a data analyst. There are a 1950 piece written about Mitchell, the more famous 1953 "controversial" essay, and a 1953 article, "Choice, Change, and Personal Distribution of Income."

Of some importance to the matters at hand, the New Classical School (NCS) appears in Figure 1.2. It follows from Friedman and Mitchell, in the case of business cycles only, and from probability as found in classical statistics, Frank Knight's views, and a 1963 essay by John Muth. It is included in part as an aide in distinguishing Friedman in his 1946-1976 decades at Chicago and other views represented at Chicago, by Frank Knight in the early years and later by the 1995 Nobel economics prize-winner Robert Lucas.

The Chicago I, II, and III designations refer to distinct schools of thought regarding mainly economists that appear at Chicago from its first year of operation in 1892 through Friedman's last decade. Schools I and II connect to Friedman, but not always directly (Frazer 1988, 281-325). Friedman's tie to Chicago I is through Mitchell, who published a part of his dissertation in 1903 under the title *A History of Greenbacks with Special Reference to the Economic Consequences of Their Issue: 1862-1865*, and to John Dewey and Thorstein Veblen through Mitchell. Friedman's tie to Frank Knight at Chicago concerns more of a reversal of direction. Just the opposite of Friedman, Knight did not see prospects for economics as empirical science and he advanced a classical probability by viewing risk as actuarial probability and uncertainty as incomplete information. The NCS adopts the Knight view of risk and uncertainty and only the business cycle part of Friedman's orientation with its connections to Mitchell.

That orientation pertains to Friedman's distinction between economic trends and cycles as departures from trends, as illustrated in Figure 1.3. There, I present a hypothetical time series for income, Y (or some composite, coinciding indicator for income), and show it to have a trend (or permanent) component and a transitory (or cyclical) component. Such a trend is obtained by FS by using the method of the triplet (Frazer 1988, 750; FS 1982, 74-75, 78, 308-309). The points A, B, and C are obtained by an averaging procedure concerning points at and between the trough (T) and the peak (P), at and between the peak and the trough, and at and between the trough and peak, respectively. With them a line denoting trend may be obtained.

Returning to Knight and the NCS, the trend in Figure 1.3 is a rational state in NCS/agent-expectations terms. The cycle in Figure 1.3 is viewed as a state of incomplete information in those terms.

Figure 1.2
Selected Approaches and Uses of Statistical Methods (including probability)

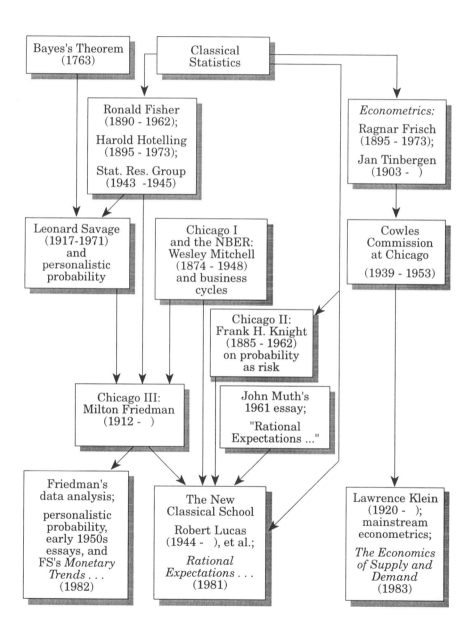

ALTERNATIVE APPROACHES TO ECONOMIC ANALYSIS

As regards the deductive part of economics, known most commonly as economic theory,[3] the Friedman connections are again extremely wide ranging, even as they appear as a unified whole. Starting in Figure 1.4, at Cambridge University, where economics gained a high regard, we have Alfred Marshall, on the left of Figure 1.4, and a Cambridge view of the equation of exchange, on the right. From such roots emerge what became main tracks in economic analysis, which in popular terms include the theory of price (later encompassed as so-called microeconomics) and monetary economics as taken up by J. M. Keynes.

These price-theoretic and monetary matters both are encompassed in Friedman's economics, although there are a few schisms along the way. From Marshall on the left side of Figure 1.4, the theory of price is combined with a wide range of theories of market structure (including mainly monopolistic and imperfect competition) to culminate in microeconomics with an antitrust emphasis. The theory of price exclusive of the added theories of market structures is connected to Friedman with a twist suggested by theory as an engine of analysis and later the special variant of instrumentalism I call Friedman's instrumentalism (Frazer 1984a).

The monetary line of analysis I connect to J. M. Keynes follows several routes. First, there is on the left Keynes's link to Friedman via Keynes as monetary economist. Second, there is a Keynes link to what is popularly

Figure 1.3
The Cycle and Trend Components in the Time Series

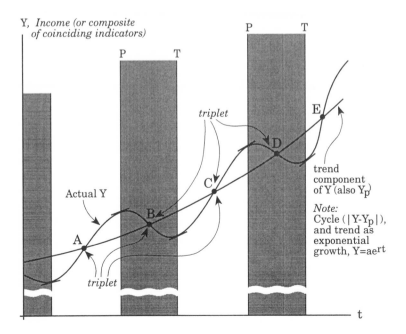

Y, *Income (or composite of coinciding indicators)*

Actual Y

triplet

triplet

trend component of Y (also Y_p)

Note:
Cycle ($|Y-Y_p|$), and trend as exponential growth, $Y=ae^{rt}$

t

known as macroeconomics. And, third, there are links extending from macroeconomics and from Keynes's original work to post-Keynesian economics.

Cells representing Chicago I, Wesley Mitchell and the NBER, and George Katona appear in the center part of Figure 1.4, disconnected from Cambridge. The Mitchell/business-cycle/NBER link to Milton Friedman is direct, but along it pass some elements of thought found at Chicago I. In total, three direct lines of thought go to the Friedman cell (here called a Chicago III cell, to be consistent with Figure 1.2). Further, five fairly direct lines go to the cell for the NCS's rational expectations. They are from the Mitchell concept of a business cycle, Walrasian general equilibrium, the Friedman (or FS) cycles and trends distinctions, microeconomics, and macroeconomics.

A "Friedman system" cell appears among the last cells at the bottom of Figure 1.4, with links to only three of the other cells. They are the George Katona cell I have superimposed in Figure 1.4, the more crucial link to Milton Friedman, and a link to Keynes as monetary economist. The Katona link gets explicit treatment for a combination of overlapping reasons. On the one hand, there was his pioneering effort with Gestalt shifts, although with rather loose connections to the mechanical apparatus of economics, and, on the other hand, there are asides I give in *The Legacy* (1994a, 236).[4] They are that "the [group] does not change its orientation at random but only in response to a cause" and "an episode or shock . . . causes some reorientation of the [group] thought processes." I especially connect episodic change to Friedman, FS, and information contained in time series.

In constructing *The Friedman System* I have drawn on my major efforts to deal with the totality of Friedman's work (including with Anna Schwartz), and especially my early connections to Columbia University (including those through James Angel, Joseph Dorfman, and Arthur Burns), separate fellowships in mathematics and statistics, and an interest in J. M. Keynes as a philosopher and a monetary economist. Indeed, my early interests in Keynes, business conditions, Friedman, and ultimately the prepublication copy of FS's *Monetary Trends* (1982) led to numerous visits to England, to extended stays in London during the school years 1989–1990 and 1991–1992, and to the spring term 1994 as professor at the London School of Economics. The combination of early interests and FS's 1982 work was the basis for my series of books over the 1988 through 1995 period (including *The Florida Land Boom* with John Guthrie).

EXPECTATIONS

Anticipations of business conditions and even more specific magnitudes for the myriad actual and imagined time series in economics fall under the rubric "expectations." Scholarly awareness of their presence has existed for some time, as evidenced by Irving Fisher's 1896 interest-rate equation (1896, 8–11, 66–67). Reference to the equation appeared in J. M. Keynes's *General*

Figure 1.4
Alternative Approaches to Economic Analysis

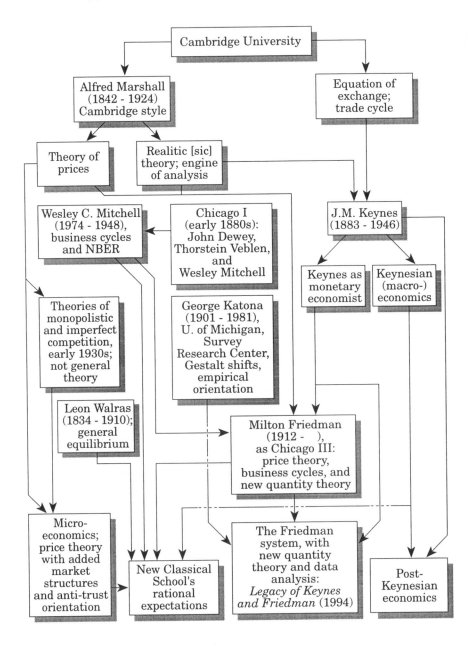

Theory (1936, 141–142), but he in fact set it aside and very little attention was given to it at a time when deflation was viewed as the problem and empirical research remained meager by comparison with later standards, such as those set by Milton Friedman and the "big-model" builder Lawrence Klein. As Friedman's work emerged, the Fisher equation appeared in the prepublication copy of *Monetary Trends* (FS 1982), in some proceedings (Friedman 1968, 11–27), and in Yohe and Karnosky's 1969 paper at the Friedman-friendly Federal Reserve Bank of St. Louis (1969).

Another emphasis on expectations appeared in G.L.S. Shackle (1952), but it was rather limited in its orientation and largely exclusive of the mathematical discipline of probability. Also, an edited volume of conference proceedings titled *Expectations, Uncertainty, and Business Behavior* appeared in the United States in the late 1950s (Bowman 1958). Even though a number of well-known economists participated in the Bowman volume, the Friedman system of economic analysis offers dramatic and far reaching treatment, by comparison.

Coming later the NCS's rational expectations, to which we turn in Chapter 11, gained enormous visibility in the 1970s, but it contained fatal restrictions. Among them it connected to Frank Knight's distinction between risk and uncertainty, and "agent rationality" called for behavioral units to adopt almost the entire mechanical apparatus of economics in the formation of expectations, as we will see. Contrary to positions in *The Friedman System* and more to specific theoretic topics, the received statements of the mechanical apparatus would lead to predictions of behavior along the following lines: (a) bond traders would place large amounts of capital on positions they would take in the market on the basis of the prevailing uses of the apparatus in economics, (b) large industrial concerns would place larger proportions of capital spending at risk when the economy is moving into recession (or at the same time interest rates are falling, as in recession), and (c) internationally mobile capital would move toward countries with the relatively high interest rates, even when those rates reflect the probabilistically weighted outlook for inflation and economic instability.

Once Friedman introduced the permanent income hypothesis for consumption (1957) and resurrected the Fisher equation for his treatment of interest rates and the liquidity preference demand for money (1968; Frazer 1994a, 40–52), all the old structure changed. The issue Keynes introduced in regard to liquidity preference resurfaced in the hands of Sir Roy Harrod (1971), Keynes's official and first biographer. Keynes had asserted an absence of the inflation-rate effect on the interest rate (actually the long-bond rate i_L) à la $i_L = i(\text{real}) + \dot{P}^e$. Here i(real) is the real rate of interest, (Frazer 1994a, 170–181), $i_L = \dot{P}^e$, and $\dot{P}^e$ is the expected inflation rate.[5]

Keynes, we recall, had adopted the view of his time whereby the central bank controlled "the" rate of interest (meaning the long-bond rate). In addition, in dealing with this policy matter, Keynes treated the value of capital expenditures (CV) as being obtained from the discounting of a flow of future returns (say, R_1 for year 1, R_2 for year 2, etc.). It was such that $CV = R_1/(1 + i)^1 + R_2/(1 + i)^2 + \cdots + R_n/(1 + i)^n$. And, indeed, with the separate probability weighting of the expected returns, as on page 6, $Pb[R1]$ R_1 for just R_1, $Pb[R_2]$ R_2 for just R_2, and so on. So, in any case, from the presumption of direct control over the rate of interest the central bank got its presumption of awesome and direct control over value.[6]

Now, when the central bank is viewed as losing its direct control over the rate of interest ($\pm\Delta i_L$) by way of inflationary expectations, the bond analogy does not hold in its restricted form (i.e., the given flow of returns and the control over the interest rate). Indeed, the expected inflation may affect the perceived purchasing power of money balances, the value of bonds, a different value for equities, and even numerous time series such as those for exchange rates and capital spending.

So, Pandora's box was opened. Identifying with Keynes's position, Harrod said:

What the new-found anticipation does is to change the relative values of money-denominated assets on the one side and equities and real estate on the other. The idea that a new-found expectation can alter the relative value of two money-denominated assets is logically impossible, and must not be accepted into the corpus of economic theory.

The occurrence of a new-found belief firmly held, that a certain rate of inflation will occur, cannot affect the rate of interest. But the growth of uncertainty about what rate of inflation, if any, is in prospect, can send up the rate of interest. (1971, 62)

As this edifice that Harrod defended would fall, numerous related topics in economics fall with it. To be sure, even as we add the language of uncertainty (in this case, $Pb[P^e]$) we get what I call the bond market equation, $i_L = i(\text{real}) + Pb[P^e]P^e$. Thus, an increase in uncertainty about the inflation rate (that is, a decline in $Pb[P^e]$, to the extent that it approaches zero) leaves the nominal, market rate of interest lower. This is just the opposite from Harrod's view of uncertainty regarding inflation. It is true that far reaching effects on the mechanical apparatus of economics and its interpretation follow when expectations enter.

As I indicate, in the expectations field the area most extensively addressed has been inflation, as Friedman's work and numerous references attest (Bomberger and Frazer 1981; Frazer 1980, 159–164). Friedman, however, linked his efforts concerning expectations to the mechanical apparatus of economics more broadly viewed. He did so with regard to Marshall's demand curve and groups of agents, the consumption function, the utility of income, and the liquidity preference demand for money. In addition, Friedman connected the latter to Fisher's 1896 equation, and he introduced the Maurice Allais notion of psychological time (Allais 1965).

By comparison with George Katona's efforts and those of others to introduce psychology into the apparatus of economics,[7] the "Friedman system" offers herculean jumps toward a behavioral economics that may be extended along the lines of interdisciplinary research in the social sciences, which we turn to in Chapter 14. Of no small significance, this interdisciplinary extension preserves major parts of the mechanical apparatus of economics. It achieves this with reference to the "Friedman system" along the lines we later indicate. The major parts of the mechanical apparatus which are retained include the following: the reoriented Marshallian demand curve, where Friedman gives attention to group behavior and the price index (Frazer 1994a, 13–14); a slightly altered liquidity preference demand for money with motion (Frazer 1994a, 40–49, 63–68); the consumption function with motion (Frazer 1994a, 165–170); and a reoriented Keynes/Keynesian link between interest rates and capital expenditures.

In the first instance, Friedman makes no distinction between the way groups of households and overall spending respond to episodic impacts, and, in the latter instances three major building blocks from J. M. Keynes's economics are redirected in terms of their potential relevance to accommodate the Friedman system. Redirection comes about in place of rejection, and a matter so fundamental as psychological time enters.[8]

I extend analysis regarding it to encompass neutral and nonneutral states for psychological time. When economic growth is smooth along a trend path, as illustrated in Figure 1.3, we have the neutral state. As business conditions depart from the trend state, nonneutral prospects come about. As in regard to turning points in business conditions (P's and T's in Figure 1.3) agents form expectations by looking back and making analogies to prior turning points. More generally, psychological time as variously embellished has to do with episodes that impact the economic system. Here, in the reformation of expectations, agents process new information and look back at the effects of comparable events and episodes in making analogies bearing on the behavior of groups and the future states of markets and business conditions.

In contrast to the central banks (or even the bond markets) raising and lowering interest rate to get smooth movement along a fixed curve that relates the interest rate to capital outlays, we have prospects for a recession of growth in capital spending as interest rates decline and for acceleration of growth as they rise along with more buoyant business conditions. As business conditions change from recession to recovery phase, the questions raised by the turn to the more favorable condition concern the "locking in" of new financing and the matter of refinancing as low interest rates appear. To judge this condition, agents make analogy to prior conditions regarding the appearance of low rates of interest and turning points in rates of interest.

GENERALITY

Economists have set great stock in the generality of the theory (or analytical system). Alfred Marshall, to whom we turned in Figure 1.4, is commonly said to have offered a system with partial equilibrium, as with equilibrium (or supply-curve/demand-curve balance) in a single product market. Leon Walras, to whom we turn in Chapter 11 and the Appendix to Chapter 1, is said to have offered a system of general equilibrium whereby balance is attained in all the current-product and even secondhand markets (including the market for common stocks or equities).[9]

In Walras's case, a system of simultaneous equations is offered whereby we have the equality of a supply and a demand function for each market. There is in that case early evidence of mathematical elegance, to be sure. Even Milton Friedman went so far as to refer to Walrasians as those who sought mathematical/endogenous elegance over fruitfulness and substance. He saw Marshall as searching for a fruitful empirical hypothesis that suggested a juncture of facts and theory.

Turning to J. M. Keynes, whom we show alongside Marshall in Figure 1.4, Keynes's economics, by some account, appears more general than neoclassical (or pre-Keynes) economics because it encompasses the less-than-full-employment state and not simply the full-employment state implicit in Marshall and neoclassical economics. Keynes's interest was said to focus on instability, disequilibrium (or absence of balance), and the "short run." In contrast, Marshall's economics was said to treat the "long run," where supply-demand forces were in balance at a full employment level of production. This neoclassical economics offered satisfactory market-structures theories of perfect competition and monopoly on Friedman's accounting.

Milton Friedman, in his early days as a professor at the University of Chicago, came to see these theories of market structure as adequate for his purposes of prediction, with emphasis on the theory of relative prices, as opposed to the main purpose of so-called microeconomics, which we come to see as antitrust rather than empirical economics (Frazer 1988, 306–323). As appears widely known, economics was set on a two-track, micro-macro route after Keynes and the disputes he had with the essentially micro/Marshallian/neoclassical economics.

At this juncture two special analytical problems arise as Friedman enters upon the scene with rather special views of Marshall, as elucidated by Roger Alford of the London School of Economics (Frazer 1994a, 13–16), and with the purpose of economics as being prediction (or *modus tollens*, i.e., prediction with error being passed backward in terms of a system of logic). In the first instance, Friedman does not embark on the separate micro-macro tracks which were embraced on the more visible front of economics. Instead, he starts to deal with the behavior of groups (say, even in Marshallian-market terms) in response to outside shocks (or what we call Gestalt shocks in the present work). These responses and the relevant prices in the Marshallian markets for Friedman are tied to a price index for a group of markets. It may extend to Keynes's interest in the economy as a whole, to all the markets for the output of goods and services (also known generically as income, Y, and on some occasions as gross national product, and on others as gross domestic product), and to the Cambridge price-theoretic equation. In the latter, as it pertains to Keynes and Friedman, the money stock (M) is some variable proportion [k(. . .)] of income, namely M = k(. . .)Y. So the money stock and monetary phenomena enter especially as determinants of prices and income (the product of a price index and the total output, i.e., PQ), where the price index links to Marshallian markets.

The second special analytical problem that arises as Friedman enters the scene extends to theories of market structure that are embraced under the labels "the theory of monopolistic competition" and "the theory of imperfect competition." In the former case, Harvard's Edward Chamberlin had claimed to have offered "a general theory" (Frazer 1988, 306–323), which in fact Friedman saw as a set of special cases and not as a general (encompassing) theory.

Now, turning to some of the topics at hand, we may ask about the generality of the theoretic systems (say, as they may regard the New Classical School [Figures 1.2 and 1.4], "the Friedman system" [Chapter 9] and analysis "with undertones of George Katona").

The NCS's system, to which we turn in Chapter 11, embraces the main mechanical apparatus of economics and, via special definition of agent rationality, extends this special rationality to the formation of inflationary expectations. The NCS system ends with a set of Walrasian equations. These are said to represent agent rationality in the long run (also, in Friedman's economics, a secular trend concept). Departures in the data series from this NCS long run are phases of business cycles, which we connect to Wesley Mitchell in both Figures 1.2 and 1.4.

In Friedman's economics, the departure from the secular trend for income are transitory states ("irrationality" in NCS terms) and "the business cycle," to use Wesley Mitchell's term. The final research/interpretation problem Friedman encounters when doing research with Anna Schwartz on the FS *Monetary Trends*, which we turn to later (Chapter 5), is twofold. First, there was a lag in the effect of money-stock growth on income that in effect directly determined the transitory conditions. Second, FS were put in the position of both viewing the lagged effect as stable and predictable for much of the 1865–1975 period covered by *Monetary Trends* and of reporting on a change in the structure regarding the formation of "rational" inflationary expectations beginning in the mid 1960s and coinciding with the onset of the greatest peacetime inflation in U.S. history.

This becomes the point of entry of the variable lag and what I call New York's revenge (Frazer 1994a, 68, 180; 1994b, 24–25). It is the phenomenon addressed in various chapters where agents in the money and financial markets learn quite quickly about inflationary prospects and even rumors emanating from Washington, D.C. in the formation of expectations. Forming these expectations the bond markets respond without lags in the effects of inflationary actions and inactions, and they do so without a "money illusion" (not the same as "irrationality"). The personalistic probability of agent learning enters. Since this class of probability encompasses both the classical notion of "uncertainty" as incomplete information and the idea of "risk" as actuarial probability, I see the analysis I call the Friedman system as more general than economic analysis in which classical probability receives the emphasis.

So, to emphasize the generality I associate with the Friedman system, I note the following:

1. Friedman's economics makes no distinction between shocks to Marshallian markets and shocks to the economy overall where the price index enters. The relative prices which come from the theory of the perfect market still enter the analytical system, and the respective market prices (say, p_1, p_2, . . . ,p_n) enter the price index (P), but they do so while avoiding strong emphasis on the detailed, descriptive truth of axioms as in the so-called theory of monopolistic competition (Frazer 1994a, 53–89).

2. The Friedman system encompasses both trends and states of business conditions (i.e., more-or-less-than-full and full-employment states up to the noninflationary rate of unemployment).

3. Stability in the Friedman system ends with a system of Marshallian-markets, supply-demand equations and unknowns (parametric prices, as it were) rather than a system of Walrasian equations. In addition to the way the price index enters in Friedman's view of the Marshallian demand curve (Frazer 1994a, 13–17), the system adds motion to the more ordinary mechanical apparatus of economics and time rates of change for stock and flow quantities such as the money stock and income. Further, if these particular quantities grow at the same rate, the interest rate and the velocity of money [the inverse of the variable constant, $k(. . .)$] enter as levels rather than as time rates of change (Frazer 1994a, 75–81). The anticipated problem in introducing the stock market to a system of Walrasian equations is that at equilibrium (balance along trend lines) stock prices may grow with the assets and earnings of the firms where equities depict ownership. The Marshallian/Friedman concept of a system of final equations for the current output is different from that set forth in the NCS view (Chapter 11).

NOTES

1. This introduction to the probability of outcomes in the three instances referred to may be illustrated. First, as regards the utility of income, $U(y)$, and the probability weight, $Pb[U]$, I note the values (F) for his utility function (Frazer 1994a, 73–75, 159–160),

$$F = \sum_{i=1}^{n} Pb[U_i] \, U(y_i)$$

Second, as regards the nominal long-bond-rate of interest (i_L),

$$i_L = i(real) + Pb[\dot{P}^e] \, \dot{P}^e$$

where $Pb[\dot{P}^e]$ is the probability of the outcome and $\dot{P}^e$ is the expected inflation rate (Frazer 1994a, 113, 135). Third, for consumption, C, as some function of permanent income, Y_P, we have, $C = k[(i(real), Wnh/W, u)]Y_P$. Here Y_P is expected income, and $k[i(real), Wnh/W, u]$ a variable factor of proportionality. The variable factor itself is a function of the real rate of interest, a measure of liquid wealth (namely, the ratio of nonhuman capital to total capital or wealth, W), and u is a portmanteau variable (Frazer 1994a, 14, 165–174).

In the last instance we could signify the expected-trend value, T, and restate the previous consumption relation,

$$C = k(...) Y_T^e$$

and, for the purpose of refinement, we could even include the product of the probability of the expected trend and the expectation, $Pb[Y_T^e] Y_T^e$.

2. For one month hence, an index value of 1 (1.00 times 100 = 100 percent) may mean great certainty and a subsequent value of 76.3 (0.76.3 times 100) by comparison may mean a considerable decline in certainty.

3. The term "theory" has a special connotation in this most common use. In it, the term connotes a body of abstract thought with no intention of empirical relevance to economic policy or operations. An example of this connotation is found in the title "The Theory and Practice of _____" (Reader fill in the blank). In such an orientation, one encounters a mechanical structure, as it were, built upon axioms (or assumptions) and definitions, but as distinct from practice. In other words, there is a disconnection. This separation and setting aside of theory and practice trivialize economics by conveying the idea that the theory has nothing to do with the facts, policies, or operations, and vice versa.

Other connotations in the use of the term "theory" in economics view it as argument in support of a policy and/or as a mechanical structure that generates conclusions as well as often conveying links between instruments and policy. Actually, in some cases, the term is synonymous with "hypothesis," which means a statement or conclusion to be tested against the empirical data and/or statistical results from the data. The hypothesis, however, may be tested by comparing alternative hypotheses for conformity with the data and statistical results. To be sure, the alternative may be a naive view, in which case the testing loses some of its force.

In economics one may follow a parallel to mathematics in which a structure is obtained by deducing theorems, propositions, and rules from axioms and definitions. However, special analytical/empirical problems arise here where we encounter in economics terms like *modus ponens* (passing truth forward from axioms/assumptions to conclusions/predictions) and *modus tollens* (passing error backward to assumptions, as where the theory fails in its prediction). On the one hand, the rather strictly mathematical process is reversible (i.e., theorems and conclusions may become axioms and axioms become theorems or conclusions), but, on the other hand, any search to find compatibility with the mass of data details ends in a description without the necessary abstraction called for to qualify as an empirically/factually based theory which by its nature must be a simplification of the mass of detail.

Also, following the mathematics parallel in economics, we may find references to "pure theory" and "applied theory" where we encounter the implications that the theory can be applied when in fact one may be left to his/her own ingenuity to find a fruitful theory. Issues surrounding such complicated prospects arise in Friedman's discussion of Henry Schultz's *The Theory of Measurement of Demand* (1938). Friedman says, "Schultz took the theory as fixed and given," and "tried to wrench the data into a pre-existing theoretical scheme, no matter how much wrench was required." (Friedman in Stigler 1994, 1200)

4. Katona was a European immigrant to the United States who had studied psychology at the University of Göttingen. The author of his entry in the Palgrave

dictionary says: "His Ph.D. was on the psychology of perception. While at the University of Frankfurt, he wrote a prize-winning monograph on the psychology of comparison, with an empirical orientation. Hyperinflation drove him to work for a Frankfurt bank and he wrote a widely quoted article on the mass psychological aspects of inflation. There followed a period in Berlin studying Gestalt psychology" (Morgan 1987a, 15).

Morgan also summarizes thus:

Katona developed the theory and substance of psychological economics, with particular attention to the effects of national events on the confidence, expectations, plans and ultimately behavior of masses of individuals. From a background in Gestalt psychology, he noted that there can be major restructuring of the way people interpret their world and their future, leading to sometimes dramatic shifts in behavior. And he had a firm belief in people's capacity to learn and to adjust their goals, so that behavior was more than a simple response to stimuli.

For a list of Katona's works, see Morgan (1987a, 16).

5. In some later context, the dot over the variable signifies time rate of change (x 100 = equals percent change (e.g., text page 149, n.10). One must judge from the context.

Fisher actually added another term to the right-hand side of the original equation. This third term was the interest that could be earned (or forgone) on the increment (decrement) in the nominal interest payment as a result of the price adjustment. For Fisher's derivation of the original equation, see Irving Fisher (1896, 8–11, 66–67).

6. To be sure, this approach has led to much mischief, where we even find expectations impounded and an entire formal, elegant work on wealth effects (Pesek and Saving 1967). Possibly this was done in the name of rigor and what Joseph Schmpeter called "scientism." In any case, I applied the term quite early to Karl Brunner's work (Frazer 1973, 389), to whom we return in Chapter 9, and efforts to surpress the role of expectations.

7. Although Katona's main point was "that there can be a major restructuring of the way people interpret their world and its future, leading to sometimes dramatic shifts in behavior," he moved in only a very limited way to relate such shifts to consumer spending and less rigorously to the mechanics of supply and demand.

8. Psychological time may readily be distinguished from chronological time, in that the looks backward and forward are not of a fixed lag or even a fixed distributed lag. The backward and forward looks rather concern the assessment of the effects of episodes and business conditions and the analogies made with respect to them.

9. Although Friedman used the label "Walrasian" to refer to those with special interest in the mathematical elegance of a theory (Frazer 1988, 564–565, 696, 724; Friedman 1974, 146), and although I share his usage, Walker (1987, 852–863) sketches a different picture of Walras and his work. However, we should note that Friedman is confronting economists of his era, where "abstractness, generality, and mathematical elegance became ends in themselves."

Chapter 2

The Big Picture: Economics as a Systematic Way of Thinking

Much has been written about Friedman's economics and the Friedman system's embrace of his data analysis views and his instrumentalist variation of economic theory—all with the view to conveying to others the Friedman-system variation of economics. The main problems with conveying this existence are several and we turn to them now. Quite frankly, however, many dismiss Friedman's work (including that with Anna Schwartz) because it has ideological overtones, because the structure underlying important parts of it broke down, and/or because major central banks encountered difficulties in implementing policy along lines Friedman prescribed, with the possible exception of the Bundesbank. In any case, analyses of data and empirical testing in economics at the most authoritative levels have not moved economists as a group toward clear statements of any empirically based economic theory. Rather, the results from the era of intense data analysis and econometric work ushered in with the modern computer appear to have driven economists back into heavy reliance on a priori arguments and constructs; into studies of limited, time-period parts of history (even if given an econometric tone and appearance), and into increasingly narrow areas of specialization with increasingly stronger boundaries of separation and inconsistencies across boundaries.

Simply put, we have returned in many respects to economics as a way of thinking more than toward economics as empirical science and/or with widely held principles. So, this chapter is about economics as ways of thinking. Of course, I may hope that a student of the subject will consider all of them and choose the "best" or most fruitful route. There is a warning: thinking has an influence on the mind for better or worse.

SOME PERSPECTIVE

Adam Smith (1712–1790) presented the first of the major works about what we may view at the end of the twentieth century as a rather large picture of a market-oriented economy (Smith 1937). In most respects, from an economic/theoretic point of view, it may be seen as argument for social and economic reform—for an open economy with trade and rivalry in markets that would enhance "the wealth of nations." Making connections among Smith, his friend David Hume (1711–1776), and the monetary matters Hume introduced (Frazer 1988, 41–45; Hume 1963) provides a comprehensive view of an economy with a monetary presence and interrelations between the parts and the whole. This connection between the parts and the whole is most explicit in Smith's famous statement of the invisible hand: "As every individual . . . endeavors as much as he can both to employ his capital . . . to produce the greatest value, he is in this, as in many other cases, led by an invisible hand to promote . . . the society more effectually than when he really intends to promote it" (Smith 1937, 423).

After Smith economics waxes and wanes at the hands of David Ricardo and others, but especially so at the hands of John Stuart Mill, whose two-volume *Principles* (1895) was widely read for over a half century after its first publication in 1832. However, Mill was a reformer, who sacrificed what may be seen with hindsight as logical rigor in order to gain style and to argue for his social and economic concerns (Frazer 1988, 50–52).

In this comprehensive view of economics, Alfred Marshall sought to add rigor and to give explicit form to demand and supply curves (Frazer 1988, 55–57). In doing so, he relied strongly on ceteris paribus and some mathematical foundations to offer a logically consistent view, even though, as Milton Friedman adds, the theory was intended to be relevant to the real world and fundamentally based on observation. As Friedman said of both Marshall's principles and Frank Knight's *Risk, Uncertainty, and Profit*: "The difficulty is that the observation is casual, unordered observation. There is no systematic attempt to marshal the relevant facts which the theory generalizes or test the theory by additional facts" (in Stigler 1994, 1202).

This is no criticism of Marshall's work. Indeed, Marshall's approach in fact sets the stage for much to come in economics. Quite explicitly, in the effort to develop economics as an important structurally sound, observationally based way of thinking, the development of logical rigor would predictably come before efforts at systematic observation because of the relatively low cost of the movement along mathematical lines. Not until the 1920s to 1950s would statistical data emerge on a sufficiently grand scale to open up the prospects for systematic attempts to marshal the relevant facts, test theories, and test the theories against additional bodies of data. And this prospect could not predictably be realized as cost-effective until after the electric computer emerged on a relatively wide scale, say, in the late 1950s.

In these data-gathering and data-analysis developments the United States was in the forefront. In the first instance, the distinct American contributions are most readily symbolized by the Wesley Mitchell/NBER connection (Figures 1.2 and 1.4), and, in the second, by the data-analysis and econometric orientations we symbolize with the work of Milton Friedman and Lawrence Klein, respectively (Figure 1.2). However, what we come to is not entirely the hoped for success at empirical verification, the setting out of a stable statistical relation, and the testing of the latter against various bodies of data that yields widespread agreement.

Rather, there is the matter we have already associated with Rose Friedman, and several almost fatal failures warrant emphasis. In the Friedman case, the first failure came with a change in the structure underlying the formation of inflationary expectations (said differently, a change in the lag in the relation between the central bank's monetary policy—whether accommodative, neutral, or disciplined—as in Frazer 1994b, 39–47). In any case, in the wake of Friedman's research, agent learning, improved communication, and greater efforts at anticipating the future came about.

The second failure in Friedman's case stems not from Friedman's contribution but from the varying ability of the central banks (and especially the inability of the Federal Reserve and the Bank of England) in fact to hit targets for money growth, in combination with allowances for changes in the income velocity of money and within the immediate-, short-, and medium-term contexts in which the central banks and financial markets most frequently operate.

In Klein's case failure also appears in the instability of statistical relations, and especially inability to formulate a solution equation for gross national product GNP or gross domestic product GDP with right-hand-side variables that are independent and controllable directly by the central bank and/or the government in other respects. However, as we have emphasized, Klein's and Friedman's approaches differ markedly.

Overcoming these failures remains formidable without altering the respective perceptions of economics as theoretic/data-analysis science. In my argument, however, the Friedman system best sets the stage for a way of thinking about a world in which markets, trade, facts, and money matter. But that is not the main point about the economics generally. Rather, it is a compounded set of points: first, we have an abundance of data (more in fact than economists can fruitfully analyze); second, economics as science must be empirically oriented; third, its structure need not be abandoned if we follow Friedman's instrumentalist leanings; fourth, psychological concerns, as taken up by George Katona (Figure 1.4), gain in importance and relevance as well as come to the forefront in the Friedman system; and, fifth, at the close of the twentieth century we are in many ways thrown back to viewing economics not so much as a successful science but as a way of thinking about the world.

This chapter traverses selected parts of the foregoing introduction and focuses on economics as a way of thinking. In it economics retains its distinguishing structure, at least as recast by way of Friedman as well as his influence. It does so in a way that invites connections with other social sciences. It also retains features of Adam Smith's great work—namely, its breadth, the connection between the parts and the whole, and the emphasis on theory as argument in support of policy. As we should already see from Chapter 1, psychological analyses, the economic outlook, and a predominance of episodic impacts on data series come to the forefront.

ANTICIPATORY-DATA SERIES AND THE FRIEDMAN SYSTEM

Economics as a systematic way of thinking takes much of its enduring character from the course set at Cambridge University by Alfred Marshall's *Principles of Economics* (eighth edition, 1920) and J. M. Keynes's *General Theory of Employment, Interest and Money* (1936). A most distinguishing feature of the Cambridge style, as found in Marshall and implied in Keynes's great book, is that of reasoning in terms of schedules (mildly static, partly zero time relations, simplified by the use of ceteris paribus). As a part of this style, logical completeness has been valued, although informally, with the exception of some parts, such as Marshall's mathematical appendix (1920, 838–859). Further, the authors bring to the respective works casual and relatively unordered observations, although Keynes gave attention to very different observations and classes of phenomena.

As I have recognized (Frazer 1988; 1994a), Friedman drew on both of the famous Cambridge authors and, by common standards in economics, recast key, essentially static constructions along more dynamic lines, as he added more ordered observations, specific roles for time, and income and inflationary expectations. To do this, he drew on his mathematical and statistical background, as did Keynes at an earlier date, and used his experience with the great abundance of numbers that had become available in the United States, more so than in other countries. This abundance of data can have impact in itself, in that its absence provides little incentive for economists to move economics toward systematic reliance on observation.

Mathematical formulations almost devoid of even casual observations have appeared. A classic, Leon Walras's *Elements of Pure Economics* (1954), gave impetus to the notion of general equilibrium, embraced the notion of a system of many equations and many unknowns, and offered what Friedman saw as an example of mathematical elegance at the price of fruitfulness. R.G.D. Allen's *Mathematical Analysis for Economists* (1938) pulled together that part of mathematics that appeared most relevant to the pre-*eneral Theory* theoretic treatments, and Paul Samuelson offered restatements of extreme-value mathematics with some overtones of difference equations as a form of dynamics in his *Foundations of Economic Analysis* (1953). By 1958, James Henderson and Richard E. Quandt were making explicit mathematical statements of the theoretical part of economics that was being relabeled microeconomics. And in 1966 I offered (with William Yohe) a systematic, mathematical statement as regards the part of economics that came under the label "money and banking."

By the time Friedman's work was gaining its first widespread attention, much data gathering had come about for him to rely upon, which we suggest in part in Figure 1.2 by the link between Wesley Mitchell's National Bureau and Friedman. Mitchell's classic "The Making and Using of Index Numbers" was about by 1917 and was revised in 1921. More formal work was to come (Diewert 1987). Also, at Mitchell's Bureau, Simon Kuznets was at work on what would become the accounting for gross national product (Kuznets 1937), and Mitchell and Arthur F. Burns were going about measuring "business cycles" to use Mitchell's term.

The data in economics was to become even more abundant, as pioneering work led to the reporting of sources and uses of funds data by the Board of Governors at the Federal Reserve System,[1] and as other data gathering took place. Of special interest to the work at hand, the George Katona–connected Institute for Social Research at the University of Michigan came to undertake surveys of consumer finances regarding spending plans, optimism, and confidence for the Board of Governors of the Federal Reserve System. Joseph A. Livingston, a University of Michigan Ph.D. in economics and a Philadelphia journalist, started gathering data that would lead to the Livingston data on inflationary forecast (Frazer 1980a, 154–160, 167 n.4; 1988, 199–200, 205–208). When it was later taken over by the Federal Reserve Bank of Philadelphia, Livingston's gathering of anticipatory data was broadened in scope. And, finally, the National Industrial Conference Board (later just Conference Board) began its reporting on consumer confidence.

The emphasis on these selected anticipatory-data series is especially germane because the series bear on the demand for money, even though the demand for money is not an explicit part of the data-gathering undertaking. Inflationary prospects, and confidence in the economic and political future, indeed have a pervasive influence via the money-stock and velocity routes on the wide range of economic time series generated by the market economy of the United States. This demand for money appears in Freedman's economics and in *The Friedman System* as the velocity of money—all in connection with an identification problem (text pages 55-57), Keynes's motives for holding money and thus an extended definition of money (Frazer 1994a, 47–51). And as a consequence, the selected anticipatory-data series lend themselves to the study of the impact of episodes via uncertainty about the future income, inflation/deflation, and so on.

Hence, we should see, in the important areas we address, that there should be few apologies for an absence of data with which to evaluate economic theories. They beckoned for analysis. In some instances the data have been analyzed, and in others statistical results from analyses are ignored. Quite possibly, in some instances, the meager attention the results receive in any extended length of time simply reflected the higher value placed on the techniques that may be unfavorably brought into question. In fact, *The Florida*

Land Boom (with Guthrie 1995), I find myself pointing to the roles money and its velocity share in booms (or even ordinary phases of business conditions) even as we stress the nonrepetitive nature of the comprehensive events such as the Florida boom (1915-1925), the Great Depression (1929-1939), and the Keynesian era of prolonged inflation in the United States (1962-1980).

EPISODIC IMPACTS, INDEPENDENCE/DEPENDENCE, AND SYSTEMATIC THINKING

As suggested from the perspective of a search for stable relationships, episodic impacts on the data series are troublesome, as regards the prospects for empirically verifiable statements that may be generated by theoretic economics, once time is introduced. The historical use of "ceteris paribus" was essential to the main structure we inherit from such dissimilar economists as Marshall and Keynes. In a Friedman system view, this need not be abandoned, but the place of ceteris paribus (or its statistical counterpart the assumption of independence in time series and policy-connected variables) and its retention are catastrophic once time is introduced. To deal with the catastrophe, I later argue for broadening the search for repetitive phenomena by first giving due recognition to nonrepetitive, episodic change.

Independence

Although troublesome, the term "independence" takes its rather ordinary meaning from mathematics. It carries the somewhat commonplace meaning of being free of influence, control, or determination, and also of not being dependent (i.e., not controlled or influenced by something else).[2] Where the condition of zero influence by something else may be quite rare in economics, we may try to create it artificially (i.e., in the imagination, as we suspend disbelief). The most common historical way of doing this in economics is through invoking "ceteris paribus." It is a sort of hammer and tongs way of forcing what may not in fact be the case. And, at the same time, it permits reasoning to proceed with some rigor, even if at the price of possibly losing touch with reality.

Although there are problems in gaining statistical support, we may invoke a distinction between the short and long runs and make statements such as the following: that changes in the money stock are exogenous (to invoke a technical term) before they impact with some lag on income and before the income impacts on the money stock and that changes in the money stock operate with some lag before impacting the expected inflation rate and thereby raising interest rates. On the other hand, we may simply gain a touch of reality and avoid the statistical problems surrounding the use of the term "endogenous" by simply asserting that responsibility for controlling the money stock lies with the authority extended to monetary officials regardless of the statistical correlation between the money stock and any error term in a stochastic equation (say, multiple regression equation, for an example). Further, if the money stock is not directly controllable, in contradistinction to the theory, we may find a surrogate route for defending its controllability. And yet when we engage in some of these improvisations, we may gain understanding but at the price of losing rigor in the sense that the statistical method is not directly applicable. So, there are tough choices about the route one wishes to go—whether fruitful or elegant but less fruitful.

As already introduced, there are other terms in economics that are closely related to "independent" and "dependent," such as "exogenous" and "endogenous," respectively. In this extended context, the exogenous variable may be controlled, independent of other forces, or simply outside the equation system context, and the "endogenous" variable is said to be determined within the equation system context. Accepting the belief, even imaginatively, that we can construct a system of equations that model the economy, we have the extended, parallel notions of forces operating from outside the imagined economic system and of forces internal to the economic system itself.

The terms may be used rather casually or even rigorously. Later, in the present work, we encounter "degrees of exogeneity and endogeneity" in Chapter 10, "Endogenous/Exogenous Money Supply Theory." The thought process becomes more strained.

In the ideal/disbelief–suspension context, we would think of the economic system as being modeled by a system of equations where we had distinct exogenous and endogenous variables and a rather straightforward model adhering to mathematical rules and economic-policy prospects. Going this route we get the so-called big models that were ably pioneered by Lawrence Klein (Figure 1.2) and others (Frazer and Yohe, in Frazer 1973, 287–311). In these models we encounter a fundamental mathematical rule (actually not always valid) and the equally basic economics concept of a reduced-form equation. The mathematics rule is that there should be as many nonredundant equations as variables (actually, in economics, endogenous variables).[3] Where this is the case, solutions exist for each of the endogenous variables. A solution equation for one of the variables may be called a reduced-form equation. It may consist of parameters (e.g., a_o, a_1, a_2, . . ., a_n) and exogenous variables (i.e., independent variables). An example I have used with specific real-world content is as follows:

GNP and/or GDP $= a_o + a_1 i + a_2 M_{US}/M_{UK} + a_3 \$/\pounds +$ fiscal policy (or central bank support policy with respect to it) $+ \ldots$ (1)

Here, "the idea . . . is that interest rate (i) effects, money–growth (M) effects, exchange-rates (\$/£) effects, and so on, can be manipulated by political agencies to put GNP on target as far as convention and economic policy are concerned." However, there is a problem here with the uses of statistical methods to provide numerical values for the parameters and thereby separate the effects. It is also a problem regarding the way we think about the actual separation of the effects and the real world. Namely, the effects may not be in fact separable because the right-hand-side variables are interdependent, for example, "accelerated money growth may cause inflation, inflationary prospects, higher interest rates [via i = i(real) + $\dot{P}^e$], a declining dollar exchange rate [$\Delta(\$/\pounds)$, $\Delta(\$/DM)$, etc.], and so on with respect to numerous other time series" (Frazer 1994b, 56).

On the one hand, suspending the matter of whether independent or not, we get a false rigor of sorts, albeit rigor. And, on the other hand, we invision an economy with enormous interdependence in the time series it generates for our examination. In the latter instance, the demands in terms of thinking and technique are actually greater than the false ones we achieve with forced independence. Introducing the real world comes at a price.

Consistency

In searching for truth in economics, however, whether at an open-economy macro level [including as to its parts à la Friedman on Marshall's demand curve (Frazer 1994a, 13–16) or at a price-theoretic micro level, the presence of consistency in the thought process gains in importance, especially in the light of economists' various inabilities to establish and agree on a predominantly empirically based, theoretic economics, whether à la Lawrence Klein, Milton Friedman, or others. Fulfilling Klein's ideal and/or Friedman's criteria for a stable statistical relation over time (including tests of the theory by facts additional to the scope of the investigation) is appealing, to be sure. But in the presence of the failure to achieve these ideals and meet the main criteria after the years of effort in the presence of the modern computer we are, it seems, thrown back to the main pre-Keynes effort to work out and embrace at a personalistic level at least a way of thinking that is consistent, although now also extending along empirical lines.[4] The essentially clinical view I adopt of agent rationality (Figure 1.1; Frazer 1994a, 55, 73–75) would seem no less applicable to analysts than to agents. It does seem that one may hope and suspend disbelief only for so long before abandoning all efforts at seeking understanding of mysteries and/or embracing the most fundamental of religious views.

AN OVERVIEW

Three prominent and rather visible ways of thinking in economics may be pointed out and illustrated against the background of the foregoing review and definitions. The three are sketched in Figure 2.1, in the first row of cells, along with the variations shown below them. As earlier definitions may indicate, "independence" and "consistency" are crucial to the discourse. Both are connected to mathematics. As almost the total body of mathematics itself enters, three general areas may be distinguished—namely, (1) calculus (sometimes called analysis, although the term "analysis" may have looser uses, as in "analysis of data," which may connote uses of statistical methods), (2) matrix algebra, and

(3) probability. The matrix algebra provides a means for solving systems of equations. At a mathematics/theoretic level, where the systems of equations can be quite large, analysts may be reduced to counting the number of nonredundant equations and the number of variables (say, with unknown values as to mathematical solutions, although time series generated from the real world correspond to the variables).[5] However, as equation systems of the sort Lawrence Klein worked with grew quite large, and as the modern computer gained a greater role in the 1960s, actual solutions using matrix algebra became possible (Frazer 1973, 462–467), even though we may question their real-world relevance as guides to policy.

Probability also enters along the lines introduced earlier (pages 4, 6–7, 14 and Figure 1.2). As pointed out, this may take on the role given to it by Frank Knight or a more general role. In the Knight case, probability was mainly actuarial (meaning like coin tossing, card playing, and games of change) and uncertainty meant incomplete information, as where agents simply lacked information. Even as the more general meaning of probability as both games of chance and uncertainty came to prevail, the Robert Lucas–led NCS embraced the Knightian view, in which actuarial probability was viewable as independent of background occurrence and generalized learning. Thus, the Lucas–led approach was viewable as being manageable in the most straightforward mathematical/actuarial terms. When one takes this approach to probability and combines it with an economic structure such as Walras introduced in 1874, (the n-equations and n-unknowns matter), then one has a body of work that can readily be manipulated in rather strict mathematical terms.

Mathematical Predominance

Now this is what we place in the left-hand subcell of the first column in Figure 2.1; there are twists that receive more attention in Chapter 11. Most notably, behavioral units of the economy are claimed to be rational ("agents," we say) in the long run, as regards the mechanical structure of economics, even to the extent of knowing (or even simply intuiting) actuarial probability distributions about outcomes. The long run this NCS adopts is a trend concept such as we illustrate in Figure 1.3. The cyclical part of Figure 1.3, in this NCS view, is incomplete information, so agents are lacking in the information to be rational in this state. A main policy connected conclusion is that agents can be thrown into this out-of-synch/transitory state only by being tricked by government policy. Once agents achieve rationality, they cannot be tricked, they see the future in terms of the "best economics," and government stabilization policy is unnecessary.

The New Classical School's Rational Expectations (NCS's RE) approach offers no systematic attempts to marshal relevant facts nor to test the theory by

Figure 2.1
Schema for Systems of Economic Thinking

Mathematical predominance (formal modeling, with heavy reliance on ceteras paribus and/or independent variables)	Econometrics (multiple regression equations and more)	Friedman's economics as a variant of instrumentalism; motion and a mechanical structure as change in time approaches zero at the limit

Positive Economics: New Classical School, Robert Lucas et al., but without ordered observations, systematic attempts to marshall the relevant facts, and so on, as in the right-hand column

Normative/positive economics à la Jan Tinbergen, *On the Theory of Economic Policy* (1952), *Centralization and De-Centralization in Economic Policy* (1954), and *Economic Policy: Principles and Design* (1956). For example: "Proposition 4: Part I. The number of non-redundant policy instruments (i.e., instruments whereby two or more targets) available to the policy-maker do not influence precisely the same must be at least equal to the number of independent targets..."

(continued)

Atheoretical economics: David Hendry and Neil Ericson, "An Economic Analysis of U.K. Money Demand..." (1991). This is "fashionable econometrics" but without economic theory.

Facts and theory à la Lawrence Klein: big models, number of non-redundant equations equals number of unknowns (i.e., endogenous variables)— a. relevant nonpolicy variables endogenous to the model, b. independent variables on the right-hand side of a solution equation.

Friedman's economics:
a. ordered observations
b. systematic attempts to marshall the relevant facts
c. test of a theory by additional facts
d. no facts without theory, no theory without facts
e. psychological time
f. episodic change
g. analysis of a few variables at a time before proceeding to multiple regressions
h. average time lag in the effects of monetary policy
i. change in structure underlying expectations in mid 1960s.

Friedman system— all of the above but with additional features. These include a. personalistic rationality.

(continued)

(continued)

A solution to a model may be assumed to exist if the model consists of n independent variables and n nonredundant equations (Frazer and Yohe 1966, 616 - 617). Note that the matter of independence arises and that the number of nonredundant policy instruments must equal the number of independent targets.

(continued)

b. psychological time tied to personalistic learning; c. consistency as regards (a) and (b), as well as overall; d. a predominance of episodic impacts; e. Gestalt prospects via a substantially enlarged and extended review of economic theory with undertones of psychological economics; f. a pervasive role for bond-market perceptions of monetary policy with allowance for variations in lags in the effect of monetary policy g. change in time approaches zero at limit (i.e., "open ended" closeness).

additional facts. In other words, most of what the NCS achieves is the prospect for a mathematically elegant statement of large amounts of rather formed economics. One may choose to enter upon that route of thought.

Going back to earlier post–World War II work of a highly mathematical sort in economics, we find policy–oriented contributions in the Jan Tinbergen subcell of the first column in Figure 2.1. It was a time of fairly high hope for uses of mathematics to serve the formation and conduct of economic policy as regarded economic stabilization.

Jan Tinbergen, who also appears in Figure 1.2, went about model building of the sort we label in column 1 as normative/positive economics. The normative part is about how the policy ought to be formulated and conducted, but noting the reliance on essentially mathematical formulations, we encounter the notion of n-equations and n-unknowns, and the presumption of independent variables and independent targets (such as targeted employment and inflation rate, more or less economic growth, and targeted exchange rates).

So all is well and a nice, normative mathematical exercise appears. But then a dangerous part enters, most notably, since the posited conditions do not conform to the real world, the next step (actually not taken by Tinbergen) is that the government should make the world conform to the model, so that then it can be manipulated to achieve policy goals in the real world (note: positive, how-the-world-works economics is achieved).

The prospect of this latter phase of conducting policy escaped me at first when I encountered it and viewed it as an attempt to introduce more mathematical concepts that did in fact imply real economic variables. Along the way I became suspicious of such economic constructions and encountered people in economics who in fact advocated the last step of making the world conform to the model with no more than a mathematical argument for doing so. That amazed me.

In fact, I encountered a real person of some prominence, who was known to me from graduate school days of the 1950s and on intermittent occasions since. The chance encounter was at breakfast during a conference in Geneva, Switzerland, in the spring term of 1990. It was a time when the James Baker–led move to bring down the exchange value of the dollar (Frazer 1994b, 129–130) was leading to a Bush inflation approaching four percent, and when the economy was moving into the 1990–1991 recession. The condition appeared to contribute to Bill Clinton's 1992 election, in part because the March–1991 trough was not reported until after the November elections and because the Bush administration appeared to offer no plan for improved economic performance. Even so, the U.S.'s economic performance entered as a campaign issue in the United States in 1992, and Alan Greenspan at the Federal Reserve was poised to advocate deficit reduction and reduced inflationary expectations as means of lowering interest rates and stabilizing the economy (Frazer 1994b, xiv, 8–9, 51–58, n.2, 94). Reappointed by Clinton as Chairman at the Federal Reserve, Clinton's support of Greenspan and Greenspan's strategy appeared to pay off for Bill Clinton and the Clinton campaign of 1996.[6]

In any case, the spring-1990 breakfast meeting came about as my highly talkative roommate and I sauntered into the coffee shop, to encounter the less talkative, Sphinx-like William Vickrey and together settled in for breakfast. The roommate immediately asked the future president of the American Economic Association (1992) and 1996 shared-prize winner of the Nobel award in economics, what was the source of the inability of U.S. economists to advise the government properly and get the economy performing. The answer (a paraphrase): Well, if the government does not give us the proper (implied Tinbergen proper) number of instruments to achieve the n-number of targets, then there is little we can do as economists. So, we have still another way of thinking about the world. Namely: change the world to fit the model.

ECONOMETRICS

Returning to Figure 1.2 we point to lines along which econometrics develops. Central to that part we link to Lawrence Klein are, first, Keynesian/theoretic economics and, second, a simultaneous equation system that appeared at Klein's hands as an extension of the earlier Klein–Goldberger model (Frazer 1994a, 206–213; Klein 1966). Especially linked to the latter was the view of the estimation of the parameters found in the equations by means of the multiple regression technique.

This earlier extended Keynesian model consisted of twenty equations (sixteen with statistically estimated coefficients and four definitional equations or identities) and twenty endogenous variables. So we have a juncture of the economic theory that led to the equations and the time series corresponding to the variables. The system grew in size, and the prospect of actually obtaining and further estimating solution equations from the system became realistic.

The story has been widely written about. Suffice it now to say that data sets were added (e.g., "sources and uses of funds" accounts) and the system was extended along international lines. The exercise did not work out entirely as hoped—relationships were not stable, the solution equations did not serve exactly as guides to policy (Frazer 1994b, 160 n.10), Klein reduced the claims for his modeling techniques to these of forecasting aids, and the use of the multiple regression technique with the statistical testing did not serve to affirm the economic theory.

During the same period Friedman's uses of statistical methods and the idea that the use of the regression technique could proceed without any link to economic theory emerged. The idea was to keep searching the data series until strictly statistical criteria were met regardless of economic theorizing. Indeed, such an idea is formally embraced by Hendry and Ericsson (Frazer 1988, 735–760; HE 1991), as they proceed in 1983 to challenge Friedman and Schwartz's *Monetary Trends* (FS 1982), by presenting the paper "Assertion without Empirical [actually they mean econometric] Basis: An Econometric Appraisal of *Monetary Trends in the United States and the United Kingdom*, by Milton Friedman and Anna Schwartz."

This paper culminates eight years later in HE's *American Economic Review* article "An Econometric Analysis of U.K. Money Demand in *Monetary Trends* . . . by Milton Friedman and Anna J. Schwartz" (HE 1991, 8–38) and in FS's reply to HE "Alternative Approaches to Analyzing Economic Data" (FS 1991, 39–49). What HE do is to assume authority for the use of multiple regression technique, embrace a fixed standard they call "modern econometric methods," and apply it until they obtain a statistical relation that they claim to be at odds with the FS results (FS 1982). Reinforcing earlier charges and my reactions to them (Frazer 1988, 735–760), some points and counterpoints from the 1991 confrontation between HE and FS in the *American Economic Review* proceed with "specification analysis."

The central idea is that the regression equation that enumerates the particulars in the right–side variables is specified properly when it survives tests to detect misspecification. After this they look for an economic rationale for their finding. They conclude:

On a substantive level, the empirical consistency of our model is consistent with a structure in which nominal money is endogenously determined by demand factors, conditional on prices, incomes, and interest rates. Undoubtedly, the model proposed above is not the end of the story since, for example, parameter nonconstancy is evident during 1971–1975. That it is not perfect is less than surprising, as the data span a century during which financial institutions altered dramatically: witness the growth of building societies and, after 1970, the introduction of Competition and Credit Control regulations and of floating exchange rates. Even so, the evidence suggests that substantial benefits are available in practice from a progressive research strategy exploiting tests in both model design and model evaluation. (HE 1991, 33)

As on the occasion in 1983 (Frazer 1988, 755–757), HE make no distinction between trend and transitory components in the data series (Figure 1.3) and they avoid analyzing a few variables at a time to determine the true bounds on a regression coefficient (Frazer 1994b, figures 3–1 and 3–3). Central to doing this is the "regression effect" (also "regression fallacy") last illustrated by Friedman in 1992 and presently taken up in Chapter 7.

NOTES

1. Recognizing that funds are bookkeeping entries (and not specifically money) there is a basic rule regarding sources and uses of funds. With the exception of deposit-creating fractional-reserve banks, the basic rule is as follows: an increase (decrease) on the asset side of a balance sheet is a use of (source of funds) and an increase (decrease) on the liabilities side of a balance sheet is a source of (use of funds). Deposit-creating, fractional-reserve banks are an exception because increases in bank credit (an asset of the banks) leads to a growth in bank deposits (a liability of the banks), so an increase in liabilities by this route is not a source of funds to banks as a whole. Of course, banks of this sort may move reserves, bank credits, and bank deposits about among themselves and from one region of the country to another.

2. Referring to statistics:

The common-sense interpretation of independence is analogous to that of zero covariance or correlation. For instance, a formula relating the covariance between X_2 and X_3 to their correlation coefficient is

$$\rho = \sigma_{23}/\sigma_2\,\sigma_3$$

where ρ is the correlation coefficient, σ_{23} is the covariance, and σ_2 and σ_3 are standard deviations for X_2 and X_3 respectively (Frazer 1973, 9 n.7).

To illustrate the problem:

[C]onsider four variables, X_1, X_2, X_3, and X_4, which are related in some way. Without defining specific relationships the present ones may be denoted: $X_1 = f(X_2, X_3)$, $X_2 = g_1(X_4)$, and $X_3 = g_2(X_4)$. Here the variable X_1 is dependent on X_2 and X_3, and X_2 and X_3 are each influenced by X_4 in some fashion. In anticipation of subsequent constructs, one may think of X_4 as an expected rate of inflation, X_2 as the cost of funds for capital expenditure (or interest rate), X_3 as the rate of return on capital outlays, and X_1 as the amount of capital expenditures. Now, if X_2 and X_3 are both influenced by X_4, and if X_4 is operating, then only a misleading interpretation of the cause(s) of observed changes in X_1 can result from, say, impounding X_4 in ceteris paribus (treating it as a constant, as in a laboratory experiment). Proper mathematical analysis will call for the use of the function of a function rule which would bring out the dependence of X_2 and X_3 on some common force.

This problem is carried over to the classical least squares statistical method. Employing that method, one may wish to estimate parameters and view X_1 as dependent on X_2, X_3, and X_4. But the ceteris paribus assumption is intrinsic in the assumption of zero covariance or correlation between any two of the so-called independent variables. The problem in statistical method is that of multicollinearity. In the presence of multicollinearity, analyses of data are not useless, but they require a different interpretation (Frazer 1973, 9–10).

3. For an outline of the proof of the existence of a solution and the assumptions involved, see Baumol (1961, 311–316). Also, on solutions, see Allen (1938, 278–281) and possibly others.

4. The two main parts of this view of agent rationality are Bayesian learning as it relates to probability and data analysis and the price-theoretic axioms of completeness and ranking and transitivity. As we may recall, the agent faces the subjective choices of ranking preferences and selecting from alternative A and B, B and C, and so on, and then on being consistent by ranking A over C when A is preferred to B, and B is preferred to C (Frazer 1984a, 55, and 73–75).

5. There is a vast literature on this subject, it relates to the economics at hand, see Frazer (1973, 91–92, 297–298, 287–311, 462–467); Frazer and Yohe (1966, 39–48, 89–91, 621–624); Vickery (1964, 118–124).

6. *Deja vu*; it appeared as another case of the political business cycle. Episodic as to impact, the definition of "political business cycle" has taken various related twists. It was first seen in terms of instabiity in the economy that was cuased by shifts in political administrations and the economic policies their varying ideologies would give rise to. Some later emphasis moved toward changes in the elected officials that would coincide with the public's dissatisfaction with the economy's performance.

Raising the question whether politics and economics mix, Merrill Lynch Chief Economist Donald Straszman (*The Advisor* November 1996) writes thus:

One of the most popular questions asked voters during a presidential campaign is: "Are you better off now than you were four years ago?" Challengers use this question to discredit a candidate saddled with a weak economy. Incumbents use the same question during good times to promote themselves.

Is there any economic indicator that can reliably forecast election results? The University of Michigan's index of consumer sentiment—a measure of consumers' *perception* of economic conditions, such as employment, spending and interest rates—turns out to be the best economic indicator of an incumbent's "re-electability." Voters might not be able to quote the latest economic statistics, but they do know how they feel.

An incumbent has never failed to win re-election reading near 100. Likewise, when sentiment was low at election time, incumbents have been summarily turned out of office. The late-October 1996 reading on the sentiment index was 96.5.

Chapter 3

Beyond Neoclassical Economics

Abraham Hirsch and Neil de Marchi are the authors of *Milton Friedman: Economics in Theory and Practice* (Hirsch and de Marchi 1990). A welcome addition to the literature on Friedman, it deserves some attention here in part because its title and substance are misleading. The title suggests that the book may contain some biography, but there is very little of that, and the subtitle suggests that there is an emphasis on "theory and practice," while contrary to that, even the authors point out that Friedman took for granted "the continuity between pure science and application [practice]" and draws no such distinction (Hirsch and de Marchi, 1990, 141–142).

The Hirsch/de Marchi book treats methodology (138 pages), Friedman's practice (116 pages), and the methodology of political economy (27 pages). The book's major contribution lies in the area of the methodological discussion set on a course by Friedman's famous 1953 essay (Frazer and Boland 1983; Frazer 1988, 107–136, 164; Friedman 1953a). By the term "methodology" Hirsch and de Marchi mean the philosophy of science and not, as has crept into usage, the uses of statistical methods. Even so, James Wible (1984, 1049, 1057–1058, 1061–1062) suggests that Friedman's uses of statistical methods should be drawn upon in casting him as a philosopher of science (also see Frazer 1988, 133–135). To be sure, this is the case, as the next chapter should affirm.

Hirsch and de Marchi make much of the published title of what we embellish in the next chapter as the famous essay (Hirsch and de Marchi

---

This chapter first appeared as a review of the Hirsch and de Marchi book (Frazer 1992). It is slightly altered to fit *The Friedman System*.

1990, 12, 70, 82, 271), "The Methodology of Positive Economics" (Friedman 1953a). The title implies the distinction drawn from J. N. Keynes (1891), the father of J. M. Keynes, but the prepublication title of the essay is more indicative of what Friedman had in mind. The working title as taken up on page 52 was "The Relevance of Economic Analysis to Prediction and Policy."

Hirsch and de Marchi are aware that Friedman was more interested in doing economics and could have had only a superficial knowledge of Karl Popper's and John Dewey's works, which enter into the discussion. As I suggest, Friedman's contacts with Popper were probably more relevant to the influence on Friedman than his study of the philosopher (Frazer 1988, 117, 173). And, to be sure, Friedman could have been influenced only in the most indirect way by John Dewey (say, via Wesley Mitchell), as indicated in Figure 1.4).

The thrust of the Hirsch/de Marchi contribution is to view Friedman as a philosopher of science in relation to John Mill, John Dewey, Wesley Mitchell, Frank Knight, and Karl Popper. A main criticism I make in this regard, and I do not think it detracts from their contribution, is that the authors (1990, 40 n.10; 72, 91–93; 106–107 n.23 and n.28) draw on the Frazer/Boland essay about Friedman's methodology (Frazer and Boland 1983) but incorrectly say that Frazer and Boland "consider Friedman" a short-run instrumentalist and [but] a long-run Popperian" (1990, 40, 92). In a section of the Frazer and Boland essay we [I] said, "Friedman's views on methodology are instrumentalist in the shorter run where policymakers reside" (Frazer and Boland 1983, 141). The short run here was viewed explicitly as opposed to some philosophical concept of an almost never-ending dialogue. The point (also in Frazer 1988, 132–133) is that Friedman was not interested in one true theory as some philosophers may be. His instrumentalism is his own variant, which I disassociate from the controversy between Hirsch and de Marchi and Boland (Frazer 1984).

Hirsch and de Marchi are inclined to relate detailed discussion of methodology to Friedman's early pieces, whereas I look to these antecedents and assume a more forward looking perspective. In it I seek links between the early works generally, Friedman's "Marshallian Demand Curve," the closely related 1952 piece on Wesley Mitchell "The Economic Theorist," and the 1953 essay. Not only does the essay on Mitchell (Friedman 1950) say a lot about the way time should enter into economics, it reflects the early dissertations written under Friedman's direction at the University of Chicago (Frazer 1988, 153–55).

Hirsch and de Marchi see Friedman's paradigm in Thomas Kuhn's sense as neoclassical, Marshallian, and normative science (1990, 157, 152–153, 160, 171–173, 207–208), whereas I see Friedman's work as revolutionary in terms of Thomas Kuhn's canons of revolution (Frazer 1988, 171–173). Yet, Hirsch and de Marchi note five points about Friedman's use of Marshall as distinctive (1990, 168–171). A clue to this stretch of their position is that they never see that Friedman is really departing from the standard statistical regression model (Frazer 1988, 110, 112, 134–135, 542, 560–561, 776 n.69; Friedman and Schwartz 1991), to which we turn in Chapter 4. Clearly, when Hirsch and de Marchi come to the position of Hendry and Ericsson versus Friedman in the multiple regression area (Friedman and Schwartz 1991; Hirsch and de Marchi 1990, 170), they in effect say that Friedman got it wrong. Continuing, they state, "two important problems" (171–172), namely, (1) "Friedman at times goes beyond empirical analysis and intrudes his own political or value preferences," and (2) "Friedman is not able to come up with predictions that are quantitatively accurate enough for policy advice."

My first reaction to these two points is that Friedman offers a total analytical system (extending to his uses of statistical methods). This system has variously been called monetarist and, by me (Frazer 1994a, xix–xx, 120; 1994b, xiv, 6,56, 66), "the Friedman System." I call it thus because the system is encompassing, extending to microeconomic foundations and open economy/exchange-rate matters, as well as uses of statistical methods. Furthermore, this Friedman/policy-oriented/behavioral system is an alternative to the Keynesian one with the central focus on interest rates and fiscal policy. Also, the choice of Friedman's system reduces to a choice between a government policy that facilitates adjustments in the private sector and a government policy that intervenes directly. Such a choice is hardly apolitical. And, indeed, I offer Hotelling's line to deal with the classification of technical topics in economics, whether politically centrist or right-wing (Frazer 1994a, 82–84; 134, 203–204; 1994b, 77–79, 105–106, 156–157; Hotelling 1929).

Further, the predictions—say, of an average lag time between money acceleration and a rise in interest rates—may not have been so bad if the change underlying the formation of inflationary expectations had not changed in the mid-1960s (text page 17), possibly due in part to Friedman's impact to begin with. And, finally, in redirecting economic though along policy-guiding lines, he did set in motion some factual/institutional-based ideas that ultimately bear fruit. Among these I would point to the statetment of Friedman's law (text page 142) which brought attention to the interaction of monetary and fiscal policy. It was such that the two could be viewed as substitutes and that the effects of government budget deficits on spending could be shown to depend on monetary accommodation, discipline and neutrality (Frazer 1994a, 94–112; 1994b, 39–50, 87–93).

In any case, in the second case above I note problems of central bank operations in implementing a Friedman policy (first, text pages, 23–24, and later 146–147; Frazer 1994b). And, in either case (1) or case (2) we now see choices between alternatives as to how to proceed (Frazer and Boland 1983, 130; and later text Figure 4.1). The political/economic alternatives may be viewed best in terms of the superiority of one system over the other, and not in relation to some naive alternative.

Cutting through the details and possible inconsistencies of the sort Hirsch and de Marchi note (1990, 153, 271), I offer the following positions that differ from theirs: (1) In his soaring flight, Friedman, like J. M. Keynes, underwent "a struggle to escape from habitual modes of thought and expression." (2) The key to this struggle lies in his statistical and Mitchell-Bureau connections, as well as in the monetary work. (3) Moving to the topics found in Keynes's 1923 *Tract* and the *General Theory*, Friedman ties into Keynes's view of the quantity-theoretic expression (with its price index), the consumption function, and liquidity preference demand for money. Here, the price index is not unlike that in Friedman's demand-curve paper (Frazer 1994a, 13-23), and Friedman's approach shows that Keynes failed to escape the quantity-theory expression in the liquidity-preference model (Frazer 1994a, 31-52).

All these points are tied to the time frames passed along by Friedman, as illustrated in Figure 1.3, and there is much more. Taking the time frames and more (Frazer 1988, 112, 123, 132, 153; Frazer and Boland 1983, 130), Friedman backs away from the "economic man" axioms of neoclassical economics (Frazer 1994a, 6, 13, 55, 68). A symbol of this backing away is the "as if" principle, to which we turn in Chapter 4. The principle, nonetheless, appears in various forms (Frazer 1988, 126-27; Hirsch and de Marchi 1990, 14, 135, 148 n.6).

Following the foregoing route, Friedman's work was as much of an attack on neoclassical economics as was Keynes's, and, to be sure in both instances, there was no separation of the theory of money and the theory of production such as we find in the neoclassical economics which Keynes attacked. In fact, Friedman's integration of the theory of money and production is so clear as even to bring into question the separation of money in the new classical school's economic (text pages 171, 182-183), and in the so-called micro- macro-economics distinction as far as positive economics is concerned (especially Frazer 1994a, 13-15, 63-67).

A difference between Friedman and Keynes lies more in Friedman's strategy of appearing to be orthodox, and what I call Friedman's "valid orthodoxy." Namely, Friedman finds some outstanding thinker from the past—such as Adam Smith, Alfred Marshall, or Irving Fisher—as a source for some idea that in fact is more Friedman than the orthodox figure he credits. So, I view this as a strategy for getting a view accepted that may otherwise seem radical and draw attention to Friedman as a controversial figure. Friedman's Marshallian demand curve paper fits into this scheme of doing things a particular way.

In Friedman's economics there is no separation of the theory of money from the theories of production and employment, as in neoclassical economics, and, to be sure, there is no neoclassical synthesis of the monetary and value theories such as we find at the hands of Don Patinkin (1956). Friedman's approach meets the criteria for a scientific revolution in the Kuhn sense (Frazer 1988, 711-731).

Had Hirsch and de Marchi pushed more into Friedman's uses of statistical methods and gone on to Friedman and Schwartz's *Monetary Trends* (1982) and the controversies that grew from that (Frazer 1988, 68–87, chap. 18; Friedman and Schwartz 1991), they might have found some clue to the monetary revolution and the uses of statistical methods.

Having dwelt at some length on Friedman's 1953 essay and comparisons with Mill, Dewey, Mitchell, Knight, and Popper, the authors add chapter 12. Although that appears as an effort to distinguish the methodology of positive economics from the polity, there are difficulties in doing this, because the choice is not between "value-free generalizations about the way in which economic [analytical] systems work." Rather the alternative analytical systems offer a choice between one role for government and another, as later chapters indicate.

Part II

The Famous Controversial Essay

The introductory essay to Friedman's *Essays in Positive Economics* (1953a) has been called "the best known piece of methodological writing in economics" (Caldwell 1982, 173) and referred to as the "famous essay" (Frazer and Boland 1983, 129). Its published title was "The Methodology of Positive Economics," which went well with Friedman's 1953 collection of reprinted essays. However, the essay's prepublication title is more indicative of its content, as I introduced it with Boland (1983): "The Relevance of Economic Analysis to Prediction and Policy" was the title of the preproduction copy Arthur Burns read and commented on as late as November 1992 (Frazer 1988, 164). Indeed, the essay makes more sense when seen in terms of the working title and Friedman's larger effort at research, writing, and persuasion. The published title comes from the passage Friedman quotes from John Neville Keynes (Friedman 1953a, 3). But this connection to John Neville, the father of the famous J. M. Keynes, both sidetracks the discussion and relates to what I refer to as "the valid orthodoxy" in Friedman's work (Frazer 1988, 119). It subsumes Friedman's tendency to offer radical ideas but to package them in accepted authority. Whether that tendency is conscious, unconscious (as I think), the published title of the essay indicates Friedman's means of improving its chances of entrance.

In any case, the famous essay induced waves of controversy both before and after Lawrence Boland and I shifted the grounds for discussion to the logical content of the essay in its own terms and to the "Foundations of Friedman's Methodology" (Boland 1979; Caldwell 1982, 173; Frazer and Boland 1983, 129–144; Frazer 1988, 107–136, 735–760; Wible 1984, 1049–1070). The gist of the first of the papers just cited was that the essay was free of logical error; the Frazer/Boland paper connected Friedman to a variant of instrumentalism (Frazer 1984a) and to Wesley C Mitchell (Figure 1.2 and 1.4); and Wible both drew a parallel to the instrumental pragmatic American philosopher John Dewey (also Figure 1.4) and noted that much of Friedman's methodology as philosophy should be sought in his uses of statistical methods. Indeed, not only had the Frazer/Boland paper taken up Friedman's use of mechanical apparatus in terms of policy connected instruments for prediction and tests of theories against one another, Frazer and Boland went on to Friedman's use of apparatus, to his mathematical statistical background, and to a blend of "a priori constructions (such as Marshall's demand curve and Keynes's liquidity preference schedule) and statistical methods" (Frazer and Boland 1983, 133-141).

Further, immediately before the Frazer/Boland paper (1983), Friedman and Anna Schwartz published their classic—now known by the short title *Monetary Trends* (1982)—which somehow attracted attention to Friedman's uses of statistical methods even though these had been apparent much earlier. As late as December 1982, articles appearing in the *Journal of Economic Literature* by Charles Goodhart and Thomas Mayer offered general reactions to the uses of statistical methods (Frazer 1988, 540, 544). Goodhart said, "As Thomas Mayor has noted . . . F-S are out of tune with current trends in econometrics," and Goodhart characterized the statistical evidence as presented in a "somewhat *idiosyncratic* manner."

Concurrently, David Hendry and Neil Ericsson were undertaking an assessment of *Monetary Trends* in a paper first presented in 1983 to the Bank of England's Panel of Academic Consultants (Frazer 1988, 736-741), with a view to assessing the work from the point of view of "the prevailing fashion in econometric work" (FS 1991, 40). Thus, as it turns out, after almost a decade, a variant of Hendry and Ericsson's 1983 paper appears in the *American Economic Review* (HE 1991), with a response by FS (1991). Parallel to this development, other works appeared on issues set in motion by the Frazer/Boland paper, the Wible paper cited earlier, and the philosophical dimension of Friedman's orientation in general.

Part II of the present book returns to FS's uses of statistical methods as they have been dealt with by Frazer and Boland (1983), Frazer (1988), and Hendry and Ericsson (1991). An important strand of thought is that stated by Wible, that one must look to Friedman's uses of statistical methods to gain insight into the philosophical/methods dimension of Friedman's work. Indeed, Part II's contribution is that of returning to the famous essay and viewing it in terms of uses of statistical methods, Friedman's "indirect method" generally, and the controversies set on course in the early 1980s by Friedman and Schwartz, Frazer and Boland, and Wible.

Part II in effect comprises an elaborated walk through Friedman's 1953 essay with the hindsight of Friedman's background and the larger body of his work. The main relevant features of his background are the early experiences in uses of statistical methods (Frazer 1988, 155-159); the empirical science connection to Wesley C. Mitchell (Frazer 1988, 107-136; Friedman 1950), the teaching of "price theory" at the University of Chicago, which Friedman took over from Jacob Viner (Frazer 1988, 180, 182), and his early contacts with Karl Popper at meetings of the Mt. Pelerin Society (Frazer 1988, 107, 115, 117, 119-124, 172-173).

As the larger body of Friedman's work emerges there is a Friedman variant of instrumentalism (Frazer 1984a). Most notably there is a backing away from "economic man axioms" (*modus ponens*) and the move toward the review in which the purpose of the economic apparatus is prediction (*modus tollens*). By way of Mitchell there is a view of testing theories against one another in terms of their explanations and predictions about going from points A and B to the economic goals (Figure 4.1).

In the 1953 essay, Friedman emphasizes "the class of phenomena the hypothesis is designed to explain" (1953a, 13–14) and notes the implications of hypotheses as well as their axioms (synonymous with assumptions). He raises questions about whether the axioms (assumptions) are "sufficiently good approximations for the purpose in hand" (1953a, 15). He says that whether they are depends on whether the theory works and on the predictions it yields. Friedman then goes on to offer some positive remarks under three headings about the significance and role of assumptions—(a) as an economic mode of stating a theory, (b) as an indirect test of a theory, and (c) as a convenient means of specifying the conditions under which the theory applies in a valid way. Under the "economic mode" heading, we note references to "crucial assumptions" as a means of getting at key elements of an abstract model. However, there are different possible sets of postulates, definitions, and even undefined words which imply a model or are implied by it that are logically equivalent. Consequently, the axioms and definitions of a model from one point of view may be regarded as conclusions or theorems from another, so, given this possibility of interchanging theorems and axioms, there is some flexibility in viewing the model and in judging its assumptions indirectly from overall performance (Friedman 1953, 23–24). Even with his overall review of the concept and role of "assumptions" Friedman says, "The very concept of the 'assumptions' of a theory is surrounded by ambiguity" (1953a, 23).

Against this background to the essay, it would be inevitable that Friedman would address arguments about truth in positive economics as it bore on the detailed descriptive truth of axioms and the popular practice of the early post-World War II years of looking for the truth content of price theory in terms of a detailed microscopic view of its axioms. This would be the case particularly in two areas: that of the institutional economics rooted in Thorstein Veblen's attacks on neoclassical economics and another that focused on the question of the truth of the homogenous-products axiom from the theory of the perfect market (Chamberlin 1948; Frazer 1994a, 68–71; Friedman 1953a; 38 n.33; Robinson 1933).

In fact, Friedman has a good bit of interest in institutions as traditions and practices, and in behavior as I link it to John Dewey, Thorstein Veblen, and Wesley Mitchell, as well as in the "economic psychology" I turn to. But over the post-World War II years, through the latter phases of controversy surrounding "the famous essay," that was not what the special group of institutional economists perceived. A paradox emerges and comes forward in Chapter 4, namely, that the institutionalists who claim roots in the work of John

Dewey, Thorstein Veblen, and Wesley Mitchell come to attack vehemently Friedman's advancements of the economics found in his Mitchell-connected/NBER work. We ask why and turn to the paradox of Chapter 4.

In Chapter 5, axioms and predictions are presented to elucidate further the famous essay. There I turn to James Tobin's liquidity preferences demand for money and the Friedman-system view I offer. Attention is given to the phenomena the alternative theories address, and even to institutional considerations. I add to Friedman's work the relevance of central bank operations in the monetary area, to which Friedman turns in the famous essay (Friedman 1953a, 41–42) and in later research.

Two hypotheses related to these operations and theoretical works are as follows:

H_{CB}. *The central banks*: Traditions, operating procedures, and accounting controls influence the choice of economic theory on which government bases its central banking financial markets policies. (Note: The choice of a theory on which to implement policy may have not only political overtones but dependence on accounting arrangements, for accounting control purposes, and on past practices and traditions, including constitutional and statutory matters.)

H_{TW}. *The theoretical works*: Underlying the theoretical works, such as Keynes's *General Theory* and Friedman and Schwartz's *Monetary Trends*, are implied views of central banking arrangements, policy approaches, and the means of intervention into the money market (Frazer 1994b, 3).

In the famous essay, Friedman makes points about the "indirect evidence" in support of a theory. He is actually quite eclectic here as regards history and a host of other sorts of information in Chapter 6, we will introduce indirect evidence and "expected returns," as taken up in the famous essay, and the bond trader I turn to after Friedman and Schwartz report structural changes underlying the formation of inflationary expectations. The points found in Friedman's essay regarding indirect evidence are as follows: a theory is accepted because it works, direct evidence is strengthened by indirect evidence, evidence is scattered in "numerous memorandums, articles and monographs," evidence supporting one class of phenomena may be supported by evidence from a very different class of phenomena, and choice among alternative assumptions depends in part on their capacity to bring indirect evidence to bear on the validity of the hypothesis (Friedman 1953a, 20, 22–23, 28, 40–41).

Not to be dated by the essay, the points are repeated in Friedman's rebuttal (with Schwartz, 1991) to charges regarding FS's evidence raised by David Hendry and Neil Ericsson (1991) to which I turn in Chapter 7, "Analyses of Data." In Chapter 8 I address Friedman's critics as they react to the famous essay and my article (with Lawrence Boland, 1983). In particular there is an interplay of the philosophy and Friedman's special uses of statistical methods, even when we accept Webb's definition of "philosophy of science" (Webb 1987, 396), as I do (Frazer and Boland 1983; Frazer 1988, 107–136): namely, the formal meaning of "methodology" concerns the philosophy of science and not, as often occurs in economics, the use of statistical methods (Webb 1987, 314–315). However, as indicated earlier and as pointed out by Wible (Frazer 1988, 134–136; Wible 1984, 1057–1661), one must look to Friedman's unusual uses of statistical methods in economics to discern a philosophy of science. Indeed, the philosophy resides in what he does.

I agree with Webb the critic (1987, 329), who says, "There is no indication that Friedman had much acquaintance with the then–contemporary issues in the philosophy of science." Especially in the case of the philosopher John Dewey, with whom many link Friedman as a philosopher (Hirsch and de Marchi, 1990; Wible 1984), there is only an indirect link via Wesley Mitchell, as shown in Chicago I (Figure 1.3). From this perspective and others, I will turn later to James Webb's critical piece, which (according to Wible 1987, 355) argues in support of institutional economics as the preferred economic ideology.

Chapter 4

Institutional Economics, Friedman, and Selected Critics

Referring to the founders of American institutional economics, Philip Klein (1978, 252) names a few and quotes Paul Samuelson, who pointed to Thorstein Veblen and Wesley Mitchell as the greatest institutionalists. By no coincidence, these two are identified in Figure 1.4 under the heading "Chicago I." Most short lists of the early institutionalists would also include John R. Commons. Indeed, in the spring of 1940, the Friedmans were pleased to anticipate the move to the University of Wisconsin, where Friedman taught during the 1940–1941 school year. The assignment at Wisconsin appeared ideal at the time: "Good teaching jobs coming out of the 1930s were scarce, and . . . the department of Wisconsin had been brought to a level of national prominence through the work of John R. Commons in the areas of institutional and labor economics." These areas had some compatibility with Wesley Mitchell's and the National Bureau's orientation during the Mitchell/Friedman era at the Bureau. Indeed, the names Commons and Mitchell are commonly linked with what may be described as "the American contribution" to economics before World War II (Frazer 1988, 163).

The professional organization for more-contemporary American institutionalists became the Association for Evolutionary Economics (AFEE)—a name taken from Thorstein Veblen's essay "Why Is Economics not an Evolutionary Science?" (Frazer 1978, 345). The *Journal of Economic Issues* (*JEI*) began in 1966 as the principal organ for the association. However, the ties to the institutionalists roots have not been very strictly adhered to, with the consequence that the earlier prospects fractured and went in different directions as many identifying with the early institutional economics became more uniquely ideological and less directed at influencing the main body of economics.

Among the highly visible post–World War II figures who could readily identify with the institutionalist beginnings were John Kenneth Galbraith (Frazer 1988, 140, 194–204, 240, 265–269) and Milton Friedman, via his direct ties to Mitchell, Simon Kuznets, and the National Bureau, on the one hand, and an indirect identification with the American philosopher John Dewey, on the other. While Galbraith gained reputation as a skilled and persuasive writer and remained somewhat of a debunker of pretentiousness, Friedman's efforts were directed at influencing the direction of mainstream economics as were Wesley Mitchell's.

In 1978, the AFEE group's president lamented the absence of a coherent view among American institutionalists and said, no doubt with justification, "We mostly are ignored" (Klein 1978, 254–255). Indeed, James Wible (1987, 438) mentions a "preferred economic ideology—institutional economics"—after encounters with some critics (Liebhafsky and Liebhafsky 1985; Webb 1987).

From the perspective of a preferred economic ideology, institutional economists confront Milton Friedman on three fronts with which AFEE members are identified. Although Friedman removed himself from the identification with so-called economic man axioms and Robinson Crusoe economics as his career got under way (Frazer 1988, 30, 34, 118–122, 125, 277, 293; 1994a, 6, 13, 68), a main front for the institutionalists has been criticism of axioms in economics which could readily be attacked by them because of the identification of those axioms with "economic man" and neoclassical and Robinson Crusoe economics (Frazer 1988, 306).[1]

In an invited lecture before an AFEE group, Rexford Tugwell mentioned studies, noted the outdated axioms, pointed to "the intense study of economic behavior," and paradoxically pointed to analysis led by Wesley Mitchell (Tugwell 1978, 243), with whom Friedman is closely identified. On the subject of the axioms Tugwell said:

Early in this century the studies of certain psychologists—E. L. Thorndike, J. B. Watson, Walter Cannon, William McDougall, L. M. Terman, and A. A. Brill, to name only a few—undermined the assumptions of laissez-faire economics. When individuals were closely observed, they turned out to behave not at all in the rational manner required to support the marginal utility theory. . . . The idiosyncrasies of individuals would have made severely logical behavior unusual. . . . The necessary assumptions of laissez-faire were left in tatters, and economists began to speak of "administered" prices. (Tugwell 1978, 243)

Confronting an outdated emphasis on economic man axioms, a sizable portion of AFEE economists chose to direct even more intense criticism at the axioms of the perfect market and, by so doing, to cut a niche for themselves in the highly political area of microeconomics and antitrust. Especially this group embraced government regulation via such theories as those of Edward Chamberlin in the United States (1948) and Joan Robinson in England (1933). In doing this, they began to attack Friedman aggressively as a neoclassicist. They chose to see his backing away from the economic axioms as nothing more than a defense of neoclassical economics, which itself had become an institutionalist "whipping boy." At the same time these institutionalists ignored the routes Friedman had taken to depart from the axioms and move into behavioral economics, as influenced by Wesley Mitchell's general orientation and special work on business cycles and money. Convenient though the false image of Friedman may be, it is inaccurate and does not reflect Friedman's response to the Marshallian demand curve, Keynesian liquidity preference demand for money, and the Keynes/Keynesian consumption function.

Another front on which the ideological institutionalists in effect confronted Friedman presented itself much later, in regard to the exogeneity of the money stock. Taking a Keynesian and post-Keynesian stand on the endogeneity of the money stock, ideological institutionalists both embrace the post Keynesian work of Nicholas Kaldor (Frazer 1994b, 87–91, 103–104; Hodson, 1991) and larger roles for detailed intervention into the economy by government.

We may ask why this group of institutional economists chose to ignore the behavioral component in Friedman's work. The answer is that the ideology regarding the traditional *modus ponens* is more important to them in their attack on neoclassical economics than the study of behavior, particularly where uses of statistical methods may enter (as taken up in Chapter 5).

Even as some fringe institutionalists identify Friedman with the behaviorist John Dewey (Hirsch and de Marchi; Wible 1984, 1987), albeit indirectly, they are unable to give up the false charge that Friedman is a neoclassical economist. Doubtless the reason is that they still cling to the charges Veblen made about economics in the nineteenth century and to the status he gained in doing so.

Among the critics of Friedman, the one to mount a lengthy charge against his famous 1953 essay is James Webb (1987), who also questions even the indirect identification of Friedman with Dewey. Taking a strong institutional-economics AFEE stand (as we indicate in Chapter 8), Webb and others look narrowly at Friedman's essay and thus avoid any engagement with the sophisticated uses of statistical methods and the larger picture of his life and work, which sheds some light on the essay.

In light of continued controversy, this chapter takes up the essay again in some detail. In the next chapter, I discuss the uses of statistical methods. In Chapter 8, Webb's views about Friedman's famous essay are discussed.

Friedman's 1953 essay (Friedman 1953a; Frazer 1988, 695, 724, 731) was quite widely written about (Boland 1979; 1980; Caldwell 1980; 1982; Frazer and Boland 1983; Rotwin 1980), even before the spate of controversy that appeared in response to Frazer and Boland (Boland 1984; Hirsch and de Marchi, 1984; Hoover 1984b; Liebhafsky and Liebhafsky 1985; Webb 1987; Wible 1984; 1985; 1987). Regarding the pre-1979 mass of responses to

Friedman's essay, Caldwell said (1980, 366) it "is probably the best-known piece of methodological writing in the discipline [economics]."

After the Frazer and Boland piece appeared some responses (Hirsch and de Marchi; Hoover 1984) reviewed some of the philosophical positions that were rather more specific to Boland and philosophical issues in general than to Frazer and Boland (Frazer 1984).

In 1984 and later (Frazer 1988, 107–136, 172–180), I pointed out the following: that Milton Friedman did not himself advocate the formal philosophical positions that were surfacing; that he preferred doing economics to talking about it; that the links to the philosopher Karl Popper were partly through personal contact via the Mt. Pelerin Society; and that to enlarge upon the philosophy of science that was sketched in the essay one must examine what Friedman actually did in economics.

As I have pointed out, the working title of the famous essay was "The Relevance of Economic Analysis to Prediction and Policy" (Frazer 1988, 36, 112, 139).   To be sure—in relation to economic analysis, prediction, and policy—Friedman's uses of statistical methods enter in a major way, as I will illustrate step by step. From the perspective obtained in the illustrations, I will turn later to James Webb's critical piece, which, Wible (1987, 355) says, supports institutional economics as a preferred economic ideology.

Further, the essay, which took its final title from the subject matter of John Neville Keynes's work (1891), is not so much about the distinction Friedman drew between positive economics ("what is") and normative economics ("what ought to be") in the early pages of the essay as it is about his indirect approach to the use of mechanical apparatus and statistical methods. The title of *Essays in Positive Economics*, in which the essay appears, more accurately reflects the collection of essays, because the distinction J. N. Keynes drew (1891) needed restating at the time of the collection and because the final reprinted essay "Lerner on the Economics of Control" called for the distinction between Lerner's book (1944) and the study of observations about "what is." Indeed, in a 1953 class taught by Abraham Bergson at Columbia, the Lerner book was the text and the distinctions Friedman makes were omitted. In an introductory paragraph to his review of Lerner (1944), Friedman says:

Most of the book is devoted to the formal analysis of the conditions for an optimum. The institutional problems are largely neglected and, where introduced, treated by assertion rather than analysis.   This disparity in the attention devoted to the formal and institutional problems is, however, obscured by an intermingling of the formal and institutional analysis. Formal analysis takes on the cast of institutional proposals, and conclusions about institutional arrangements seem to be derived from the formal analysis and supported by it, though, in fact, the formal analysis is almost entirely irrelevant to the institutional problem. (Friedman 1953b, 301)[2]

POLICY A, POLICY B, AND THE GOALS

After the one-page introduction in the essay to the work of John Neville Keynes (1891), Friedman turns to a discussion of the role of positive economics in relation to normative economics, which he got from Wesley Mitchell. Relevant passages regarding the next three pages of the essay are, first, from Frazer and Boland (1983, 130):

Given alternative policies A and B (for example, a Keynesian interest rate control policy vs. a Friedmanian monetary aggregates Policy . . .), the question was which policy should be selected. Such question of how we get from where we are to the policy goal was thus seen as an empirical question, as one of selecting the most useful theory among available competitors.

A relevant passage from Frazer (1988, 112):

The essay . . . suggested an alternative to conventional methodology, and gave rise to the indirect method (a) in the uses of mechanical constructions found in economics and (b) in the uses of statistics.

The question of "what ought to be" in terms of the choice between policy A or policy B as a means of getting us from where we are to where we want to be was viewed primarily as an empirical question (i.e., as a question of having the most valid theory).

When taken up in Frazer (1994a, 7), we get Figure 4.1 and the following paragraph:

In particular, Friedman saw statistical methods as a means of resolving differences of opinion among economists about how to achieve the economic goals. There would be alternatives A (say, for i-regime, which is identified later) and B (say for M-regime, also identified later) as shown in . . . [Figure 4.1]. The matter was reduced to the best means of achieving the goals. The notion has a parallel to that of testing one hypothesis against another rather than against the naive model, such as encountered in econometrics.

Here we come to the effects of using the mechanical constructs from economics (say, instruments) to predict the effects of policy. Theories are arguments for using one alternative or another to reach the goal. Statistical methods aid in making the choice between the alternative policies for reaching the goal(s). An emphasis on the prediction of effects enters, as does the relevance of the logical alternatives introduced first by Lawrence Boland (1979). Principally, in regards to the famous essay, Boland made note of *modus tollens* as opposed to *modus ponens*. Relevant passages from the essay which bear on these points follow:

Figure 4.1
Policy Alternatives and Economic Goals

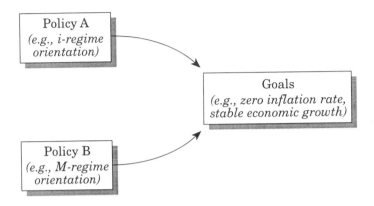

Normative economics and the art of economics, on the other hand, cannot be independent of positive economics. Any policy conclusion necessarily rests on a prediction about the consequences of doing one thing rather than another, a prediction that must be based—implicitly or explicitly—on positive economics. . . .Two individuals may agree on the consequences of a particular piece of legislation. One may regard them as desirable on balance and so favor the legislation; the other, as undesirable and so oppose the legislation.

I venture the judgment, however, that currently in the Western world, and especially in the United States, differences about economic policy among disinterested citizens derive predominantly from different predictions about the economic consequences of taking action—differences that in principle can be eliminated by the progress of positive economics—rather than from fundamental differences in basic values, differences about which men can ultimately only fight. (Friedman (1953, 5)

Reflecting essentially the Mitchell-connected position about the relation of positive to normative economics, Friedman writes of progress in economics and agreement about "policy" (say, A and B in Figure 4.1):

If this judgment is valid, it means that a consensus on "correct" economic policy depends much less on the progress of normative economics proper than on the progress of a positive economics yielding conclusions that are, and deserve to be, widely accepted. It means also that a major reason for distinguishing positive economics sharply from normative economics is precisely the contribution that can thereby be made to agreement about policy. (Friedman 1953, 6–7)

Now, in his early pages, Friedman hints thus:

Laymen and experts alike are inevitably tempted to shape positive conclusions to fit strongly held normative preconceptions and to reject positive conclusions if their normative implications—or what are said to be their normative implications—are unpalatable. (Friedman 1953, 4)

THE USES OF STATISTICAL METHODS

To be sure, Friedman's idea that the resolution of arguments supporting policy A or B in Figure 4.1 would come about through his uses of statistical methods was highly idealistic. In fact, the uses of the statistical methods themselves become highly controversial (Friedman and Schwartz 1991). Although Friedman's uses initially emphasize the simple, few-variables-at-a-time, regression method, they have a considerable amount of sophistication, familiarity with topics such as "the regression fallacy," experience with the use of statistical methods, and a background of observations that led to Friedman's positions and to philosophical twists.

Observing post–World War II controversies and the frequent lack of resolution by either theoretic argument or statistical results (as considered in Chapter 5), I offer the following:

I am reminded of Rose Friedman's challenge (Frazer 1988, 288), which I partly paraphrase, namely, economists' empirical, data-analysis views are readily predicted from knowledge of their political orientation and, she says, "I have never been able to persuade myself that their political orientation was a consequence of the positive [empirical-economic] views." To be sure, I recognize that political and social orientations on the part of economists and others may be significant (and indeed overriding in many cases) in the selection of one or the other approaches of policy oriented economics. (Frazer 1994a, 203)

Predictions Not Yet Observed

Friedman's next major point in the essay regards "predictions about phenomena not yet observed." Here we find a call for predictions outside the sample period (Frazer 1994a, 167, figure 6–6). This statistical matter is perhaps made even clearer in Friedman and Schwartz's response to Hendry and Ericsson (HE 1991): "As already indicated, the real proof of their pudding is whether it produces a satisfactory explanation of data . . . for subsequent or earlier years, for other countries. . . . One example of such a test . . . dramatically illustrates how misleading a multiple regression can be for predictive purposes, even though it satisfies all the standard test" (Friedman and Schwartz 1991, 48).

Identification

The next turn of some substance in the essay is to the strictly statistical problem of identification, which Friedman illustrates most simply in terms of ordinary supply and demand relations for "the final market for a consumer good, on the one hand," and "day-to-day fluctuations of prices in a primarily speculative market," on the other (Friedman 1953a, 7–8). In the first instance, as regards identification (say, the locus of points making up an ordinary demand schedule), Friedman says, "There is a clear and sharp distinction between the economic units that can be regarded as demanding the product and those that can be regarded as supplying it." Continuing, he says, "There is seldom much doubt whether a particular factor should be classified as affecting supply, on the one hand, or demand, on the other." But then, he notes, the generalization is not always valid, as he points to the speculative markets:

Is a rumor of an increased excess-profits tax, for example, to be regarded as a factor operating primarily on today's supply of corporate equities in the stock market or on today's demand for them? In similar fashion, almost every factor can with about as much justification be classified under the heading "supply" as under the heading "demand." (Friedman 1953a, 8)

Now, in choosing which of the cases applies, only factual evidence can show which is right or wrong, and such empirical evidence may be difficult to interpret, as Friedman says, "It is frequently complex and always indirect and incomplete." The interpretations of such data in economics, as opposed to physical sciences, "generally requires subtle analysis and involves chains of reasoning, which seldom carry real conviction."[3] Taking note of disturbing outside (or episodic) conditions, Friedman says (1953a, 10), "No experiment can be completely controlled, and every experiment is partly controlled, in the sense that some disturbing influences are relatively constant in the course of it."[4]

Some of the difficulties plaguing empirical science then fall under the technical problem of identification of the phenomena and episodic impacts such as a rumored "excess-profits tax, among others." So, as Friedman turns to the identification of money demand as opposed to the money supply (a stock), he proceeds "indirectly" to deal with the problem of pinning down the apparatus empirically (FS 1982, 32–36). This is in lieu of identifying an ordinary Keynesian liquidity preference curve, which is simply presented with the presumption of a central-bank-controlled, long-term bond rate (i) and a money-demand function of that rate, $M = f(i)$, ceteris paribus (Frazer 1994a, 33–37). Generally, locked up in ceteris paribus is income (Y), so that variously we have a money stock (M_d) demanded in one case and a money stock supplied in another (M_s). With the income constant (i.e., locked up in ceteris paribus, where some other variables may also reside), changes in the long-bond rate parallel changes in the velocity of money ($\pm\Delta_L \rightarrow \pm\Delta Y/M$, causation implied). Now, this view is no earthshaking matter, except it implies that the long-bond rate is controlled, directly and exclusively of any prospect of inflation and more specifically the expected inflation rate ($\dot{P}^e$). Further, there is an idea that the curve [or function, $M_d = f(i)$] has some counterpart in the real world that can be isolated.

To be sure, this carries no conviction for Friedman, and, consequently, as with the Marshallian demand curve, he proceeds "indirectly" to deal with the identification problem, as well as with policy and causal matters. The policy here resides in a presumption about the central bank's direct control over the money stock (M) and a fairly complicated money demand analysis, although by comparison with conomics, Friedman kept it simple.[5] Most notably, as regards identification, the central bank controls the nominal money stock (M), and households control the real, price-level (P) adjusted money stock (M/P) by turning over the stock of money balances faster ("actual M" greater than "desired M," and $\Delta Y/M$) or slower ("actual M" less than "desired M," and $-\Delta Y/M$). So here money demand is identified with household spending more or less until the turnover of the money stock is constant (Y/M = constant).

This money demand is dependent on all the motives J. M. Keynes attached to the holding of money balances (Frazer 1994a, 47–49),[6] and on expected rates of return on four classes of assets (Frazer 1994a, 40–47).[7] Also, special time frames enter (such as cycles of the Mitchell-related NBER sort and secular trends, as in Frazer 1994a, 23–26), and, initially, Friedman reported lags in the impact of accelerated (decelerated) money growth on income and interest rates, where the rate on long-term bonds is equal to the real rate of interest plus the expected inflation rate (Frazer 1994a, 40–47, 170–175).[8]

So, the policy links were changed and the analytical apparatus of liquidity preference was redirected. This change was in part also directed at the statistical identification of money demand as distinct from monetary policy (Frazer 1994a, 94–116).

FACTUAL EVIDENCE AND FRIEDMAN

Recalling that Friedman thought factual evidence would lead to a choice between alternative hypotheses for the economists he had in mind (those who shared his values, et cetera), in two important instances Friedman changed his position when he confronted changes in the factual evidence. To provide background to the first, I draw on the 1946 correspondence of Friedman and E. B. Wilson (Stigler 1994), who was a prominent physics and statistics professor who was also revered by the economist Paul Samuelson during his student days at Harvard (Frazer 1988, 88). In November and December 1946 Wilson wrote to Friedman in response to the latter's review of a 1944 book by Oscar Lange (Friedman's review was about methodology; it is reprinted in *Essays in Positive Economics,* (1953b, 277–300.) Wilson also inquired about good empirical works in economics that Friedman could recommend.

In responding to Wilson's request, Friedman limited himself to works he was most familiar with at the time. Three of the five he listed are the following:

1.   W. C. Mitchell, *Business Cycles* (1913) in contrast to the 1927 book which is pretty neutral.

2.   A. F. Burns and W. C. Mitchell, *Measuring Business Cycles*, National Bureau of Economic Research (1946).

3.   A. F. Burns, *Production Trends in the United States*, National Bureau of Economic Research (Stigler 1994, 1200).

However, after research on the United States and the United Kingdom in *Monetary Trends* (1982, 588–620), FS reported that the omission of monetary phenomenon they found cast a negative light on Burns's work and some of the latter studies on long swings in business conditions (Frazer 1994a, 219–225). FS said that Burns and the others had stayed in "well-worn ruts" and thus had omitted the predominance of "decidedly larger amplitude of the swings in money and nominal income than in real income" (FS 1982, 602).   Thus Friedman changed his favorable position about Burns's *Production Trends* work.

Friedman went on in his December 16 letter to Wilson to express uncertainty regarding Henry Schultz's "measurement of demand" study, although Friedman had "rendered invaluable assistance" to Schultz on the study in the school year 1934–1935 (Schultz 1938, xi).   Friedman said:

It [the Schultz work] is an exceedingly careful and systematic attempt to put empirical content into a pre-existing theory. I have excluded it because there seems to me no reverse influence of the empirical work on the theoretical structure. Schultz took the theory as fixed and given, and tried to measure what he thought were essential functions in the theory. He imposed extremely high standards of care and thoroughness in the measurement process—but he nowhere attempted what seems to me the fundamentally important task of reformulating the theory so it would really generalize the observable data; *he always tried to wrench the data into a pre-existing theoretical scheme, no matter how much of a wrench was required* (Stigler 1944, 1200).

As the post–World War II period proceeded, there were, to be sure, many examples of economists' "wrenching the data into a pre-existing theoretical scheme."

A second example of Friedman's changing prior positions in response to factual evidence (and examples are not limited to two) appears in FS's *Monetary Trends*.   There FS had sought repetition as to the impact of accelerated money growth on income and interest rates.   For the most part, there was a lag in the impacts and this entered into the framing of the theory; in other words, the empirical science they wanted depended on the lag in the impacts.   But now FS reported that to their disappointment the lag structure changed in the mid-1960s: that is, the structure underlying the formation of inflationary expectations changed (Frazer 1988, 447; FS 1982, 11, 478, 479–480, 558–573). This meant especially (1) that the bond traders who set the price (and therefore the interest rate) on the long-term bonds became more responsive and sensitive to the processing of information regarding the inflationary outlook and (2) that the inflation-rate-related shifts in the money stock and income (in other terms, M/Y) occurred more immediately. To elaborate, the crucial interest rate and money-turnover rate were both responding to inflation prospects more immediately. The door was opened in fact for a much more immediate analysis of expectations, which I have called "the Friedman system" (1994a, xx; 1994b, xiv) and which I treat in *The Friedman System.*

TESTING IMPLICATIONS OF HYPOTHESES, EXPLANATIONS, AND REALITY OF ASSUMPTIONS

We see best the way Friedman proceeds to establish a philosophical base for the rather complex subject of economics, as he viewed it, by first restating aspects of his background. With respect to the background, the mathematics statistics component via Harold Hotelling, the Statistical Research Group, and Leonard Savage is highly visible in Figure 1.2, in combination with the Mitchell/institutionalist/empirical-science background sketched in Figure 1.4. In addition, we have given note to the "engine of analysis"/instrumentalist component of the background and to Friedman's view of the unanimity regarding "basic values" as opposed to Rose Friedman's challenge.

First, in regard to the mathematics, it gives rise to tautologies (Friedman 1953a, 7, 11, 26)—axioms, theorems, proofs, and, indeed, the logical process may be reversed, hence the tautologies.[9] However, this process of reversing the logic is disrupted when one turns to the mechanical structure of economics, opts for simplicity in the hypothesis/theoretic statements, and adopts Friedman's instrumentalist view (as in Frazer 1984).[10]

Further, the mechanical structure of economics lends itself to serving simply as "disguised mathematics" (1953a, 12). Analysts sensing the difficulty of conducting fruitful economic experiments can readily be drawn into this mathematical haven.

Sensing a way out of this misleading circle with its emphasis on disruptive details, Friedman introduces the fruitful empirical hypothesis which may be tested by its implications and, at the same time, notes that the disguised mathematics may give rise to efforts at detailed descriptions of the world rather than relatively more simple (and hence abstract) and fruitful notions. In breaking the cycle of the disguised mathematics and avoiding descriptive detail, Friedman leans on the "engine of analysis"/instrumentalist part of his background; in doing so, he opts for hypotheses as predictors and shifts away from strong reliance on the truth of axioms which economists had adopted. Friedman says that the difficulty in finding the fruitfulness in the implications of the hypotheses in the social sciences gives rise to the prospect of another way of proceeding. It is that of supposing that hypotheses have assumptions and "that the conformity of 'assumptions' to 'reality' is a test of the validity of the hypothesis *different from* or *additional to* the test by implications" (Friedman 1953a, 13).

Furthermore, Friedman was surely aware that assumptions in economics could not apply in his strictly empirical sense and that extremely unrealistic or arbitrary axioms would not guarantee a significant theory (Friedman 1953a, 12, 14). But, in the first sense, assumptions could give rise to fruitful and useful prospects. One assumption found in Marshall was that of the measurement of utility and the derivation of the demand curve in terms of the declining marginal utility of additions to the household's purchase of a given commodity. In Friedman's empirical sense, he could point to the ordinary and the compensated demand curve and relate the distinction to a price index and the terms of the index (Frazer 1994a, 13–19). Here a rise (decline) in the index represented the loss (gain) of real income to the household, and these losses (and gains) were measurable in the price-index terms.

Another assumption, that of the "homogenous product," was related by Friedman to various groups of firms making up Marshallian industries. Firms in these industries could have differences in products as revealed by detailed descriptions and retain an industry classification (Friedman 1953a, 38). Where efforts were to be made to view small product differences as leading to separate products and separate industries for each product, an industry and groups of firms making up industries could not be identified in the sense of statistical categories (say, transportation, automobiles, and so on).

Now, especially in this latter instance of the "homogenous product" axiom, we get the theory of the perfect market (Frazer 1994a, 68–71) with which we can, in turn, identify the theory of relative prices (p_1, relative to p_2, p_2 relative to p_3, and so on, for goods that may substitute for one another). By Friedman's standard this theory is abstract and predicts in a fruitful way. It says, for example, that if the price of one brand of automobile declines relative to that of another brand, the quantity demanded of the reduced-price brand will increase. The price relatives say a lot about the production and allocation of goods, especially in instances where inflation (deflation) does not distort the messages being sent by the relative prices (Frazer 1994a, 63–68).

Once considerable detail regarding the so-called homogenous product is introduced and once product differences make for numerous distinct industries for which we have no statistical category, then the theory loses its simplicity and fruitfulness. The analyst is set on a course of descriptive detail. Meaningful empirical counterparts to the theory and understanding of it are forgone.

The understanding of the theory centers upon "the class of phenomena the hypothesis is designed to explain" (Friedman 1953a, 13, 14). For Friedman the purpose is "empirical science" (prediction à la relative prices, and so on). For another body of economics noted earlier as "microeconomics" in a bottom cell of Figure 1.4, the purposes are antitrust, government intervention in markets, and maximizing of the allocation of consumer surplus to households. Also, at this point, different views of the public's welfare enter as well as ideological differences, as illustrated in Frazer by the introduction of opposing Chicago and Harvard views (1988, 281–325).

Presently, I offer no new description of these views. However, as Friedman went about his business, Lawrence Boland provided an effective logical defense of Friedman's views on axioms and predictions in Friedman's famous essay (Boland 1979; Frazer, 1988, 114–115). He presented the concepts of logic and reverse logic by introducing the terms *modus ponens* and *modus tollens*; the latter identified with Friedman's empirical orientation. Boland also clarified somewhat Friedman's "as if" methodology, as it was called. Correctly stated, a prediction is "as if" the predicted behavior followed from the axioms (and not "as if" the axioms were true).

As to simplicity, the theory of the perfect market was surely that, and the possible fruitfulness of the theory of relative prices appeared acceptable for Friedman's purposes. In addition, for Friedman the basic Cambridge expression that accompanied the quantity theory of money and passed through J. M. Keynes's hands had potential for empirical study. Indeed, Friedman was to remedy the matter of its weakness by proceeding along the liquidity preference lines introduced earlier. But in 1953 he said the following:

The weakest and least satisfactory part of the current economic theory seems to me to be in the field of monetary dynamics, which is concerned with the process of adaptation of the economy as a whole to changes in conditions and so with short-period fluctuations in aggregate activity. In this field we do not even have a theory that can appropriately be called "the" existing theory of monetary dynamics. (Friedman 1953a, 42)

Whatever restatements of the quantity theory eventually emerged, a paragraph in Friedman's essay gave rise to considerable controversy and conflicted with vested positions taken by many economists. That paragraph follows:

In so far as a theory can be said to have "assumptions" at all, and in so far as their "realism" can be judged independently of the validity of predictions, the relation between the significance of a theory and the "realism" of its "assumptions" is almost the opposite of that suggested by the view under criticism. Truly important and significant hypotheses will be found to have "assumptions" that are *wildly inaccurate descriptive representations of reality* [italics added], and, in general, the more significant the theory, the more unrealistic the assumptions (in this sense [of descriptive detail]). The reason is simple. A hypothesis is important if it "explains" much by little, that is, if it abstracts the common and crucial elements from the mass of complex and detailed circumstances surrounding the phenomena to be explained and permits valid predictions on the basis of them alone. To be important, therefore, a hypothesis must be descriptively false in its assumptions; it takes account of, and accounts for, none of the many other attendant circumstances, since its very success shows them to be irrelevant for the phenomena to be explained. (Friedman 1953a, 14–15)

The major areas of the conflict with vested interests were twofold, and Friedman introduced both as examples of bad economics. The first concerned market structure notions identified with Edward Chamberlin of Harvard, in which he had called into question the axiom of the homogeneous product in the theory of the perfect market. Questioning the truth of axioms in terms of descriptive detail, Friedman saw the new market-structures works as examples of bad economic theory. However with hindsight we may say that Chamberlin, Joan Robinson, and their legions of later followers had purposes different from Friedman's. Their purpose was normative/regulatory economics and not the search for fruitful, empirically valid hypotheses.

John Kenneth Galbraith—an erstwhile student of Thorstein Veblen's work, a price controller for a time during World War II, and a long-term tenured professor at Harvard (Frazer 1988, 191–204)—provides a good example of an early reaction to the truth of the axioms found in the neoclassical theory of price. Confronting them, he backed away entirely from the usefulness of the received economics and went on to write persuasively about institutions, economics, and economists. On the other hand, confronting the same axioms and the new market-structures works, Friedman went on to write his famous 1953 essay. He then backed away from the truth content of the economic man axioms entirely and–in so doing–offered an instrumentalist/ *modus tollens* view with added attention to observed behavior.

Friedman and his followers aside, the AFEE institutionalists and some others coming out of the Thorstein Veblen era and beyond made careers debunking the "economic man" orientation, as Veblen did. So, as another example of the criticism of economic theory as unrealistic, Friedman turned to Veblen (1898) and Oliver (1947) using material from Veblen and then Oliver:

Economics is a "dismal" science because it assumes man to be selfish and money-grubbing, "a lightning calculator of pleasures and pains, who oscillates like a homogeneous globule of desire of happiness under the impulse of stimuli that shift him about the area, but leave him intact"; it rests on outmoded psychology and must be reconstructed in line with each new development in psychology; it assumes men, or at least businessmen, to be "in a continuous state of 'alert,' ready to change prices and/or pricing rules whenever their sensitive intuitions . . . detect a change in demand and supply conditions"; it assumes markets to be perfect, competition to be pure, and commodities, labor, and capital to be homogeneous. (Friedman 1953a, 30–31)

Now, Friedman's approach, which incorrectly came to be seen as a defense of neoclassical economics, departed dramatically in fact from it, including as it relates to the behavioral psychological notions and the role of money.[11] Indeed, as the Friedman system unfolds, it introduces more psychology into economics than AFEE/institutional economists perceive, even in their own institutional/Veblen based orientation. However, in order to maintain their perceived superiority over economists as dismal scientists they could not abandon their perceptions. Instead, they insisted on seeing Friedman's 1953 essay as a defense of neoclassical economics, and thus falsely dismissed him as a neoclassical economist, while failing to see that he had in fact moved economics in the direction of behavioral/interdisciplinary study in the social sciences as set on its course by the Chicago I group (Figure 1.4).

NOTES

1. "Economic man axioms" are largely the extreme-value axioms of economics such as utility maximization and profit maximization. At a time when some special truth was thought to reside in the assumptions of economics (*modus ponens* and all) the implication was that the resulting structure of economics found its truth content via the truth of the assumptions (syn. "axioms"), and that the axioms extended to the view of the human as greedy, atomistic Homosapiens. Friedman departs from this by adopting an instrumentalist view whereby the purpose of economics is prediction (say, predicting the effects of accelerated money growth on spending after allowance for velocity ratio, or predicting the effects of an episode on the spending behavior).

As one may guess, the label "Robinson Crusoe economics" (Frazer 1988, 306, 445) is a reference to the hero of Daniel Defoe's 1719 novel about the sailor who, shipwrecked on an island, survives by various ingenious contrivances. In economics the label applies to the view of man with a ready-made cultural background, habits of thought and all, who operates somewhat in isolation (atomistically, say). The American philosopher John Dewey and the economist Thorstein Veblen, and Wesley Mitchell who followed them, saw behavior differently.

In the extreme we could apply the label to that body of economics that is locked up in ceteris paribus ("all other things," including episodic changes as well as traditions, operating procedures, and means of control such as encountered in Frazer 1994b, 3, 76, 77, 80, 135, 168, 172–173, 179, 206, 239–240 n.12), as it considers prices, production, and much more.

2. The paragraph indicates Friedman's interest in "institutional problems" and "institutional analysis." The institutional economists considered in this chapter would, to be sure, prefer to ignore such interests.

3. In Chapter 12 I deal with bond traders and interest rates in linking President Clinton's health care reform plans to interest rates. The account, I believe, is quite accurate, but it does entail chains of reasoning. As the chapter may indicate, I do not think "truth" will be simple and direct when and if it is ever found in economics.

4. For the 1970s and 1980s, for which I have analyzed U.S., U.K., and F.R.G. data, I conclude that unfortunately disturbing outside conditions are more the norm than controlled experiments (Frazer 1994a, 1994b). For a list of important episodes in these decades, see Frazer (1994a, 88).

Simply focusing on the results for these decades is adequate to suggest the virtual impossibility of finding stable statistical relations using conventional—and possibly any—econometric methods that rely on a controlled experiment environment, over any extended periods, such as found in FS's works.

5. Friedman's approach to keeping the economics simple was different to be sure, but perhaps not really so simple. First, the traditional way of keeping the economics simple is the method of ceteris paribus, and/or the invocation of the presumption of "independent" variables (Frazer 1994a, 14–15, 20–21, 50, 63, 88, 138–139) where we encounter what I call the separation-of-effects problem (Frazer 1994a, 29, 49–51, 134–135, 146, 165; 1994b, 55–57.

Second, the Friedman approach was to analyze a few variables at a time, to package a marid of simple results, to rely in part on independent evidence, and to arrive at a simply stated rule (e.g., inflation is everywhere and everyplace a monetary phenomenon). To this approach the Friedman system adds learning on the part of economic agents, makes more explicit the place of psychological time, and adds "open-ended closeness" (as defined on later occasions) to obtain a cross-section and virtually timeless state among other features.

6. These motives may be listed:

1. Transactions motive (tide agent over from one pay period to the next)

2. Speculative motive (realize gains, avoid losses—bonds, stocks, real goods; also probability as uncertainty)

3. Precautionary motive (probability as uncertainty: means of dealing with an uncertain and unforeseen future)

Of course, "[T]here is no known way of directly separating and/or identifying the pools of money that may correspond to the transactions (M_T), precautionary (M_P), and speculative (M_S) motives for holding them. Rather, there is the concept $M_T/Y + M_P/Y + M_S/Y = M/Y$," where Y is income, M/Y is the Cambridge k, and k is the inverse of the velocity-of-money ratio. This is such that

changes in velocity can simply be said to occur for one or another reasons that most likely relate to episodes. For FS in *Monetary Trends*, changing financial sophistication in the United States before 1903 would be an example of a change in the transactions demand. The precautionary demand may arise over some government induced uncertainty, or military encounters such as the Iraqi invasion of Kuwait and the rise in oil prices in August of 1990, just when the U.S. economy was on the brink of a possible recession. (Frazer 1994a, 47–48)

7. The money demand prospect may be denoted $M/P = f(Y/P, w; \ldots; u)$. The "w" is a measure of liquidity, M/P and Y/P imply the inverse of velocity [$(M/P)/(Y/P) = M/Y$, and $M/Y = 1/(Y/M)$], w is a measure of liquidity, u is a catch-all variable for matters of secondary importance, and the three dots "$\ldots$" represent expected rates of return on four classes of assets:

r_m^e the expected nominal rate of return on money

r_B^e the expected nominal rate of return on fixed-value securities, including changes in their prices

r_E^e the expected nominal rate of return on equities, including expected changes in their prices

r_R^e the expected rate of return on physical or residual-claim assets in terms of any direct income they yield (or storage costs they impose), plus the expected rate of change of prices of goods and services (i.e., the expected inflation rate, $[1/P][dP/dt]$*

8. The equation is denoted $i_L = i(real) + \dot{P}^e$. The factor $Pb[\dot{P}^e]$, the probability of the expected outcome, is added to the last term in Frazer (1994a, 113, 135; 1994b, 25, 106). The equation then in effect reads $i_L = i(real) + Pb[\dot{P}^e] \dot{P}^e$.

9. On the tautological nature of the mathematics, see also Frazer (1988, 718–719).

10. As regards Friedman's variant of instrumentalism, there is a weak connection to the philosopher Karl Popper.

11. For further statements along this line, see Frazer and Guthrie (1995, 87).

Chapter 5

Analysis, Axioms, and the Liquidity Preference Constructions

Although the use of static constructions known as schedules has been a source of strength in economics since Alfred Marshall's work, an analytical/statistical problem arises from it. First, there is a phase where initiatives are undertaken to gather and collect data. This is best represented as judged by later results and initial efforts by Wesley Mitchell and the NBER of his era (Figures 1.2 and 1.4). Not only did Mitchell promote the first efforts at reporting price indexes in the United States, the Bureau also supported the development of national income accounts by the later Nobel laureate Simon Kuznets (Frazer 1988, 99). Of course, Mitchell's goal and that of his Bureau was not simply to gather and promote the collections of data, but do this with the view to confronting the a priori constructions of economics with the facts. I note that this phase of the Bureau's work culminated in Milton Friedman's publications (often coauthored with Anna Schwartz).

Second, there is an econometric phase (identification and all that, text, pages 55–57). Although it gained considerable fashion and popularity in economics curricula and even appears as a fashionable way of thinking (Figure 2.1), I have singled out the Nobel laureate Lawrence Klein as a representative (Figure 1.2).

Its heavy reliance on the assumption of the independence of the right-hand-side variables in single simple and multiple regression equations and/or in solution equations to the multiequation/multivariable models no doubt sustained this fashion in econometrics. This assumption, I have pointed out, has a compatibility with the use of the term ceteris paribus in the common, static a priori constructions encountered in economics. Consequently, econometrics in its early stages offered to some the twofold prospect—that even the act itself of going through the econometric way of thinking imposed good mental discipline and that the effects of selected variables could be separated and found to support effects implied in the static a priori constructions. For example, we encounter the Marshallian demand schedule, where the quantity demanded of a commodity is a function of the commody's price, q = f(p, ceteris paribus). Also, as appears in James Tobin's liquidity preference construction, the stock of money balances demanded depends on the rate of interest, M = f(i), where a choice between holding money balances or bonds is confronted by agents, and where there is said to be switching from cash to bonds as interest rates rise, ceteris paribus.

Third, the modern computer comes on the scene in the post-World War II years, as reflected in Friedman's data analyses and Klein's move from the early Klein–Goldberger model of twenty equations and twenty unknowns to Klein's superbig models of over fifteen hundred equations and the required number of unknowns (Frazer 1994a, 210–213; Klein 1983).

Friedman saw the problems of pinning down empirically the static a priori constructions early on, including initially the Marshallian demand curve (1949; Frazer 1994a, 13–27), where the quantity demanded was treated as a function of price, say $q_1 = f(p_1$, ceteris paribus), with all other things locked into ceteris paribus.   Taking note that all other things could not be equal because raising (lowering) the price meant a loss (gain) in utility, Friedman went on to do two things: First, he offered two demand curves (the ordinary curve and the compensated demand curves, where utility was constant). Second, he related the prices regarding the demand curve to the terms of a price index, where we could in fact measure the loss (gain) in purchasing power of nominal income resulting from inflation (deflation). There was the implied view of the indexation of income (Frazer 1988, 118–119, 221–226; 1994b, 15–17). For instance, the behavioral unit could be compensated for a loss of income due to inflation. Moreover, group reactions appear in this demand-curve paper as elucidated by Roger Alford (1956).   These group reactions, say to a tax-rate change, are such that similarities in responses by the behavioral units comprising the groups are more important than differences among   them   for   the   purpose   of   movements   over   time   and   a theoretic/empirical, policy/oriented economics.

Now, a very similar problem to that which Friedman addressed in the demand curve paper (Friedman 1949) is confronted by James Tobin almost a decade later (Tobin 1958) when critics take note of the liquidity preference demand curve for money. As shown in Figure 5.1, such a curve may follow from an equation for an equilateral hyperbola. However, the equation simply depicts the curve exclusive of any rationale behind it, and that is where conflicting views arise.

Two explanations regarding liquidity preference could be recognized in Keynes's *General Theory*, as the later Nobel laureate James Tobin saw it (1958, 67–70). In one Tobin saw Keynes's original intention, and he saw the

Figure 5.1
Liquidity Preference Demand Curve as Equilateral Hyperbola

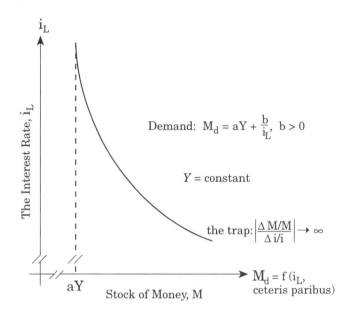

other as receiving the greatest emphasis by Keynes. The latter contained an inconsistency (Tobin 1958, 70–71), most notably, there were a normal or "safe rate" and a central bank controlled rate, as it were. This was such that the strength of an expected return to normality was thought to increase as the control rate departed from the normal or safe rate, even though expectations were held constant in the *General Theory* during the short-run period for policy purposes. As reviewed by Leijonhufvud (1968, 366-383), much of Keynes's policy-oriented analytical results followed from defining the short run as a period of constant expectations.

TOBIN'S VIEW OF LIQUIDITY PREFERENCES

In order to offer a consistent theory, Tobin (1958, 70) made a distinction about probability: that between uncertainty as "disagreement among investors concerning the future of the rate [of interest]" and uncertainty as "subjective doubt in the mind of an individual investor." (The first we show below in illustrating Tobin's reconstruction of liquidity preference.) However, I have discussed (1994a, 232-239) differences of opinion regarding the forecasting of inflation rates (and hence interest rates in the style of the bond market equation, $i = i(real) + Pb[\dot{P}^e] \dot{P}^e$) as a part of uncertainty as regards personalistic probability.

Now, in response to the inconsistency, several alternative routes exist. These include Tobin's explanation and the Friedman-system explanation I state later. Tobin's route relies on agents having different opinions about interest rates (or, in operational terms, bond prices, since changes in the long-bond prices of traded marketable issues are the market means of changing the long-bond rate of interest).

Even so, in achieving this interest-rate orientation with expectations constant as interest rates change, Tobin assumes that the expected value of capital gains (or losses) from holding interest-bearing assets will always equal zero. Indeed, this is very much at odds with the way bond traders orient themselves in actual bond markets and it contains the message of a special orientation toward central bank policy.

As the control rate varies in the Tobin context, it simply changes the opportunity forgone from holding money balances for different bond-buyer/investment units. It is such that at different threshold interest rates the bond-buyer/investment units simply hold all the money-bond assets in either money balances or bonds. Going this route one encounters no changes in expectations as interest rates vary with respect to the liquidity preference curve. Indeed, the financial markets are unaffected by any messages the central bank may send by raising and lowering interest rates, assuming it has that power to begin with.

In Tobin's construction, individual bond-buyer/investor demands for money balances are different, as illustrated by points A, B, and C in Figure 5.2, when differences of opinion about bond prices (and hence interest rates) prevail. Taking into account these differences, a smooth, downward sloping curve is obtained by adding the horizontal/geometric distances suggested by points A, B, and C: hence, the liquidity preference curve constructed by Tobin's difference-of-opinion approach.

In the construction shown in Figure 5.2, the central bank is thought to control the rate of interest directly and thereby control the quantity of money demanded. One may argue along the lines of some strict supply-demand-quantity mechanism that the rate is controlled by increasing (decreasing) the money stock and that increasing (decreasing) the money stock along the horizontal axis of the final part of Figure 5.2 lowers (raises) the rate of interest. There may even be the implied or stated view that the central bank engages in open market purchases (sales) of securities to bring about this control (following the Federal Reserve's open market operations in the United States, Frazer 1994b, 79–100). But here several problems arise. The Federal Reserve has not successfully exercised this power to peg the interest rate via open market operations at levels that are opposed by the bond market itself (Frazer 1994b, 68-99); the Fisher-equation variation, as presented earlier, treats with some empirically grounded authority the prospect whereby the bond market processes inflationary/deflationary information in a way that determines the rate of interest; and the Friedman system, money-stock control view is an alternative to the Keynes/Keynesian interest-rate and fiscal-policy view (Frazer 1994b, 79–100). In fact—and very much at odds with the Tobin perspective, as expressed by the Fed's chairman, Alan Greenspan—interest

Figure 5.2. The Difference of Opinion Approach to the Liquidity Preference Curve

Note: The smooth curve part of Figure 5.2 is obtained from adding geometric distances, $\overline{iA} + \overline{iB} + \overline{iC}$.

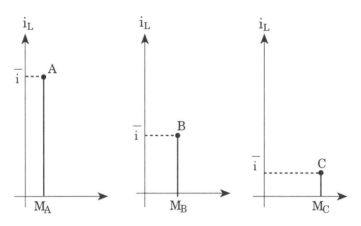

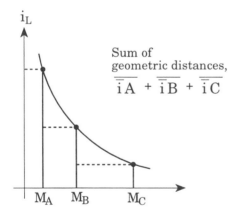

rate targets are best brought about by controlling the prospect of inflation (Frazer 1994b, xiv, 8–9; 57–58 n.2, 75–76, 79, 94).

In one scenario I offer selected time series—such as those for gold, labor market conditions, and wholesale prices—that may be tracked for early signs of expected inflation with the view to reacting against inflation before it appears in consumer and gross domestic product (GDP) measures. The idea is actually a reversal of the Tobin/interest-control view. The reversal occurs along two lines: first, that by achieving by open-mouth-credible means the prospect of a zero inflation rate, a real rate of interest will emerge from bond-trader responses; second, that at this real rate, i(real), the proper noninflationary growth will occur in the money stock, even with built-in allowance for the velocity ratio (Frazer 1994b, 225–231). Also, this latter state unfolds in two ways, namely, that the public holds just the stock of money balances it wants at zero inflation (i.e., the actual and desired stocks are the same) after any allowances for technological changes in the payments mechanism; and, in the Friedman context, that the public determines the constant-dollar stock of money. Although the central bank determines the nominal stock, under the arrangements stated, the real and nominal stocks are the same.

In any case, whatever the scenario, the central bank cannot have the control arrangement in all the ways the strong, ceteris paribus statements above may indicate. In other words, the central bank cannot simply raise and lower "the interest rate" directly to get a given money stock condition, the money stock cannot be put on target to get a desired interest rate irrespective of allowing for the expected-inflation component in the interest rate and other prices. In fact, in early October 1979, following efforts to set a short-term interest rate as a means of controlling inflationary money growth, crisis conditions emerged in the United States (Frazer 1988, 262–263, 655). Reacting to them and returning from Europe, then Federal Reserve chairman Paul Volcker announced on Saturday night, October 6, that the Fed would move in an attempt to control bank reserves without the intervening step of working through an interest rate (specifically, a federal funds, target rate), which was seen as a part of the inflation-control problem. Said differently, the attempt to predict the money stock from the liquidity-preferences arrangement Tobin offered was declared a failure.

The effect of frequent reliance upon ceteris paribus statements is a part of what I have called the separation-of-effects problem (Frazer 1994a, 29, 50–52; 1994b, 55–57). Notably, such effects cannot be found and isolated is some stable parameter(s) by the "direct" use of known statistical methods.

THE FRIEDMAN-SYSTEM VIEW

The Friedman-system's liquidity preference curve comes about in reference to a trend rate of interest (i_T) to which we may expect the long-bond rate to regress. Shown in Figure 5.3 such a rate may be denoted in terms of weighted values for the past trend (or permanent, P) rates,

$$i_T = \text{const} + W_1 i_{t-1,P} + W_2 i_{t-2,P} + \ldots + W_n\, i_{t-n,P} \qquad (1)$$

This rate, I conjecture, in reference to a broad sweep of the future is likely the real rate (or expected-inflation-free rate). Further, the bond traders are into the 30-year "bellwether" bonds or out of them and into cash balances depending on their short-term prospects for capital gains (a rise in bond prices) or losses (a decline in bond prices). In terms of U.S. history since World War

Figure 5.3
Trend and Transitory Components for the Rate of Interest

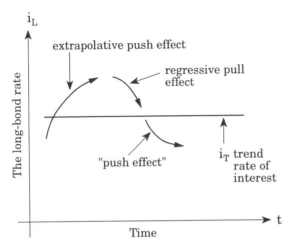

II, and Friedman and Schwartz's (1982), Yohe and Karnosky's (1969), and my own research, I view the bond market on a day-to-day or month-to-month basis as lowering long-bond prices (i.e., raising long-bond interest rates) on information indicative of inflation and as raising long-bond prices on information indicative of deflation (Frazer 1994b, xiv, 8–9; 57–58 n.2, 94, 198–200, 224–231).

Even from this perspective, however inflation-rate (deflation-rate) news may run in one direction or another at times, as I illustrate in part by reference to the extrapolative "push" effects and regressive "pull" effects surrounding the trend rates (i_T) in Figure 5.3 and indicate elsewhere for the United States, the United Kingdom, and the Federal Republic of Germany (Frazer 1994b, 35–50). So, to provide a rationale for the liquidity preference curve along the monetary-policy/bond-market lines I indicate, I offer and develop in conjunction with discussion surrounding Figure 5.3 and in reference to Figure 5.4 another of the analyses set on a course by J. M. Keynes.

First, both the final-summation curve in Figure 5.2 and the curve in Figure 5.4 can be depicted as the equilateral hyperbola shown in Figure 5.1. Mathematically and aside from senarios about how the world works in fact, it does not matter that we readily use Figure 5.1 to show how Friedman may proceed in a mechanical sense when he recasts Keynes's liquidity preference analysis. Most notably, the money stock gets accelerated, via "helicopter" money (Frazer 1994a, 40–47), which impacts on income (the asymptote aY in Figure 5.1) and moves the L-P curve outward. As acceleration proceeds, the curve moves outward at a faster rate and may even "overshoot" the rate warranted by the prior acceleration of the money stock and its inflationary prospect. With this prospect and an eye on data generated by the real world, once again I recall the bond-market equation. And once again, the probability

Figure 5.4
The Demand for Money Balances: A Bond-Market Side View

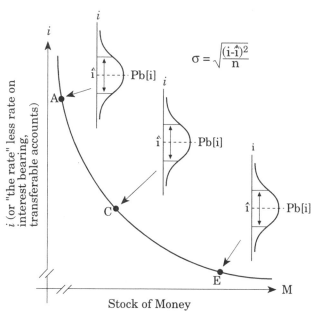

a. Interest rate as average of opinion on a
day-to-day or month-to-month basis

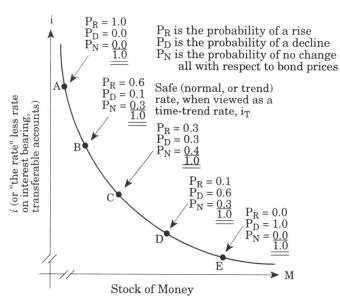

b. Rationale for the slope of the
liquidity preference curve

$$i_L = i(real) + Pb[\dot{P}^e] \, \dot{P}^e$$

here is personalistic. It may be indicated by differences of opinion as reflected in the standard deviation in forecasted expected inflation rates at a given time, just as we encounter in the current gathering of the Livingston data by the Federal Reserve Bank of Philadelphia. There the inflation rate forecasters are asked separately to forecast a price-index value for a fixed future date. These separate forecasts then may be averaged and a measure of dispersion about the mean provided (Bomberger and Frazer 1981).

Now, returning to the interest rate, the data forecast, as it were, is presently not primarily about the real rates of interest. Rather, there is a historical trend rate (i_T) for this long-bond rate. As expected inflation moves on an upward course, the "push effect" dominates for a time—interest rates rise above the trend, as illustrated in Figure 5.3. When the prospects for control of inflation come about via bond-trader reactions, the "pull effect" dominates for a time, along lines I indicate in a different context (Frazer 1994a, 232–239).

Next, the rationale for the liquidity preference curve I offer starts with the rationale for a point on the curve, e.g., point A, C, or E, as shown in Figure 5.4a. At any given time, the observed, media-reported rates of interest are averages $(\hat{i})$. These media and/or central-bank reported rates are averages for a day, a month, a quarter, and so on. Moreover, I view these as the average of opinions about what the rate should be. The opinions in question are those held by bond traders, who are located largely but not exclusively in financial centers such as New York or London.

Taking up the same curve shown in Figure 5.4a, points A, B, C, and so on, are shown in Figure 5.4b, except we now turn to the rationale for the shape of the curve itself where the time frames are essentially those reflected earlier in Figure 1.3 and presently in Figure 5.3 as regards the interest rate. The averages of opinions then become a secular trend for the rate (i_T). Although no bond traders would likely think in that time frame in their day-to-day business, I offer the rationale for the shape of the curve along two lines of reasoning: first, as taken up in the context of Friedman's pool players later, the game may be played without the players being cognizant of the mathematics behind the matters at hand; and second, in Figure 5.4b the assigned probabilities are related to the prospect of a return to the more permanent component of the time series for the long-bond rate.

Next, an additional feature of the combination of Figure 5.1 and Figure 5.4 is that the central bank has responsibility in the control of bank reserves, bank credit, and ultimately the money stock (M_S) with its predominant demand deposit component (Frazer 1994a, 96–98; 1994b, 82–91), although the round about ways of achieving this control via the use of the long-bond rate as a surrogate (Frazer 1994b, 39–50) may be n order. In any case, adopting the prospects for constant velocity $(Y/M = const)$ and money-stock growth $(\dot{M})$

at the same rate as that for constant-dollar income growth, the interest rate comparable to these growth conditions is that of the level which appears as Figure 5.3.

Going a bit further in the context of Figure 5.3, I formulate the prospects for inflation and deflation and the long-bond rate stated earlier (page 14):

$$i_L = i(real) + Pb[\dot{P}^e] \, \dot{P}^e$$

Showing this expectation as it regards the velocity ratio Y/M as well as the long-bond rate (i_L)—income growth overshoots that for the money stock as the prospect for inflation appears and as inflation impacts on the purchasing power of money balances.   These changes are such that within bounds for the inflation rate, the long-bond rate and the velocity ratio move in the same direction,   as   in   top part of Figure 5.5, but as the inflation persists and accelerates, the interest rate rises faster than the velocity ratio (Frazer 1994b, 68–77), as indicated in the bottom part of Figure 5.5.   The reason for this departure, as inflation persists, is that the absolute value of the probability-weighted expected inflation enters the long-bond rate, while inflation impacts on both the numerator and the denominator of the velocity ratio (Y/M).   As inflation comes about it penalizes the holding of money balances by a loss of purchasing power and it places a special advantage on spending as prices are expected to rise.

AN OVERVIEW

When considering the Tobin and Friedman-system views, there are fundamental differences which may be brought out by taking note of the purpose for which the theories were intended, the assumptions of the theories, and some of the hidden features of central bank operations.   In doing these things, first, I go back to the famous essay—"The class of phenomena the hypothesis was designed to explain," the implications of assumptions (whether good approximations for the purpose), whether the theory works (which depends on the predictions it yields), crucial assumptions as a means of getting at key elements of an abstract model.

First, the purpose of the theories is to serve as a guide to policy (Figure 4.1). This is mostly just implied by Tobin's view of liquidity preference, in which he was in fact dealing with a rather technical point, notably that of the inconsistency of having expectations constant when the prospect of a return to an expected rate varied as the interest rate varied. However, in the Keynesian times of the Tobin essay (1958), much could be taken for granted with regard to the widespread acceptance of the Keynesian/emerging macroeconomics. In my review of that larger picture of the emerging economics (Frazer 1994a), central bank control over the economy was seen as a major means of attaining a stable economy, albeit conditioned by the liquidity trap (Figure 5.1) and the

Figure 5.5
Schema for the Interest Rate and the Velocity Ratio in the presence of Inflation and Persistent and Accelerated Inflation

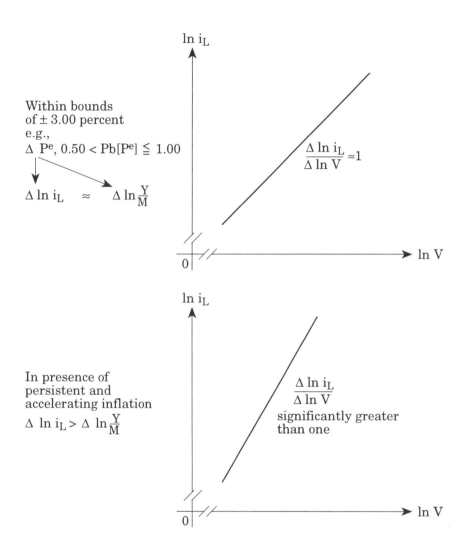

Within bounds
of ± 3.00 percent
e.g.,
$\Delta\ P^e,\ 0.50 < Pb[P^e] \leqq 1.00$

$\Delta \ln i_L\ \approx\ \Delta \ln \frac{Y}{M}$

$$\frac{\Delta \ln i_L}{\Delta \ln V} \approx 1$$

$\ln V$

In presence of
persistent and
accelerating inflation

$\Delta\ \ln i_L > \Delta\ \ln \frac{Y}{M}$

$$\frac{\Delta \ln i_L}{\Delta \ln V}$$

significantly greater
than one

$\ln V$

Keynesian preference for fiscal policy as a distinct policy instrument. In Keynesian causal linkage terms, $-\Delta i \to \Delta I \to \Delta Y$ and $\Delta i \to -\Delta I \to \Delta Y$ (where I is capital spending, not yet defined, and inflationary/deflationary expectations are constant, as indicated on text page 70). This interest rate orientation appears in J. M. Keynes's *General Theory*, especially at the Bank of England (as emphasized in Table 5-2, Frazer 1994b), and in early macroeconomics textbooks. Tobin's essay (1958) conformed with the assumption of constant inflationary expectations and the view of central bank control over the interest rate in the presence of constant expectations.

In a more encapsulated form, this comparison of views appears in Table 5.1. Turning to the axioms of the alternative views, I find mostly conflicting views about behavior, and more of an emphasis in which Tobin finds a view of liquidity preference consistent with broader statements of Keynesian mechanics. Yet Tobin's assumptions about probability I do not see as part of a behavioral system where uncertainty in the economic outlook and varying roles for expectations and alternative views about the central bank's means of control. As to empirical study, the control of interest rates, and predictions, I see no evidence of control and effects that eschew the bond market equation (text, pages 14–15), and what I introduce regarding psychological time (text, pages 15–16).

In the liquidity context I offer, Friedman's "helicopter money" (Frazer 1994a, 40–52) as an alternative approach depends on rather circutious routes (Frazer 1994b, 39–50, 95–100, 224–231). In no case do the data and the actual modes of operation lend support to the Tobin/Keynesian views of the interest rate and its control arrangements.

In any event, in Friedman's perspective, accelerated growth of the money stock impacts income and may give rise with some lag to an increase in the expected inflation rate, and so on. Turning to the Friedman system view I offer, however, bond traders set the rate of interest and process information of a general sort regarding expected inflation. This general information includes current and anticipated money growth, the bond-market surrogate for these matters, and governmental actions and inactions that contribute to it.

Drawing on Friedman's "helicopter money" concept (Frazer 1994a, 40–48; 94–102; 1994b, 21–26, 79–100), as money-stock growth accelerates (ΔM), it impacts income growth (and hence the asymptote, cY, in Figure 5.1) by setting the liquidity preferences curve in motion. Acceleration moves the curve outward faster, deceleration moves it out slower. However, once the curve is set in motion discussion surrounding the curve and interest rates centers on several points: (1) the rationale about bond prices and interest rates varying inversely to provide opportunities for making capital gains and avoiding capital losses; (2) day-to-day push and pull effects on the buyer and seller sides of the market; and (3) push and pull effects operating in the time frames of Figure 1.3, all in conjunction with time trends and the discussion surrounding Figure 5.3.

In Friedman's more abbreviated perspective, the control over the money stock entails fairly direct control of reserves, and thereby the credit and money aggregates, although this is not readily a possibility in operating contexts (for example, even for the Bundesbank in Frazer 1994b, 95–100). So, instead of the abbreviated Friedman perspective, a surrogate for the direct control of the

Table 5.1

A Comparison of Approaches by Reference to Assumptions

Assumptions and operations in the Tobin theory	Assumptions and operations in the Friedman-system theory
1. The interest rate is a direct, central-bank controlled variable. Expectations regarding changes in it are absent.	1. The interest rate is set in the bond market by traders who process information regarding future interest and inflation rates. They may do so on day-to-day and month-to-month bases, but in any case we have a trend line about which observed rates vary (e.g., Figure 5.3).
2. Bond-buyer/investment units hold all the assets in either money balances or bonds.	2. Asset structure may be diversified, depending on the maximization of the flow of returns subject to constraint, as taken up on pages 97–100, and preferences for liquidity.
3. Expected capital gains and losses are zero.	3. Making capital gains and avoiding losses are at the center of bond trading operations and consequently the setting of bond prices (and thus interest rates).
4. Uncertainty is seen as disagreement among investors concerning the future of the rate of interest, and subjective doubt is seen as distinct from uncertainty.	4. Uncertainty means personalistic probability in all instances. There is disagreement among bond traders and others who anticipate inflation rates. The interest rate data reflect averages of different opinions of bond traders on a day-to-day or month-to-month basis.
5. Utility enters as the preference for certainty of income over risk (in effect defined as actuarial probability).	5. The marginal utility of income decreases in some situations, increases in others, and may vary as to the specialties of individuals and firms. In other words, for example, manufacturing firms may take risk in one category of activity and bond traders in another, even when they hedge risks of other sorts.

money stock enters (Frazer 1994b, 39–50) via some reliance on the long-bond rate (i_L), but even this is not direct control (Frazer 1994b, 224–231).

Since we cannot in fact over time, or in the restricted-time state ($\Delta t \to 0$ at the limit), identify in the real world a locus of points such as suggested by Friedman's view of the Marshallian demand curve (text page 68) and discussion surrounding the curves in Figures 5.1, 5.2 and 5.4, what in fact do the mechanical structures with their underlying axioms and definitions provide? In answer, I say that they provide a rationale which should be suggestive of how the world and bank operations work, and they should serve as an aid to the memory about the phenomena at hand in the various contexts where the curves appear.

The constructions I offer without motion, however, should carry all of the baggage weighing on them without being inconsistent within the Friedman-system context. This may include the use of the constructs as memory devices that are at the same time consistent with the rationale behind the curves as well as their indirect use as instruments for prediction. Taking Friedman's instrumentalist view as regards the mechanical structures) and as indicated by me, 1994a), I say the purpose is prediction of economic behavior and the effects of policy, and I view any accompanying theory as argument in support of one view or another about how to proceed toward the economic goals (including economic stability and possibly a zero inflation rate).

The question about the purpose and the instrumentalist notion about the structure were uppermost for Milton Friedman, as they are for me. With the monetary sort of economics Friedman reflected upon in his essay, he makes a "cursory expression" of a personal view "about static monetary theory" which has had a form of the quantity theory of money as its basic core in all of its major variants from David Hume to the Cambridge School, to Irving Fisher, and to John Maynard Keynes" (Friedman 1953 41–42). He then goes on, first, to say that we do not have in 1953 a theory "that can appropriately be called, 'the' existing theory of monetary dynamics," and, then, in the subsequent years, to link a basic quantity-of-money/theoretic expression to liquidity preference demand for money, as set on course by J. M. Keynes. This quantity-of-money/theoretic feature also appears in the statement of the money demand function, where we introduce the identification problem (text pages 56–57). It does so in terms of the left-hand member, and the first right-hand member where we encounter M/P and Y/P and thus $(M/P)/(Y/P) = M/Y$ or the inverse of velocity, $1/(Y/M)$, where the inverse is the Cambridge k, in M $= k(\ \ldots\ )Y$.

In the Friedman system, and in this chapter, I see the monetary theory in terms of mechanical apparatus with motion. This is no doubt dynamic analysis, since it relies so strongly on time rates of change, group perceptions, and group reactions, "such that the similarities in terms of reactions among groups" are "more important than the differences among them when it comes to the effects of some stimulus"—a common change in the demand for firms' products, and so on. Although not introduced explicitly in the theoretic/

mechanics context, thus far, the term "open-ended closeness," as suggested by Professor Shogo Doi, is suggestive of a key feature of the Friedman system. As reintroduced later the structure is left in tack as a change in time approaches zero at the limit. Going beyond that limit, changes in time and notion enter to move the structures about as do the episodic impacts on the data series and the behavior they reflect.

Chapter 6

Indirect Evidence, Bond Traders, and Expected Returns

The shared banking, Bank of England, Keynes, Keynesian view of interest rates has lasted a long time, given its context; that is, the tortuous analyses surrounding it, as found in Tobin's 1958 paper; the history and institutional prospects that contradict it (Frazer 1994b, 65–100); and Friedman's notion that evidence from experience is "frequently as conclusive as that from contrived experiments." By this route, Friedman says, the evidence in economics "is far more difficult to interpret" than that in the natural sciences. According to him:

It [the economic evidence] is frequently complex and always indirect and incomplete. Its collection is often arduous, and its interpretation generally requires subtle analysis and involved chains of reasoning, which seldom carry real conviction. The denial to economics of the dramatic and direct evidence of the "crucial" experiment does hinder the adequate testing of hypotheses; but this is much less significant than the difficulty it places in the way of achieving a reasonably prompt and wide consensus on the conclusions justified by the available evidence. It [the mythical prospect that some crucial experiment may be performed to render prompt and wide consensus] renders the weeding-out of unsuccessful hypotheses slow and difficult. They are seldom downed for good and are always cropping up again. (Friedman 1953a, 10–11)

But, in any case, being denied the crucial experiment, we turn to indirect, quantitative and institutional, and historical evidence regarding the absence of direct control by central banks over the long-bond rate of interest. I state shortly two hypotheses and later contrast evidence supporting each. As a first step in doing this I recognize later that even in J. M. Keynes's view of the central bank's control by way of liquidity preference theory there existed a view of the term structure of interest rates behind it (Keynes 1930, 142–147). Turning to this and an alternative position, I cite quantitative evidence and institutional practices that deny support for Keynes's "backwardation" and related supply-demand-quantity views of the yield curve (Hicks 1946, 136–139; Keynes 1930, 142–147; Leijonhufvud 1968, 288–289).[1] As one may recall, in this view of yields on government debt instruments, the central bank is seen as extending changes in yields in the short-dated segment of the securities market to the long-dated segment and as moving these yields in the same direction.[2]

However, I see that Tobin in his exposition (1958) was moved to introduce the predominance of risk aversion in an area where economic survival depends on the successful realization of capital gains and avoidance of losses as bond traders take very high risk positions. To be sure, there are those other than bond traders who hedge risk from capital losses in the U.S. government securities market, but these are groups specializing in the confrontation of risk of another sort, such as those from manufacturing and distributing products, and none plays the crucial role the traders play in setting bond prices as a response to various sources of timely information. Further, along bondholder, risk-averse lines, the U.S. Treasury Department announced in May 1996, for the first time, plans to offer a bond tied to an inflation index, with the view to attracting retirement savings. The view is that the yield will fluctuate with inflation and thereby protect the bond's value from declining when inflation arises. Hopefully this is not an ominous sign of the government's plans.

Thus I turn to questions about risk and income and those who play the game and enter the lottery of life at less than fair actuarial odds (Frazer 1994a, 159–164). I go nearly a full turn from the strict "backwardation" and related supply-demand-quantity views to general matters of liquidity found in Keynes's famous *General Theory* and also in an extended discussion of Friedman's use of profits to illustrate the "as if" method of the famous 1953 essay.

The bond trader hypothesis may be stated thus:

H_{BT} *The bond traders:* Bond traders process information (especially that bearing on inflationary/deflationary prospects emanating from the central bank, the larger government entity, and other sources), and, in doing so, set the prices (and hence yields) on long-term debt instruments. This may come about without the respective quantities of short- or long-dated issues changing for the traders as a whole. In other words, we are left with an information processing orientation, and not a supply-demand-quantity mechanism for the bond-trading group as a whole.

The liquidity hedging hypothesis, which I will address later, goes as follows:

H_{LH} *Liquidity hedging hypothesis:* The groups supplying funds to the government securities market seek, on the average, maturities that correspond to their respective needs for funds in the future. In other words, there is a hedging, or avoidance of risk, not by expressing a preference for short-dated securities to avoid losses but in choosing instruments with maturities that coincide with an anticipated need for funds.

THE TERM STRUCTURE OF INTEREST RATES, TREASURY/DEBT-MANAGEMENT PRACTICES, AND LIQUIDITY HEDGING

There are many theories of the term-to-maturity structure of interest rates (Frazer 1980a, 411–417), which appear in connection with the Treasury yield curve. As illustrated in Figure 6.1 it is the curve resulting from the plots of interest rates at a given date on different maturities of the marketable debt instruments that are issued by the U.S. Treasury in the case of the United States. The idea is that the yields (as percentages) are plotted for securities that are homogeneous as to risk of income and default on principal in every respect but one, notably the time to maturity. The long-bond rate (i_L) in such a context, is what I call the riskless rental value of capital funds. Most notably liquid funds may be in effect placed in the government securities market by holders of marketable, nonindexed debt instruments with less risk than in any other homogeneous class of debt instruments. When the government approaches default on its payment of interest and principal, other securities may be subject to default by an even greater margin in most instances.

Yet, in all the instances save one, movements at the respective ends of the curve are viewed in terms of some supply-demand-quantity mechanism whereby demands as to the quantity of one maturity or another enter into the price (and thus interest rate behavior). By contrast, the Friedman-system view places greater emphasis on inflationary/deflationary expectations. Bond traders are key players, in the short term and possibly even the long term, and the central bank's control over the long-bond rate follows this route indirectly and largely independently of a supply-demand-quantity mechanism which I clarify further later.

In turning to the theories of the term structure and closely related theories regarding the composition of portfolios of securities I do several things: I limit my discussion to only the Keynes (or backwardation) position and the Friedman-system view of the yield curve and take up closely related views about portfolios of government securities. There is no doubt with respect to the alternative theories I consider that government security dealers make the market in government securities by standing ready to buy and sell securities at different maturities and by providing bond traders. On the other hand, when I turn to the holdings of government securities by the different institutional buyers of them who serve as intermediaries supplying the funds to the government, I question theories about the portfolios, including that of the Nobel laureate James Tobin (1958). I do so by taking up debt management by the U.S. Treasury and by considering time to maturity profiles of government security holdings of different institutional groups, albeit only for the 1962 to 1969 period for which data have been analyzed. As regards these holdings by different intermediary groups,[3] the concept of the relative frequency of different maturities with respect to time to maturity is used. This is a basic probability concept that introduces probability distributions and facilitates the standard use of mean values and moments about their means to portray the distributions and their possible stability over time.

Figure 6.1
The Treasury Yield Curve, the Bundesbank Effect, and Supply and Demand

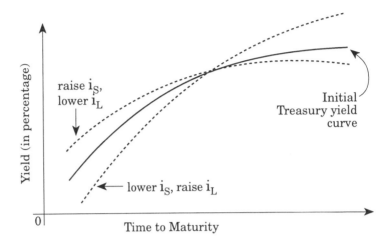

a. Bundesbank effect for increase and decrease in i_S

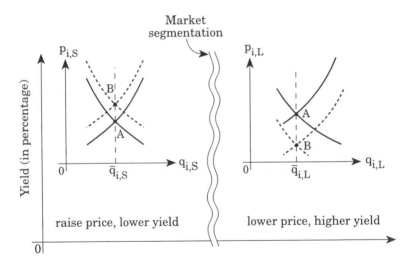

b. Supply and demand schedules, and prices and quantities
accompanying lower i_S and higher i_L

The ultimate goal is twofold: First, it is to report the finding of stability against a backdrop of Treasury debt management practices that is supportive of liquidity hedging and other views of the preference for debt instruments as they regard portfolios. Second, it is to note that the support for such a standpoint is compatible with the purer form of expectations behavior I offer in the Friedman system, as it regards phases of business conditions (Figure 1.3). In this, I illustrate the use of indirect evidence as Friedman discussed it and, at the same time, turn to the monetary interest Friedman alluded to early in the 1953 essay.

The Liquidity Preference Theory

The liquidity preference theory, as found in Keynes (1930, 142–147) and Hicks (1946, 136–139) and as dealt with by Leijonhufvud (1968, 288–289), asserts a preference for the certainty of capital over the uncertainty of income from long-term marketable bonds that experience price fluctuations, and, along that line, this liquidity preferences theory posits a predominance of an upward-sloping yield curve. It does so by way of paths: an implied supply-demand-quantity mechanism, whereby the price of the short-dated debt instruments is high (as may be illustrated by an upward demand curve shift) and the yield low as a consequence, and the reverse demand condition appears at the long end of the yield curve. This combination is thought to underlie the tendency for yields on long-dated securities to exceed those on short-dated securities. The predominance of the upward sweep gives rise to the use of the term "backwardation" in reference to the yield curve.

Furthermore, this estimation of the Treasury yield curve underlies the shared banking, Bank of England, Keynes, Keynesian view of the liquidity preference demand for money (Frazer 1994a, 33–36). In it central-bank intervention at the short-term-to-maturity segment of the yield curve is thought to move the entire curve in the same direction as the short-rate movement. The accompanying prospect is that the central bank may vary the long-bond rate by intervening with discount-rate (or federal funds rate) changes, possibly as accompanied by open market operations of the sort described in *The Central Banks* (Frazer 1994a, 84, 88, 100; 110 n.10; 169, 172–173). The yields making up the locus of points the yield curve comprises are themselves held together when the yield curve is shifted by a combination of even further prospects, notably that the shape of the curve represents a market forecast of the future movements of bond prices (and thus yields); and if a point on the curve gets out of line with the other points on the curve on the high (low) side, bond-dealing institutions may buy (sell) them and almost immediately make a capital gain (avoid a loss) as the time to maturity on the issue in question changes over the next short interval.

Now, two points raise no questions: the fact that the yield curve over a long period reflects the predominance of a backward-moving shape (such as shown for the yield curve in Figure 6.1), and the prospect that movements in the curve reflect altered anticipations by the market, since it tends historically to move upward more at the short end than at the long end during boom (or expansion) phases of business conditions. The reverse movements appear in recession phase, aside from the prospect of an inflationary recession (i.e., aside from the combination of both inflation and recession).

In dispute are the workings of the supply-demand-quantity mechanism, and the alleged link between central banking operations at the short end that bring about movements in the same direction in the short-term and long-term rates (i_S and i_L, respectively). Rather—as I outline later in the alternative Friedman-system view—information about central bank actions and inactions at the short end and overall, as it regards inflationary and deflationary processes which "bond traders" interpret, acts upon the receipt or anticipation of new information to vary the long-bond prices and hence yields via $i_L = i(real) + Pb[\dot{P}^e]\ \dot{P}^e$.

The Bond-Trader Theory, Liquidity Hedging, and the Behavior of Interest Rates

I have stated a hypothesis (H_{BT}) regarding the behavior of bond traders in the government securities market and offered text surrounding Figure 5.3 and Figure 5.4, without the elucidation of trading activity and supply-demand matters, to which I now turn. Discussion of the hypothesis is combined with the liquidity hedging hypothesis (H_{LH}), also stated previously, and factual evidence, and operations concerning the management of the marketable portion of the federal debt of the United States. This set of topics illustrates the use of indirect evidence about interest rates and the workings of monetary policy.

The time frames for H_{BT} and H_{LH} are different, as suggested in earlier discussions of Figure 5.3 and Figure 5.4. As introduced earlier, the bond traders process information on a day-to-day basis, stand ready to buy or sell securities of different maturities, and seek returns mainly from realizing capital gains and avoiding capital losses. In the processing of information, prospects for capital gains and losses arise, and prices (and hence yields) on marketable debt instruments may change, at times even widely so. In terms of ordinary supply and demand curves that make supply-demand crosses (illustrated in Figure 6.1) and that provide market clearing prices (points A and B in Figure 6.1), prices (and hence yields) simply adjust among traders. They do so as opinions on the average change over time, even though opinions at a given time differ among traders along the lines illustrated in Figure 5.4.

In this process no new quantities of either short- or long-dated issues, of any relative significance, move from the traders taken as a whole. Adjustments within the group simply occur as average opinion changes. At the end of the day some trading desk may have more or less cash and more or less short-, intermediate-, and long-term issues. Some additional securities may come on the market from central banks or new issues by the Treasury, but these are minuscule by comparison with the issues already on the market. The result is that prices may change in the short- or long-term segments of the market (say, movements from point A to B in the short-term segment of the market, and from

A to B in the long-term segment of the market), all without the quantities coming on the market changing ($\bar{q}_{i,S}$ and $\bar{q}_{i,L}$ respectively). This is what I mean when I say there is no supply-demand-quantity mechanism but rather price.

Within the larger cyclical/transitory time frame introduced earlier in text surrounding Figure 5.3 and Figure 5.4, I have time-to-maturity profiles (also described earlier, page 85). They appear in Figure 6.2 for three of eight institutional groups supplying funds to the U.S. government securities market at the end of March 1968. The mean and measures of central tendency for the profiles for such groups were studied from quarter to quarter for the end of the first quarter of 1962 through the end of the second quarter of 1969 (Terrell and Frazer 1972, 1–35). In this period there were some efforts for the U.S.

Treasury to depart from its standard orientation regarding the management of the debt, but for the most part that arrangement held firm. In determining the pricing of new and replacement issues of securities and their maturities, the issues should be tailored as to price, yield, and maturity to suit the market. In other words, there was little or no variation in the supply-side offerings as to the short- and long-term markets which I signify as market segments in Figure 6.1. Now, against this background, two sorts of developments appear. First, the maturity profiles illustrated in Figure 6.2 are stable, as indicated by the study of the properties for the profiles over time (TF 1972). This evidence supports the liquidity hedging hypothesis (H_{LH}).

Second, over cyclical time frames illustrated in Figure 1.3, yields on short-dated issues swing much more widely than yields on long-dated issues. Even so, on the average the preference for short relative to long-dated issues, or vice versa, is stable, and, in the period where data are analyzed, the Treasury is following a policy for the most part of giving the intermediate suppliers of funds the preferred maturities. In other words, the management policy and the mechanism I describe rule out the theory in which short-dated issues are predominantly high in price (low in yield) because of a greater demand for short- than long-dated maturities by the intermediate supplies of funds to the government securities market.

So, what do the developments and data results mean? They mean that with the transitory time frames and over even longer periods the bond traders are largely the group setting the security prices. This comes about mainly via an expectations mechanism and, only secondarily if at all, via a supply-demand-quantity mechanism. Said somewhat differently, analyses of expectations come to the forefront in the determination of interest rates within the transitory/cycle time frames and even at times over longer periods.[4]

Referring to what I have called the Bundesbank effect (illustrated in Figure 6.1), central bank efforts to control interest rates or send messages by way of announcements and intervention in the short-term segment of the government securities market may have just the reverse of the prospect we illustrated with the backwardation and other yield-curve views relying on supply-demand-quantity mechanisms. In sending information bearing more on long-dated than short-

Figure 6.2
Government Security Holdings by Selected Groups with Different Maturities as Proportion of Total Holdings

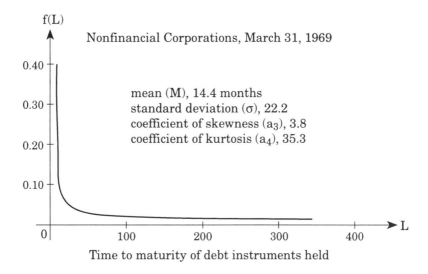

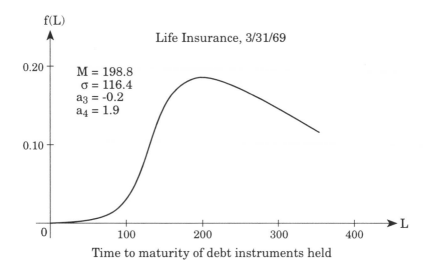

Figure 6.2 *(continued)*

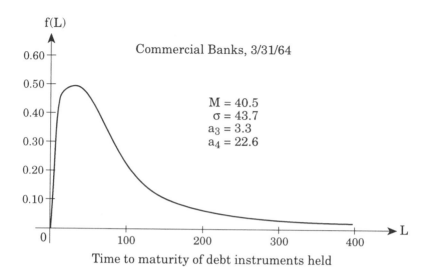

Time to maturity of debt instruments held

dated securities, the central bank moves the long-bond rate in opposition to the direction predicted by ordinary theory.

Taking such a position, then, how do I explain the tendency for the yield curve to have its backwardation shape most of the time, historically speaking. I do so in a combination of ways. Expansion phases of business conditions are of considerably longer duration than recession phases, and higher interest rates and inflation mostly occur in these rapid-growth phases, the combination of inflation and recession aside. As information about inflationary prospects comes about, interest rates rise at both ends of the Treasury yield curve, but there is more of a regressive pull toward normality at the long end of the yield curve. The predominant rise at the short-maturity end of the curve is an extrapolative push effect whereby the direction of movement pushes the yield in the direction of its movement. This effect, working in an expectations context, is stronger at the short end, where changes in rates swing in a wider range than long-bond rates, because they are not affected in the same measure by the regression to normality where more distant prospects enter.

We have, in fact, the transitory and the more permanent factors Friedman notes (1992, 2130) where he speaks of Sir Francis Galton's study of the heights of fathers and sons, and his own theory of the consumption function. In the one instance, sons of tall fathers tended to be shorter than the fathers (to regress toward the mean), and, in the other, Friedman explains why the average of spending over long periods was less than that which could be expected from timeless data or as income grew in the short term.

The Tobin Alternatives and the Utility of Income

When faced with a choice between two approaches to the liquidity preference demand for money, as recognized by Keynes (Tobin 1958, 67–70), James Tobin chose one route. I have chosen another.

Tobin chose to focus upon differences of opinion, as outlined earlier, so that he could satisfy the treatment of monetary policy found in Keynes in which expectations surrounding future bond prices (and hence interest rates) were constant when the central bank raised and lowered the rate of interest. Taking this route, the Nobel laureate Tobin had to assume that bondholders (whether traders, the intermediate suppliers of funds, or the ultimate sources of saving) held either all money or all bonds. In doing this, he adopted the liquidity preference construction in Figure 5.2. Now, having done that, he had to explain the existence of diversified holdings. To do this he turned to Harry Markowitz, who had presented a monograph written at the Tobin-connected Cowles Foundation in the mid-1950s. It offered a technique to those who held portfolios of securities and who wished to achieve two objectives, namely, a high return and a dependable return free of uncertainty (Markowitz 1959, 6). The monograph discussed how to achieve the objectives. Although certainly not empirical economics, Tobin moved to adapt the Markowitz expected-return/variance-of-return (E-V) rule to liquidity preference analysis of the demand for money as represented by Figure 5.2.

In Tobin's adaptation, we are offered the expected-return/variance-of-return plane shown in Figure 6.3. There the vertical axis depicts expected return, the horizontal axis variance of returns, and utility curves depicting agent indifference between the two variables that are imposed on the plane. As shown in Figure 6.3, the curves characterize risk averse behavior whereby a very large increment in expected return is called for in order for the agent to accept a small increment of risk (i.e., $\Delta r^e/\Delta\sigma$ increases considerably for a small increment in variance). Also, leftward/upward shifts in the U_1U_1 indifference curves depict higher levels of utility ($U_3 > U_2 > U_1$) regarding choice between two investment projects.

The idea of this analysis surrounding the selection of projects is that the agent reduces risk by selecting two securities which yield a high or perfect inverse correlation. As shown in Figure 6.3, there are three opportunity frontiers that offer choices: frontier AB, which depicts perfect positive correlation; frontier ACB, which simply depicts random returns on the respective investment projects that are therefore also independent of one another; and frontier ADB, which shows perfectly inverse correlations. It is such that the variance of one return is offset by variance of the other to eliminate risk. The virtually risk-free expected return from the portfolio is then at point D.

So, in summary, where does Tobin's theory leave us? Does it predict the effects of interest rate changes? Is the mechanism we find compatible with operations and practices at the central bank? Are those who behave along the lines Tobin posits the group that makes the market for government securities?

Figure 6.3
Risk Reduction through Diversification: Two Investment Projects

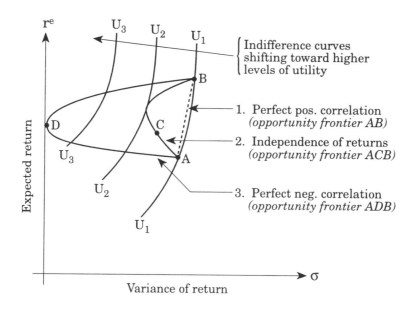

All the answers are no, when judged by the available evidence and the alternative I posit. In it, "the interest rate" is not directly controlled by the central bank. The bond traders I describe, who make the market for the "bellwether" government bonds, are not risk averse. Rather, the entire bond trading business is about putting capital at risk at less than fair actuarial odds (Frazer 1994a, 160–164) as a means of making capital gains while taking speculative positions in actuarial terms (if not in personalistic terms).

In contrast, Tobin leaves us with a package of Keynesian views. The central bank raises and lowers the rate of interest, ostensibly exclusivly of any inflationary premium (Keynes 1936, 141-142). It does so seemingly to achieve the ultimate goal of economic stability. Next, agents hold more (fewer) bonds or debt-type instruments as the interest rate is raised (lowered). The mechanism appears to be that of the opportunity forgone from holding money balances rather than bonds as yields rise. And, finally, the risk-averse assumption gains some similarity to J. M. Keynes's backwardation view of the yield curve, which is attributed to a preference for the security of capital over earnings from instruments with a longer time to maturity.

Very much in contrast to Tobin's risk avoidance, the Friedman system avoids risk aversion except in selected respects, such as for those who buy insurance. Drawing on Friedman, I find behavior where work and enterprising activity may be culturally influenced and beyond the necessity of work as a means of subsistence. Turning to Friedman's discussion of profits in the next section, I come to a rule implied by J. M. Keynes that applies significantly to what Keynes said and rnay be incorporated into the Friedman system and used in a highly relevant view of the role of liquidity shifts as they bear on instability in the economy and in part on J. M. Keynes's concept of the volatility of spending on real capital.

Taking up Friedman's remarks about profits does not mean they are the driving force to enterprising activity. Instead the outcomes Friedman suggests come about "as if" the behavior regarding profits followed from axioms and not "as if" the axioms were true. Rather, in fact, supporting arguments about the behavior in question came from pointing to Max Weber's emphasis on "living to work" rather than "working to live," and not from the ofter drawn, but limited possibility, of distinguishing between the pleasure of winning the lottery at less than fair actuarial odds and the sheer utility of income from winning (Frazer 1994a, 160–165).[5] And, indeed, I see profits and high pay for some executive officers in high-risk positions as simply prizes for playing the lottery (at less than fair actuarial odds, to be sure).

Prizes for successful engagement in business enterprises abound. Turning to such culturally influenced matters, J. K. Galbraith says, "In the affluent society no useful distinction can be made between luxuries and necessities. Food and clothing are as difficult as ever to do without. But they can be and frequently are among the most opulent of expenditure." (Galbraith 1958, 315) Thorstein Veblen himself referred to conspicuous consumption and mentioned efforts at being ceremoniously adequate. Completing the analogy of profits from business enterprise to opulent consumption expenditures, the profits are as essential as ever to the enterprises, but the behavior underlying the drive for profits is far more "ceremonial" than essential to life at a subsistence level.

The utility front is illustrated in Figure 6.4, which shows the utility function for income and units of net income from the lottery, as it were. In zone A, there is declining marginal utility of income, where an individual may buy insurance at less than fair actuarial odds. In zone B there is increasing marginal utility of income, where the game is played at greater than actuarially fair odds. Going back to what I describe as "The Lottery of Life and Social Mobility," "The Utility of Income" (Frazer 1988, 512–514; and also "The Utility of Income," Frazer 1994a, 159–165), I cite Friedman on a case of risk-prone behavior.

If all potential movie actresses had a great dislike of uncertainty [the probability counterpart to risk], they would tend to develop "cooperatives" of movie actresses, the members of which agreed in advance to share income receipts more or less evenly, thereby in effect providing themselves insurance through the pooling of risk. (Friedman 1962a, 163)

Indeed, there is more satisfaction in the ceremony of successfully generating profits and achieving high income than Tobin in particular concedes.

Figure 6.4
Working to Live versus Living to Work

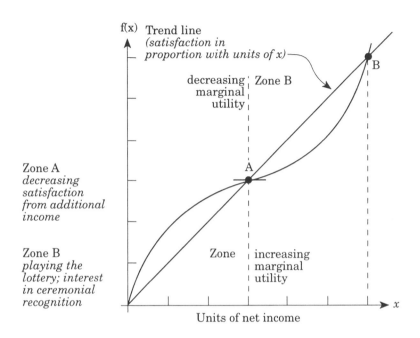

EXPECTED RETURNS, CLASSES OF ASSETS, AND LIQUIDITY

Having taken a negative stance on Tobin's theories about liquidity preference, the diversification of assets, and risk avoidance, I turn to additional features of the Friedman system. They follow from Friedman's introduction to profits and the "as if" principle which appears in the famous essay. The additional features concern the maximization of the flow of "expected" returns, classes of assets, and a role for liquidity as found in J. M. Keynes's work.

Profits, the Pool Player, and the "as if " Principle

While not viewing the profits of firms as being basic to the methodological issues of the famous essay, Friedman introduces the subject as an example of the "as if" principle (1953a, 20–23; 21 n.16). In doing this, he departs from neoclassical economics in three main respects—by introducing "expected" returns, by introducing uncertainty regarding the expectations, and by introducing maximization of "expected" returns. By 1953, moreover, Friedman had abandoned the Frank Knight distinction between risk and uncertainty for the more personalistic probability which encompassed both risk and uncertainty under the label "uncertainty" (Frazer 1988, 68–71, 722–723, 740, 744).

Now, in this as in some other instances,[6] we are left to conjecture what Friedman actually had in mind by maximization of "expected" returns. To me, on reconstruction, the route to go is that of the maximization of the flow of returns. They are net of all cost except the cost of funds, and maximization is subject to a constraint on total assets (Lagrangian mathematics, and so on, Frazer 1994a, 75–81; Frazer 1980b, 337–362).[7]

But before turning to the stream of "expected returns" Friedman himself skirts close to a neoclassical concept of profits. In this, the decision makers behave "as if" they knew marginal cost and marginal revenue curves (Frazer 1994a, 63–66; Friedman 1953a, 21–22). Friedman says of the individual firms that they behave "as if . . . they knew the relevant cost and demand functions, calculated marginal cost and marginal revenue from all actions open to them, and pushed each line of action to the point at which the relevant marginal cost and marginal revenue were equal."

Average cost (including some allowance for expected returns that attract capital to one industry, or country, in relation to another) must be met in a competitive environment in order for the firm to survive. Friedman says:

unless the behavior of businessmen in some way or other approximated behavior consistent with the maximization of returns, it seems unlikely that they would remain in business for long. Let the apparent immediate determinant of business behavior be anything at all— habitual reaction, random chance, or whatnot. Whenever this determinant happens to lead to behavior consistent with rational and informed *maximization of returns*, the business will prosper and acquire resources with which to expand; whenever it does not, the business will tend to lose resources and can be kept in existence only by the addition of resources from outside. The process of "natural selection" thus helps to validate the hypothesis—or, rather, given natural selection, acceptance of the hypothesis can be based largely on the judgment that it summarizes appropriately the conditions for survival.

Returning to the questions of evidence and uses of statistical methods, Friedman claims:

The evidence *for* a hypothesis always consists of its repeated failure to be contradicted, continues to accumulate so long as the hypothesis is used, and by its very nature is difficult to document at all comprehensively. It tends to become part of the tradition and folklore of a science revealed in the tenacity with which hypotheses are held rather than in any textbook list of instances in which the hypothesis has failed to be contradicted. (Friedman 1953a, 23)

However, as Friedman's work relating to the behavior of firms extends beyond the date of the famous essay, we especially see the marginal cost, marginal revenue, and average cost curves in motion. This comes about as Friedman illustrates the workings of liquidity preference with overshooting at the level of the firm (Frazer 1994a, 63–68; Friedman 1976, chap. 12). But when the curves from the theory of the firm are set in motion in this later writing and even in the essay, there is nothing relating to behavior that resembles neoclassical, pre-Keynesian thought regarding behavior.

Even so, in all of this there are quite flexible mathematical foundations that the more ordinary business players are not required to know. The analogy to the pool player follows:

Consider the problem of predicting the shots made by an expert billiard player. It seems not at all unreasonable that excellent predictions would be yielded by the hypothesis that the billiard player made his shots as if he knew the complicated mathematical formulas that would give the optimum directions of travel, could estimate accurately by eye the angles, etc., describing the location of the balls, could make lightning calculations from the formulas, and could then make the ball travel in the direction indicated by the formulas. Our confidence in this hypothesis is not based on the belief that billiard players, even expert ones, can or do go through the process described; it derives rather from belief that, unless in some way or other they were capable of reaching essentially the same result, they would not in fact be expert billiard players. (Friedman 1953a, 21)

Moving from profits, marginal cost, average cost, and so on, Friedman turns toward his preferred "maximization-of-returns hypothesis," which he justifies by evidence of a different character. Friedman says that it has overtones that could be a response to Thorstein Veblen's title "Why Is Economics Not an Evolutionary Science?" This evidence is in part similar to that adduced in support of the billiard-player hypothesis.

The Expected Returns and Liquidity

In a very unneoclassical gesture, Friedman introduces the potentially dynamic "expected returns," uncertainty regarding the prospects, and maximization regarding expected returns where I come to see the application of Lagrangian mathematics, with the prospect of asides to J. M. Keynes. First, for the mathematics, there are classes of assets varying from assets with a fixed, contractual claim against future sales or income (A_F), such as cash balances and near-cash liquid assets, to inventories, and residual-claim assets such as plant and equipment (A_R).

Forming a Lagrangian function $L(A_F, A_R, r)$, with total assets as a constraint ($A = A_F P_{AF} + A_R P_{AR}$), r as the Lagrangian factor of proportionality, and the total value of assets as equal to the sum of the products for the asset classes and their supply prices, respectively, I have

$$L(A_F, A_R, r) = f(A_F, A_R) + r [g(A_F, A_R) - A] \qquad (1)$$

Obtaining first-order conditions for this function, only pointing to second-order conditions (Frazer 1980b, 337–362), and engaging in some algebraic operations, we have another way of stating first-order conditions for the maximum:

$$(\partial f/\partial A_F)/P_{AF} = (\partial f/\partial A_R)/P_{AR} = r \qquad (2)$$

where $\partial f/\partial A_F$ and $\partial f/\partial A_R$ are flows of returns from the respective classes of assets, P_{AF} and P_{AR} are the respective supply prices, and, in this remarkable instance, the factor of proportionality is the rate of return on additions to the classes of assets. In words, the resulting rule is what follows: *the utility from the assets is maximized when the ratios of the marginal (extra) utilities to their respective supply prices are equal.*

Substituting different symbols for those in equation (2),

$$R_F/Value_F = R_R/Value_R = r$$

This says that the ratios for perpetual streams of returns to their respective values are equal. At these respective margins, in other words, the rates of return from additions to the classes of assets are equal under the first-order conditions. Perhaps even clearer, we have values resulting from perpetual flows of returns which are discounted by the rate of interest (currently denoted r). But these are simply means of recognizing wealth, or portions of it, as being equal to discounted streams of returns. In the J. M. Keynes sense we have the value of real capital (CV) discounted in the same way as a bond,

$$Capital\ Value = R_1/(1 + i)^1 + R_2/(1 + i)^2 + ... + R_n/(1 + i)^n$$

And, closely related, cost or supply price $= R_1/(1 + r)^1 + R_2/(1 + r)^2 + R_n/(1 + r)^n$ and as $n \to 30$ years, $CV = R/i$, and cost $= R/r$. Adding a touch of uncertainty to the future returns, $R_1, R_2, ... , R_n$,

$$Rb[R_1]\ R_1,\ Pb[R_2]\ R_2,\ etc.[8]$$

and

$$CV = Pb[R_1]\ R_1/(1 + r)^1 + ... + Pb[R_n]\ R_n/(1 + r)^n$$

So what we have here, to be sure, is neither neoclassical nor pre-Keynesian economics.

Given the flows of returns as fixed (via uncertainty and constant expectations, one year hence, R_1; two years hence, R_2; and so on), the values of additions to real capital vary inversely with the rate of interest. In both Keynes's and Keynesian frameworks, where the central bank is viewed as controlling the rate of interest directly, we have the prospect in static analysis (expectations = constant) that the central bank can implement interest-induced wealth effects (i.e., increments or decrements in capital value). This central bank view is the basis for the elementary notion of controlling capital spending (I), by raising and lowering the interest rate (text pages 76–78). To illustrate, for a reduction, $-\Delta i$ $\to$ (i < r) or CV > supply price and, consequently $\to \Delta I$. In a subtle way, in this context, a distinction is drawn between the rate of interest (i) and the rate of return (r) on additions to real capital.

However, in the Friedman system I have no such prospects for the central bank to bring this about. There are two reasons for this: central bank actions and inactions, and other governmental matters potentially connected to them, can impact on both bond prices (as set by bond traders) and the prospects held by firms for the streams of returns from additions to capital (or even additions to the additions), and, closely related, the long-bond rate is more directly determined by the prospects for the inflation rate, $Pb[P^e] \, P^e$ than by directly implemented independent increases and decreases in the discount rate.

We need not belabor this, since we have dealt with it in discussions surrounding Figures 5.4 and 5.5. The Friedman system alternative to Tobin and Keynesian economics more generally, as introduced earlier, embraces psychological time. Even so, there is a major subtlety, which I take from Keynes and retain, and there are two large differences in the way I come to the diversity of assets and portfolio holdings by comparison with Tobin's theory.

First, drawing on Keynes (Frazer and Yohe 1966, 354–356, 369–370; Keynes 1936, 225–226), the assets on a balance sheet are aligned in the order of their increasing dollar returns and decreasing liquidity to yield a schema such as seen in Figure 6.5. There (q - c), yield less carrying cost, denotes the tangible or dollar component making up the rate of return, whereas 1 denotes the liquidity premium (security and convenience) in holding the designated class of assets. As regards this schema, cash and short-term liquid assets yield very little in dollar and cents terms relative to real capital, and the real capital with highly specialized functions (such as patterns for the manufacture of automobile engines and warehouses for inventories) may be expected to yield predominantly dollar and cents returns but no liquidity of any consequence. Depending on the prospects for the flows of returns, substantial shifts into and out of liquidity may occur with considerable consequence for slower and faster growth in capital outlays and expenditures. These in turn work through to labor markets and changes in unemployment rates.

J. M. Keynes placed great stress on liquidity as a quality that could rule the roost. A shift into (out of) liquidity could follow along lines of the liquidity preference demand for money balances, as well as along lines I relate to bond traders. However, in the broader context of Figure 6.5, shifts regarding liquidity come into clearer perspective in the transitory states of business conditions (Figure 3.1). Here the shift may fall between liquidity generally and spending for additional real capital or current output. The flows of returns and forms of income are allocated to additional liquid assets (also reductions in liabilities such as bank loans) in more or less proportion than to real capital and goods and services. For example, looking at assets only, we may see assets, yielding a total and classified thus:

1. Money
2. Non-cash liquid assets such as government bonds
3. Current value of goods
4. Real capital

Figure 6.5
Asset Classes and the Liquidity Premium

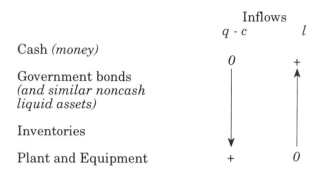

If this, then as returns flow in and growth occurs, more (or less) of the total may be allocated to cash or non-cash forms of liquidity and less (or more) may be allocated to goods and real capital.

Although not pursued further in regards to Figure 6.5, liquidity shifts readily encompass liabilities as well as the classes of assets. In sources and uses of funds terms, any increase (decrease) in assets is a use (source) of funds, and any increase (decrease) in liability-side accounts is a use (source) of funds.[9] As funds (meaning changes in bookkeeping entries) flow about they may go to more or less liquidity. Financial planning about future needs for funds may enter (Frazer 1994a, 135–143, 150–151 nn.6, 7), as where I introduced the time-to-maturity profiles for government securities and the liquidity hedging hypothesis (H_{LH}).

Within the broad picture initially set on course by J. M. Keynes, a generalized shift into liquidity means reduced spending on the current output of goods and services (and recession, as shown graphically in Figure 1.3). A shift out of liquidity has the reverse connotation. Taking note of the money stock as the most liquid of all assets (Figure 6.5), less money stock than desired by holders of money balances means a reduced velocity of money ratio ($-\Delta Y/M$), and a greater-than-desired money stock means greater spending via a rise in velocity ($\Delta Y/M$). Data analysis problems and errors in the data aside, there exist roughly inverse movements in the velocity ratio and measures of liquidity in the cyclical time frames of Figure 1.3. Even so, in special trend states—such as I identify with FS's change in the structure underlying the formation of expectations, and with trends in the 1970s and 1980s, respectively (Frazer 1994a; 1994b)—changes also occur to complicate analyses of data.

AN OVERVIEW

Friedman's famous essay generated much controversy, as I have noted, and I will turn to more of it in the next two chapters. For now, however, I ask, How could so much controversy and misunderstanding occur over what Friedman said? I answer this in several ways: (1) In 1953 the Friedman system remained in an early, even if significant stage of development; (2) the system has a divisive ideological dimension where disagreement enters (as stated earlier, and also in Friedman 1953a, 5–6); and (3) the author still had the task of communicating with a range of other economists in a language they could possibly understand. An analytical system with the motion, time frames, uncertainty, and agent expectations was no doubt beyond the vision of economists as a group in 1953.

However, there are presently but a few main points when it comes to the following subject-matter areas: the economics and central banking as set on a course by J. M. Keynes and Milton Friedman; the intermediate suppliers of funds for the businesses and expenditures on real capital (or what Keynes called "instrumental capital"); those who are prone toward risk or averse to it; and the other behavioral groups I mention. Choices and diversity of opinions exist, and individual and group practices evolve. Friedman himself (1953a, 22) refers to the process of "natural selection" in terms of evolution (also Frazer 1988, 322).

One point underscores that groups of households and firms participate in liquidity shifts and the demand for money as the most liquid of assets. The members of these groups can respond in common ways to generate business conditions and alter the trends underlying them. In both short and long periods, subtle actions and inactions by central banks enter into the formation of expectations by bond traders and firms, and into the preferences for more or less liquidity and a larger or smaller stock of money balances. In the case of the traders, we may have inflationary or deflationary messages from the central bank that are passed from the short-maturity, market segment where central banks intervene to the more crucial long-maturity market segment. Here—in contrast to actions in the short-maturity segment that are passed along in the same direction to the long-maturity segment—a reverse set of prospects referred to as "the Bundesbank effect" occurs. Here, in turn, one finds no predominant preferences for risk avoidance over earnings that underlie the backwardation view of the Treasury yield curve and the supply-demand-quantity mechanism that accompanies that view.

As to firms, even in the 1953 essay Friedman said "firms could be grouped into 'industries' such that the similarities among the firms in each group were more important than the differences among them" (Friedman 1953a, 35). Connecting this to Friedman's views on the Marshallian demand curve (Frazer 1994a, 13–17), we see that group behavior emerges over time where influences imposed on business conditions are widely shared.

Another point is that the profiles illustrated in Figure 6.2 and surrounding discussion both reflect anticipated needs for funds, which are imposed by special institutional considerations, and a predominance of the bond traders who seek capital gains from high-risk positions. In contrast to Tobin's views about a controlled interest rate, risk avoidance, diversification of the portfolio, and a preference for the safety of capital over earnings, we find bond traders who accept considerable risk and who process information bearing on the future day-to-day basis and very much set the long-bond rate in the process.

I introduce profiles of government security holdings (illustrated in Figure 6.2) of intermediate suppliers of funds that reflect liquidity hedging and special future needs for funds. Bringing out the U.S. Treasury practice of tailoring debt issues to suit the intermediate suppliers of funds,[10] I note further the presence of an expectations mechanism as it bears on short- and long-date debt instruments. In addition, liquidity hedging is not risk avoidance as far as the main business of the respective holders of debt instruments is concerned. That business may be manufacturing in the case of nonfinancial enterprises generally, or it may be life insurance and banking in the case of financial corporations. In all of these the ultimate stockholders take risk as regards earnings and principal, and the higher managers take special risk in pursuing stockholder and company objectives and even in setting out the objective.

The nature of the business, the objectives, and the traditions and practices determine the structures of assets and liabilities to a greater extent than risk avoidance. The businesses evolve into what we see. Manufacturing corporations produce goods for sale, and risks are undertaken as funds go into facilities and the marketing of products. An industry is identified with its products, as in the case of motor vehicles, apparel and related products, and fabrics, furniture, lumber and wood products, leather and leather goods, professional and scientific instruments, primary metals, chemical and chemical products, petroleum, and so on.

In the treatment of differences of opinion among bond traders (Figure 5.4), diversity among firms, and the disparity in economic outlooks generally, all may exist at a given time. The system I outline recognizes this, but when it comes to the time frames of business conditions and even trends, expectation mechanisms dominate. News and information are widely shared by the various groups. The shared influences are uppermost in the Friedman system, no matter what the differences among agents and groups at a given time. Behavior appears in the generalized shifts into and out of liquidity. The shifts are the central feature of the varying states of business conditions, where we also encounter Friedman's regressive pull toward normality.

In introducing profits as an example of the "as if" principle in the essay (1953a, 20–23, 21 n.16), Friedman rather clearly departs, as in other examples, from neoclassical economics. He does so in three main respects—by introducing "expected" returns, by introducing uncertainty regarding the expectations, and by introducing maximization regarding "expected" returns.

Now, in this as in some other cases, what Friedman actually had in mind by maximization of "expected" remains open to conjecture. The route I choose is that of the maximization of the flow of returns net of all cost except the cost of funds, subject to a constraint on total assets (Lagrangian mathematics, and so on,

Frazer 1994a, 75–81; 1980b, 337–362). In Lagrangian terms, the expected stream of returns as a perpetuity is R, the value of additions to assets is CV, and R/CV is equal to the Lagrangian factor of proportionality (r). The capital value formula, $CV = R_1/(1 + i)^1 + R_2/(1 + i)^2 + ... + R_n/(1 + i)^n$ approaches R/CV $= r$, as n approaches 30 years.

This approach is compatible with J. M. Keynes's notion of the marginal efficiency of capital and his analogy of real assets to a bond (Frazer 1994a, 77–79, 136–143), except that the expected flow of returns varies, even for monetary policy purposes, and the interest rate is not directly controlled by the central bank. Rather, central bank interventions in the securities markets may influence the flows and the long-bond rate set by the bond traders. Furthermore, uncertainty regarding the stream of expected returns may be introduced and the interest rate may be seen as having a component for a probability-weighted, expected inflation rate.

NOTES

1. As one may recall, the term "backwardation" referrs to a tendency for yields (as percentages) on long-dated securities to exceed those on short-dated securities most of the time. This upward-sloping yield curve particularly may predominate in expansion phases of business conditions, which are usually of much greater duration than recession phases.

2. So, additional to the concept of "backwardation," there is an additional bit about monetary policy; (in interest-rate control terms) it is that changes in yields in the short-dated segment of the market can be shifted in the same direction to changes in the long-dated segment of the market. Through a properly functioning arbitrage and expectations mechanism, the operations in the short-dated securities are transmitted as effects on the long-dated securities in this Keynes, Keynesian view.

3. These owners of government bonds are referred to as "intermediate" because in the underlying Keynes/Keynesian/aggregate-supply-demand block (Frazer 1994a, 122–130) they are intermediate to the flow of saving into investment. In that block we have the total of income received (Y), which goes to consumption (C) or saving (S), on the one hand, and we have total demand (Y_d) consisting of consumption (C) and investment (I), on the other. Given that consumption and saving are both functions of income, C(Y) and S(Y), that $0 < dC/dY < 1$ in the $\Delta t \to 0$ (at the limit) state, that saving is by definition that part of income not spent on consumption, and that investment is a variable constant (I $=$ constant in the Δt-zero-limit state), we have in this very basic Keynes/Keynesian building block a saving-investment equality, $S(Y) = I$. Funds in effect flow from not being spent on consumption (i.e., from saving) into investment (i.e., $S \to I$). The financial and other institutions that expedite this flow are said to be "intermediate" to the saving-investment process.

In this context questions arise about how "saving" and investment are identified when the concepts are pinned down to data or behavior (Frazer and Yohe 1966, 391). The option we take is that behavioral groups, households, manufacturing enterprises, bond traders, and so on— should be the focus.

4. Mechanisms surrounding the formation of expectations come to the forefront as the great peacetime inflation is under way in the mid 1960s. On the one hand, the information processing is continuous and short run, without the lags FS initially reported before pointing to the structure underlying the formation of inflationary expectations (FS

1982, 478, 469–573), and, on the other, it also extends for longer periods since the mid-1960s, as indicated by data results from the 1970s inflation and from the decade of the 1980s, when the inflation rates declined (Frazer 1994a, 18–21, 108–111; 1994b, 41–50).

5. Elsewhere I refer to "the lottery of life" (Frazer 1988, 512–514) when it comes to distinguishing work effort to achieve distinction from work at a subsistence level.

6. The most crucial of the "other instances" would include the mid-1960s change in the structure underlying the formation of inflationary expectations (Frazer 1988, 562, 564–565, 595–596, 652, 668–669). In my reconstruction of the Friedman system (Frazer 1994a), this gives rise to what appears later as Chapter 7.

7. Friedman, as is well known (Frazer 1988, 606, 724), was strongly opposed to efforts at mathematical elegance (or what he called Walrasian in reference to economics). Even so, he was cogently aware of the flexibility of extreme value mathematics and probability, and their uses in providing a structure for economics, and he used language suggestive of some such structure.

8. If all we had here were the probabilistic weighing of expected returns, we would have an example of a mathematical expectation. However, what we offer is not strictly that because of the presence of time and time discounting and hence the recognized preference of goods today over goods in the future (Frazer 1994a, 170–182).

9. For further discussion along this line, see Frazer and Guthrie (1995, 87).

10. The exception to this rule is the fractional reserve banking sector. It is an exception because in fractional reserve banking, reserves may arise from central bank actions or other sources and serve as a basis for multiple increases on the asset side of balance sheets in bank-loan and investment accounts (Frazer 1994b, 82–93). Thus, we have a creation of funds and not simply a use of funds.

Chapter 7

Analyses of Data

E conometric and Friedman system lines of thinking are among those introduced in Figure 2.1. Under "econometrics" alone I note two routes and point to David Hendry and Neil Ericsson (hereafter HE) as critics who engaged Friedman and Schwartz (hereafter FS) in discussion about Friedman's and FS's uses of statistical methods (HE 1991; FS 1991, respectively). Although this controversy initiated by HE is not so new (Frazer 1988, 735–760), nevertheless, appearing in the *American Economic Review* very late in the sequence of events as it did—the additional controversy both adds visibility to Friedman's critics and provides further opportunity to delineate Friedman's uses of statistical methods. They are a part of the Friedman system, as well as being rooted in his background and experiences.

These, at an early stage, lie behind Friedman's famous essay. I return to it both to continue the philosophical/uses-of-statistical-methods theme reflected in the famous essay and to enlarge on that theme. As to the background for the famous essay, I point once again to the following: (1) the exchange between Harold Hotelling (1933, 463–465; 1934, 198–199) and Horace Secrist (1934, 196–198, 200); (2) Friedman's association with Leonard Savage and the Statistical Research Group (Figure 1.2); (3) Friedman's association with Karl Popper at early meetings of the Mont Pelerin Society when its membership was quite small (Frazer 1988, 107, 119–124, 173); (4) the distinction between permanent and transitory components in time series, as illustrated in Figures 1.3 and 5.3, in Friedman (1992, 2129–2132) and in Friedman and Kuznets (1945, 331); (5) Friedman's article on Wesley Clair Mitchell (1950, 463–495); (6) Friedman's "Comment on 'A Test of an Econometric Model for the United States, 1921–1947' " (1951); and (7) the first of the articles reproduced in *Essays in Positive Economics* ("The Marshallian Demand Curve," Friedman 1953b, 47–99).

For the present purpose of taking up FS's uses of statistical methods and the critics who enter as representatives of "modern econometrics" the first and fourth sources lead to "the regression fallacy" (as illustrated later); the second leads to personalistic probability and somewhat negative experiences with multiple regression models, as well as the simultaneous equations/multiple-regression models; the third connects to Friedman's variant of instrumentalism (Frazer 1984a); the fifth links to the Friedman-led *Studies in the Quantity Theory of Money* (Frazer 1988, 155, 181; Friedman 1956) and to the later dynamic formulations found in the monetary works; the sixth reflects the skeptical outlook regarding the "fashionable econometric" models; and the seventh illustrates Friedman's approach to pinning down empirically apparatus that cannot be otherwise isolated by the direct means known as the multiple regression method (Frazer 1994a, 13–17).

Turning only to the 1953 essay itself, there are several positions in the essay that point toward FS's encounter with David Hendry and Neil Ericsson regarding uses of statistical methods. These include positions about pre-dictions of "phenomena not yet observed" (1953a, 7), about predictions based on historical data not yet "known to the person making the predictions" (1953a, 10), about disturbing influences and the inability in economics to control the experiment as a result of disturbing influences (1953a, 10), and about evidence that is complex, indirect, and incomplete (1953a, 10); the observation "Interpretation generally requires subtle analysis and involved chains of reasoning" (1953a, 11); and the prospect that phenomena are repetitive (the half-truth "There is nothing new under the sun"), and episodic and nonrepetitive (the half-truth "History never repeats itself") (1953a, 25).

In contrast, but nevertheless related to these positions via the role of episodes, is the position that on occasion the experiment "casts up evidence that is . . . direct, dramatic, and convincing as any that could be provided by controlled experiments." Here Friedman points to evidence from inflation regarding "the hypothesis that a substantial increase in the quantity of money within a relatively short period is accompanied by a substantial increase in prices." He says, "Here the evidence is dramatic, and the chain of reasoning required to interpret it is relatively short" (Friedman 1953a, 11).[1] But then— contrary to his often expressed confidence in the ability of statistical results to resolve differences of opinion—Friedman says the following:

Yet, despite numerous instances of substantial rises in prices, their essentially one-to-one correspondence with substantial rises in the stock of money, and the wide variation in other circumstances that might appear to be relevant, each new experience of inflation brings forth vigorous contentions, and not only by the lay public, that the rise in the stock of money is either an incidental effect of a rise in prices produced by other factors or a purely fortuitous and unnecessary concomitant of the price rise. (Friedman 1953a, 11)

INDIRECT METHOD

Friedman's orientation directs attention to the indirect way he proceeds (1953a, 10–11, 28) and the repeated use of the two-variable simple regression technique, including in setting bounds on the "true" regression coefficient. The indirect method appears even as Friedman approaches the overall operation of the economic system and especially before he proceeds to add variables to the right-hand member of the regression equation. There are two interrelated reasons Friedman directed attention to the simple method, and others are possible. First, as defined shortly (note 3), there is the regression effect (or "fallacy," Friedman would say). It leads Friedman and FS to utilize the concept of having upper and lower bounds on the "true" regression coefficient (illustrated late). Second, as defined later, there is difficulty in setting bounds when variables are added to the regression equation and beyond some point bounds cannot be added at all.

Further, there is the general statistical/analytical problem I call "the-separation-of-effects problem" (Frazer 1994a, 5–6, 29, 49–52, 54, 81, 165); I even refer to the man-in-the-backroom illusion (Frazer 1994a, 165, 210; 1994b, 161 n.12). It arises from adding so-called independent variables to the right-hand member of an equation as a means of separating effects when in fact the variables are dependent and even rather interdependent. The illusion is the belief of a sizable portion of students and analysts that the effects in economics may be separated by known direct means such as provided by the multiple regression technique.

Such an approach seems less acceptable when Friedman raises questions about the information contained in a single time series. I ask, "What is that information?" And following Friedman, I refer to transitory and permanent (or quasi-permanent) components illustrated in Figure 1.3. In addition, failure to make such a distinction may relate to "the regression fallacy."

I even come to refer to the impact of episodes on both components (Frazer 1994a, 24–26, 87; 1994b, 26). To allow for these component parts, Friedman proceeds to adjust the data series for the episodes and otherwise to filter out one class of information to get at another class. In the alternative, direct use of fashionable econometrics such diverse components of information are simply overlooked, are not considered, or are treated with an excessively crude approach.[2] In 1992, Friedman returned to discussion of this method.

[T]he common practice is to regress a variable Y on a vector of variables X and then accept the regression coefficients as supposedly unbiased estimates of structural parameters, without recognizing that all variables are only proxies for the variables of real interest, if only because of measurement error, though generally also because of transitory factors [e.g., transitory income, Figure 2.1] that are peripheral to the subject under consideration. I suspect that the regression fallacy is the most common fallacy in the statistical analysis of economic data, alleviated only occasionally by consideration of the bias introduced when "all variables are subject to error."

As a student of Hotelling . . . I early became aware of the regression fallacy—or, perhaps better, trap. (Friedman 1992, 2129–2132)

In 1991 FS replied:

[T]he article by Hendry and Ericsson is mislabeled. Their article is not in any relevant sense an evaluation of our "empirical model of U.K. money demand." Rather, it uses one equation from our book as a peg on which to hang on exposition of sophisticated econometric techniques. Insofar as their empirical findings do bear on ours, they simply confirm some of our principal results and contradict none. (FS 1991, 39)

They added:

We believe that there is no magic formula for wringing reasonable conjectures from refractory and inaccurate evidence. The HE approach is one way: start with a collection of numerical data bearing on the question under study, subject them to sophisticated econometric techniques, place great reliance on tests of significance, and end with a single hypothesis (equation), however complex, supposedly "encompassing"—to use one of HE's favorite terms—all subhypotheses. Another way is to examine a wide variety of evidence, quantitative and nonquantitative, bearing on the question under study; test results from one body of evidence on other bodies, using econometric techniques as one tool in this process, and build up a collection of simple hypotheses that may or may not be readily viewed as components of a broader all-embracing hypothesis; and, finally, test hypotheses on bodies of data other than those from which they were derived. Both ways—and no doubt still others as well—have their use. None, we believe, can be relied on exclusively. (FS 1991, 39)

FS then turn to questions about exogeneity, endogeneity, and "the regression effect."

On the purely statistical level, we tried throughout to avoid making arbitrary assumptions about exogeneity. For example, in the first table in Chapter 6 . . . we label one set of equations "Level of Money: Income Assumed Exogenous" and another "Level of Income: Money Assumed Exogenous" and do the same for rate-of-change calculations. Similar caution in later tables derives in large part from our trying systematically to allow for what we referred to earlier as "the regression effect." (FS 1991, 42)

Turning to the regression fallacy, and a relation between two variables (x and y) that is strictly linear, FS say:

Given errors of measurement, a sample of observed values of the two variables will yield a bivariate scatter, rather than a strictly linear relation. The calculated regression of y and x will be flatter than the "true" relation, and that of x and y will be steeper. Harold Hotelling pointed out in 1933 how potent a source of economic fallacies the regression effect can be if "errors of measurement" are interpreted to include all stochastic disturbances affecting the variables under study.

A major difference between our statistical approach and HE's is that we allow systematically for the regression effect. HE obliquely recognize this difference in their data appendix, where they note near the end that we "emphasize an 'errors-in-variables' paradigm" (HE, p. 34). Nowhere else do they mention or refer to the regression effect or seek to allow for it. In our opinion, it is often a more important source of error—because it introduces systematic bias—than is the residual error described by the standard error of estimate to which HE give exclusive attention. (FS 1991, 42–43)

FS conclude:

[HE's] estimates are the end result of trying a large number of alternative hypotheses on a single body of data. As a result, it is impossible to specify how many "degrees of freedom" have been used up in the process of reaching the final equations presented, or, put differently, to estimate the probabilities that their results could have arisen from chance. For that, one needs, in their words, "the underlying (and unknown) error variances," not "the estimated residual variance" on which they rely (HE, footnote 14). (FS 1991, 47–48)[3]

FRIEDMAN/SCHWARTZ USE OF INDIRECT METHOD

Turning to Friedman's somewhat unusual use of statistical methods, FS say, "We are more eclectic. We believe that there is no magic formula for wringing reasonable conjectures from refractory and inaccurate evidence." They continue:

[We examine a] wide variety of evidence, quantitative and nonquantitative, bearing on the question under study; test results from one body of evidence on other bodies, using econometric techniques as one tool in this process, and build up a collection of simple hypotheses that may or may not be readily viewed as components of a broader all-embracing hypothesis; and, finally, test hypotheses on bodies of data other than those from which they were derived. (FS 1991, 39)

Continuing to illustrate their rather encompassing way of proceeding, FS say it is more ambitious in that they use a wide range of evidence, "including qualitative examination of historical experience as well as numerical data for more than a century for both the United States and the United Kingdom."

A major purpose of our book [FS 1982] was to "give numerical content to some of the elements and hypotheses embedded in" "the broad theoretical framework that guided our earlier study of United States monetary history" "as well as some of the generalizations suggested by *A Monetary History*" (p. 13 passim). Accordingly, we frequently draw on evidence for the United States presented in the earlier book (Friedman and Schwartz, 1963). In particular, we use independent data for the United Kingdom to test generalizations initially suggested by U.S. experience. (FS 1991, 40)

In their conclusion regarding HE's approach, FS refer to a very real problem with econometric estimates that I see as having emerged in dramatic proportions over the 1960 to 1990 period in the United States. It is that of scrutinizing the data until a most satisfactory result appears from the points of view of analysts. This approach of gathering and interpreting evidence is analogous to the approach Friedman attributed in a 1946 correspondence to

Henry Schultz's 1938 study *The Theory of Measurement and Demand*. Friedman charged, "Schultz always tried to wrench the data into a pre-existing theoretical scheme, no matter how much of a wrench was required."

THE REGRESSION EFFECT AND BEYOND

Setting bounds on the true regression coefficient (say, the true β in $y = a + \beta x + u$) concerns the regression effect.[4] In their analysis, as in many other economic analyses, FS say the so-called independent or predetermined variables "are infected by error in a double sense" (FS 1991, 43). First, there is measurement error consisting of imprecise counterparts to the economic variables and, second, there is the use of proxy variables. In principle, the upper and lower limits FS address would be even wider if an allowance were made "for the usual standard error of estimate of the parameters arising from the stochastic element in the dependent variable."[5] However, FS say (1991, 43), they did not do this. Rather they "consistently presented t ratios, from which what is generally called the 'sampling error' can be readily calculated, so that any interested reader can combine the two."[6]

To illustrate the importance of the regression effect compared with the conventional "sampling error," FS considered an example.[7] In it, the regression effect is over eight times the standard error. Later, in going beyond measurement error in another context (Friedman 1992, 2131), Friedman mentions the presence of "transitory factors that are peripheral to the subject under consideration."

Now, FS also say they applied the computation of upper and lower bounds as a few variables were added to the right-hand side of the regressions. However, in this regard, we come to the extension of analyses to more than two variables, and, in doing so, we encounter the Leamer problem (1985): that as variables are added to the regression equation, "it's extremely difficulty to set limits on the regression coefficients . . . and that beyond some point, you may be able to set no bounds . . . at all" (Frazer 1988, 741).

The Regression Effect

The regression effect arises in a linear, two-variable context [say, x and y, $y = f(x)$], when y is first regressed on x, and x is then regressed on y (Frazer 1967, 37–39, n.3, 39; Friedman 1992; FS 1982, nn.28, 29, 173–174, 277 n.18, 224–225, 227), as illustrated in Figure 7.1a. In the first case, where the linear regression takes the form

$$y = \alpha + \beta x + u \tag{1}$$

with u as an error term, the bounds are set on the regression coefficient, β. If this coefficient were approximately one ($\beta \approx 1$), and the two regression lines virtually coincided and yielded a high correlation coefficient say ($0.85 \leq r^2 \leq$

1.00), there would be no statistical problem of any consequence in this simple case.[8] But considering results obtained for a long period as in FS's 1982 work or HE's 1991 paper, the consequence can be enormous, as Friedman suggests.

In any case, as in Figures 7.1a and 7.1b, the consequence of not setting the bounds can be very misleading, as the illustration suggests. Not only does the prospect of a false regression coefficient arise, there are the implied probability distributions in Figure 7.1b, for two selected points. In the near-ideal case (again, $\beta \approx 1$, and $0.85 \le r^2 \le 1.00$), in any event, we have in fact a bivariate distribution, as shown in Figure 7.1c. As I depart from the ideal case and take up Figures 7.1a and Figure 7.1b, the mean of the bivariate distribution is anywhere within the bounded area and, in addition, the deviations (σ's) about the means may vary to raise a further complication.

So we have implied probability distributions with variances (σ's) for the respective errors. Using money stock (M) and income (Y), FS (1982, 173–174 nn.28, 29) let P_M be the fraction of variance of M and P_Y the fraction of variance of Y. In this context, if M is measured without error, then P_M is unity $P_M = 1$, and if Y is measured without error, then P_Y is unity for the respective X and Y terms, $P_Y = 1$. But in that context, the two assumptions, $P_M = 1$ and $P_Y = 1$, cannot be simultaneously valid. Elsewhere (1991, 42–43), FS say:

Put formally, consider a relation between two variables (x and y) that is strictly linear. Given errors of measurement, a sample of observed values of the two variables will yield a bivariate scatter [e.g., Figure 7.1c], rather than a strictly linear relation. The calculated regression of y and x will be flatter than the "true" relation, and that of x and y will be steeper [e.g., Figure 7.1a and Figure 7.1b]. Harold Hotelling pointed out in 1933 how potent a source of economic fallacies the regression effect can be if "errors of measure" are interpreted to include all stochastic disturbances affecting the variables under study (Hotelling, 1933, 1934; Horace Secrist, 1934; Friedman and Simon Kuznets 1945, pp 325–328; Friedman 1957, chap. 3).

Structural Change

Of even more importance to the subjects encompassed by the present work, FS reported their regret in finding a change in the lagged relation between the time rates of change in the money stock, on the one hand, and the rate of interest, on the other. As I said (with Boland):

We encounter at this point in Friedman's work an empirical finding of special importance, namely: statistical results suggest "that the period of experience on which expectations were based shortened drastically after the mid-1960s." . . . A so-called initial impact effect of accelerated money growth on interest rates (a negative correlation) began to be overwhelmed more readily by the inflationary expectations effect (positive correlation) even for periods as short as a quarter. . . . They had expected the inflation-rate effect to be the major one for their cycle phases, but their original theoretical speculation was the liquidity effect would be important within cycles and "largely to average out for . . . cycle phases." What this finding suggests in effect

Figure 7.1
Bounds on the True Regression Coefficient and the Bivariate Scatter for a
Random Error Term

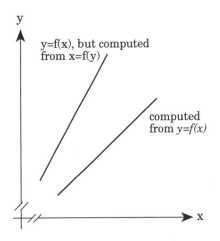

a. Bounds on true regression
coefficient

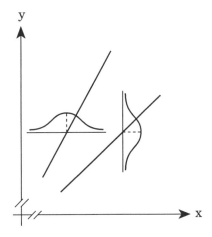

b. Probability distributions
for error terms

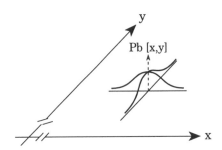

c. Bivariate scatter of a
random error term at a
single point on a single
regression line (i.e.,
identical upper and lower
bounds)

is a role in the very short time frame for a purer psychological analysis, something most economists have avoided in the past. (Frazer and Boland 1983, 138 n.13)

To illustrate a structural change for a simple relation, such as that in Figure 7.2b, a shift in the parameters α and β in equation (1) may occur. And, indeed, for each of the regression lines shown in Figure 7.2c we have a vertical least-squares fit and a horizontal-least-squares fit with bivariate scatter and all. Elsewhere (Frazer 1994b, 69–73) I show this sort of structural change with statistical results for two periods roughly divided by the mid 1960s, using an interest-rate (i_L) and a money-stock series (M) as well as income (Y). Such a structural change is shown for interest rate and the velocity of money in Figure 7.3, where in the initial context, I have changes in the expected inflation rate, P^e, impacting on both the long-term bond rate, i_L and the velocity ratio Y/M. Allowing for some probability in the formation of the expectation, Pb[P^e]P^e, as in the different context (Frazer 1994a, 244–245 n.7, figure 9.6), I see inflationary expectation as entering almost entirely into the long-bond rate i_L and affecting the numerator and the denominator of the velocity ratio differently, such that the velocity ratio reflects only a small part of the effect shown for the interest rate.

Where the probabilitic-weighted, inflationary expectation is mild and contained within bounds of ±3 percent, say, over a transitory state of business conditions, the two variables (ln i, and ln V) may simply rock in phase with the transitory condition. However, when the inflationary prospect is sustained and dramatic, as it was from the mid-1960s to the early 1980s, the two variables will drift apart as the increase in the inflation rate takes a full toll on the interest rate and only a partial toll on the velocity ratio, as on the right site of Figure 7.3

To emphasize this impact, via the expectations route, I extend the connection of the Friedman system to "psychological economics." To repeat, in revisiting the subject in 1994 (Frazer 1994b, 69–73), I illustrate dramatic changes in the relation between the velocity of money and the interest rate in the mid-1960s. In doing so, I also report changes in the bounds on the true regression coefficient. The idea is that both variables are responding to changes in expectations regarding the inflation rate, except where the change in time approaches zero at the limit. Quite possibly the agents learned more about the central bank and inflation from both experience and the work of Friedman and Schwartz (1963).

FRIEDMAN'S STORY ABOUT MULTIPLE REGRESSIONS

Finally Friedman offers as an appendix "A Cautionary Tale About Multiple Regressions." In it he recalls a research assignment with the World War II-related Statistical Research Group (Frazer 1988, 155–159), and he reviews the assignment "to serve as a statistical consultant to . . . projects seeking to develop

Figure 7.2
Distributions Regarding the Error Term and Structural Change

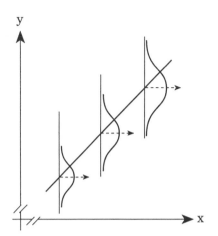

a. Probability distributions
with different variance
along regression line

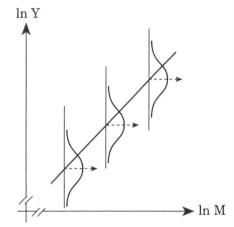

b. Probability distributions
with same variance along
regression line

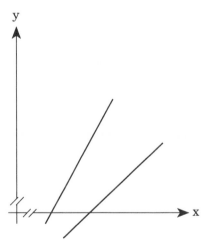

c. Change in the structure
regarding illustration in
"a part"

Figure 7.3
The Interest-Rate/Velocity-of-Money Association

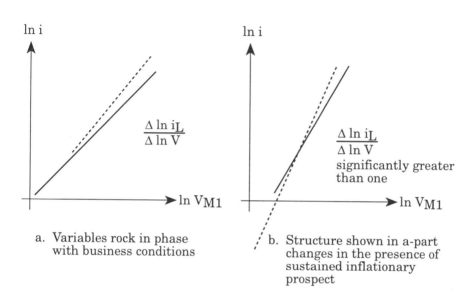

a. Variables rock in phase
   with business conditions

b. Structure shown in a-part
   changes in the presence of
   sustained inflationary
   prospect

an improved alloy for use in airplane turbo-superchargers as a lining for jet engines." The goal was to develop alloys that could withstand heat.

In his approach, Friedman ended up placing in the right-hand members of two regression equations what he believed to be the relevant factors as determined by prior experience with each variable separately. The regressions so obtained for the two new alloys were then to undergo further testing at an MIT laboratory. There specific weights were hung on standard turbine blades made from the respective alloys. They placed the rigs in a furnace and subjected them to very high temperatures to test whether the alloys would hold up under such conditions.

After the multiple regressions, which met all the statistical tests, Friedman was so optimistic that he called the alloys F–1 and F–2 (after Friedman, of course). The experiment proceeded, but, as Friedman points out, this was physics, not economics. A few days later he received the laboratory results.

Friedman concludes his story:

[M]y two alloys had ruptured in something like 1–4 hours, a much poorer outcome than for many prior alloys. F-1 and F-2 were never heard of again.

Ever since, I have been extremely skeptical of relying on projections from a multiple regression, however well it performs on the body of data from which it is derived; and the more complex the regression, the more skeptical I am. (FS 1991, 49)

NOTES

1. The wide variety of evidence Friedman points to would be that included in Wesley Mitchell's work on "greenbacks" (Mitchell 1903) and the post–World War I inflation in Germany.

Episodes of money growth and inflation appear in the Friedman directed *Studies in the Quantity Theory of Money* (1956). Other such episodes occurred in Germany in the 1957–1960 period (Frazer 1994b, 112 n.15), in Florida in its land-boom period (Frazer and Guthrie 1995), and on other occasions.

2. The common convention for dealing with episodic impacts on the data series is to include a dummy variable with a coefficient of 1 or 0, depending on the presumed occurrence of the episode. In doing this, several problems arise. For one, the episode may impact a number of the other time series under consideration and add to the separation-of-effects dilemma cited earlier. Second, episodic impacts may act as the main determinant of the data series, when in fact the dummy-variable technique assigns secondary importance to the episodic impacts. Third, the matters at hand are policy-oriented, and the practical men and women of affairs are mostly consumed by the prospect of episodic impacts and distrustful of the econometric convention (Frazer 1994a, 160 n.10).

3. In regression analysis, as a rule of thumb, the number of degrees of freedom is equal to the number of observations involved in estimating a regression equation minus the number of parameters in the regression equation in question. The number of parameters represents the degrees of freedom "given up" and used to fix points from which deviations are measured. In general, the degrees of freedom are the observations not used up in the estimating or statistical procedure involved in a given computation. They are, in other words, the number of observations in excess of the number which would prohibit any imperfection of a statistical inference made without regard to degrees of freedom (Frazer 1967, 331).

Also, the "error variances" are the true bounds on the respective regression coefficients (Frazer 1967, 37–39, 39 n.3). In the two-variable case the bounds are readily set, but as variables are added it becomes impossible to set them.

4. The regression effect arises in a linear, two-variable context (say, x and y, y = f[x]), when y is first regressed on x, and x is then regressed on y (Frazer 1967, 37–39, 39 n.3; Friedman 1992; FS 1982, 173–174 nn.28, 29, 277 n.18, 224–225, 227), as illustrated in Figure 7.1a and as discussed.

Along the same lines, a change in the structure for Figure 7.3b, as mentioned in the text (Frazer and Boland 1983, 138 n.14), is illustrated in Figure 7.3b.

5. The standard error of estimate is an absolute measure of dispersion or scatter about the line of regression, usually measured along the axis of the dependent or predicted variable. It is a form of average of deviations about the regression line, and one standard error of estimate measured off plus and minus about the regression line will include 68 percent of the observations scattered about the regression line if the scatter is normally distributed and independent of the regression line. In this respect, the standard error of estimate is similar to the standard deviation, except the standard deviation measures the scatter about the arithmetic mean of the dependent variable. In case the conditions of the classical theory of regression obtain, the standard error of

estimate is, further, the square root of the "unexplained" variance in a dependent variable:

$$\sigma_{u=} \sqrt{\frac{\sum (y-\hat{y})^2}{n}}$$

where n is the number of observations in the sample, and $\sum (y-\hat{y})^2$ is the sum of the square of the vertical differences between the observed and estimated values of the dependent variable.

As an absolute measure in the form of an average, the standard error of estimate is expressed in terms of original units of the dependent variable

6. The t-value for the text equation, $y = x + \beta x + u$, is

$$t = (\hat{\beta} - \beta) / S_{\hat{\beta}}$$

Here $\hat{\beta}$ is an estimated regression coefficient, β some hypothetical slope, and $S_{\hat{\beta}}$ the standard error of the regression coefficient.

The t-value may be used in connection with a test of statistical significance (see Frazer 1967, 341–345).

7. In two separate contexts (FS 1991, 42 n.3; Friedman 1992, 2131 n.2) Sir Francis Galton is discussed in the context of the regression fallacy. Friedman says it is "the phenomenon in question that gave regression analysis its name." With respect to Galton, Friedman says:

> Galton examined the heights of fathers and sons, and found that the sons of tall fathers tended to be shorter than their fathers, i.e., regressed toward the mean; similarly, the fathers of tall sons tended to be shorter than their sons, i.e., regressed toward the mean. This is simply the well-known phenomenon that in a linear regression of x and y, the regression of y and x is flatter relative to the x axis than the regression of x on y. (Friedman 1992, 2131)

A highly relevant condition of the classical theory is that the variance of the probability distribution is constant over the range of the regression line, as illustrated in Figure 7.2b (as distinct from Figure 7.2a). The variance is a measure of the dispersion of values for the random error term, as illustrated in note 5.

8. Such results appear in Frazer (1994b, 69–73) for the 1951:III–1965:IV and 1959:I–1985:IV periods, respectively.

Chapter 8

The Philosophical Ideological Left

Paradoxically, as I have pointed out (pages 49–51 and Chapter 4), "Institutionalists who claim roots in the work of Thorstein Veblen and Wesley Mitchell come to vehemently attack Friedman's advancement of the economics found in his Mitchell-connected/NBER work." Apparently, feeling excluded from mainstream economics, as Thorstein Veblen was (Frazer 1988, 390–391 n.14), the group turned inward and sought authority for its position in terms of opposition to the outdated psychology and view of science found in neoclassical economics and its "economic man" and perfect-market axioms (Frazer 1988, 30, 34, 118–125, 194–199, 203, 462, 476; 1994a, 6, 13, 55, 68). Taking up views of science that would oppose those inherent in neoclassical economics, the organized stream of institutionalist turned to the American pragmatist John Dewey and, following Veblen's lead and later that of J. K. Galbraith (Frazer 1988, 194–199), continued the attack on outdated axioms and neoclassical economics, which became the AFEE-institutionalist "whipping boy." They set great store in methodology (meaning the philosophy of science) as a means of pointing to a proper way of doing science.

In the meantime, Milton Friedman entered upon the scene with ties to Mitchell and the NBER's data-gathering and measurement efforts, with a rather pragmatic bent and a superb background in mathematical statistics for his day (Frazer 1988, 107–136, 155–160). To be sure, opportunities opened for him at the right time as he launched his thirty-year tenure at the University of Chicago in 1947; began attending meetings of the Mont Pelerin Society atop the beautiful Mt. Pelerin in Switzerland, where he met future political and economic leaders (including the philosopher Karl Popper); and began his cycles-, trends-, and monetarist-oriented research at Mitchell's NBER. However, in moving along these lines, he introduced the collection of his early essays (1953b) and outlined what may be viewed as the uses-of-methods

oriented philosophy for his current and future work. The first paragraph of
the introduction to the collection proceeds thus:

In his admirable book on *The Scope and Method of Political Economy* John Neville
Keynes distinguishes among "a positive science . . . a body of systematized
knowledge concerning what is; a normative or regulative science . . . a body of
systematized knowledge discussing criteria of what ought to be . . . ; an art . . . [,] a
system of rules for the attainment of a given end"; comments that "confusion between
them is common and has been the source of many mischievous errors"; and urges the
importance of "recognizing a distinct positive science of political economy." (Friedman
1953a, 3)

When considering the larger perspective of Friedman's background, the 1953
collection of essays, the early pages of the famous essay, and Friedman's
future work, this paragraph goes back to Figure 4.1 and the discussion
surrounding it. Most notably positive economics concerns the choice between
policy A and policy B (i.e., differences derived from predictions about how to
proceed [Friedman 1953a, 5]), normative economics concerns widely accepted
goals and "basic" values (Friedman 1953a, 5), and "art" concerns policy-
guiding rules for getting to the goals.

     Viewed this way, the last essays of the collection are a methodological
criticism of Lange and another of Lerner's *The Economics of Control*. Lange
and Lerner are charged with a misuse of formal methods and a failure to
distinguish between "what is" and the value systems men can only fight about.
The friction between Friedman and Oscar Lange and others associated with the
Cowles Commission for Research at the University of Chicago becomes
apparent (Frazer 1988, 705–707; Friedman 1953a, 11–14 nn.9, 11).

     As Friedman's famous essay proceeds, he underscores the direct bearing
of his plan on "the perennial criticism of 'orthodox' economic theory"
(Friedman 1953a, 30), cites Veblen and Oliver in connection with the criticism
(1898 and 1947, respectively), and then points to the theory of monopolistic or
imperfect competition as an example of theory that "possesses none of the
attributes that would make it a truly useful general theory" (Friedman 1953a,
38). In other words, coming from a somewhat American institutionalist
background himself, but with NBER connections and the added dimension of
mathematical statistics, Friedman was undermining lines of thought that served
as the foundation of the initial American institutionalist orientation and that
later would become hallmarks of AFEE institutionalists. Currently, they are
represented by the University of Texas–connected H. H. Liebhafsky and E. E.
Liebhafsky and by James Webb.

     Although much centers in this chapter on the AFEE/institutionalist
identification with Dewey, Veblen, and lines of thought emerging from the
theories of monopolistic and imperfect competition, it would be a grievous
mistake to see the famous essay as simply an attack on the Veblen-connected
"perennial criticism" of "orthodoxy" and theories of imperfect and
monopolistic competition (Friedman 1953a, 30, 38) as Webb did (1987, 411).

Indeed, it makes greater sense to single out the rift with the Abber Lerner stance in *The Economics of Control* (Friedman 1953b, 3, 301–319), the decades-long conflicts that Friedman entered into regarding a "retreat into purely formal or tautological analysis" by numerous economists (Friedman 1953a, 11–12), and "a group connected with the Cowles Commission in Economics at the University of Chicago" and even later with Yale University (Frazer 1988, 68–87, 281–325). In any case, and perhaps no great surprise— in all of the instances at hand—those groups and works Friedman singles out on technical/philosophical grounds would appear to the political/ideological left of him by the time his career in economics had played out. These behaviorist/institutionalist groups favor enlarged roles for government in the areas of fiscal policy, government regulation of business, and monetary matters.

FRIEDMAN'S OWN REVOLUTION

In going about his own revolution in economics,[1] Friedman no doubt wittingly or otherwise saw importance in disconnecting his Mitchell/NBER leanings from emerging Cowles Commission and institutionalist elements as well as in making overtures to orthodox economic theory, even as he was dramatically and in large part departing from it. To be sure, there are in Friedman's revolutionary work successful efforts at redirecting major parts of the mechanical, mathematical-based apparatus of economics rather than forthrightly rejecting them, and making promotional overtures to "a valid orthodoxy" (Frazer 1988, 119). Efforts at redirection include the liquidity preference analysis from Chapter 5 and the Marshallian demand curve work, briefly reviewed later.

Connecting my own sentiments to those of Friedman, I would point out that mathematics is a very flexible language, that it should not be judged by the way it appears in the ceteris paribus-based neoclassical economics and in selected texts on mathematical economics, and that as a flexible language mathematics can be used to rescue parts of economics that otherwise are condemned by it. Indeed, it would be a horrendous disservice to trash the mathematically based apparatus found in economics, as AFEE institutionalists would, simply because of either the past inflexibility of its uses or the added sophistication needed when the analysis moves along dynamic lines with specific time frames, psychological time, and all.

In my own efforts at interpreting and piecing together Friedman's economics, his background, and ultimately the Friedman system, I never saw Friedman's essay in the negative way Liebhafsky and Liebhafsky (hereafter L-L) and Webb did. Rather, I saw it in the light of the revolutionary economics he engaged in, and promoted, although I had been at interals a student with institutionalists such as Clarence Ayers at Texas and Joseph Dorfman at Columbia, and I had read the works of the labor economists and John R. Commons.

In 1978, I was turning my attention to Friedman's background and education in an effort to go beyond simply reading his articles and books, which I had done for years. In the winter term of 1978, I visited Friedman, shortly after Lawrence Boland's piece on Friedman's 1953 essay appeared (Boland 1979), and in November Lawrence Boland attended a session where I delivered a paper that became the 1983 article with Boland (Frazer and Boland 1983). Operating independently of us, James Wible was writing on Friedman's economics and the philosophy of science (Wible 1982). He was shortly to take note of "An Essay on the Foundations of Friedman's Methodology" (Frazer and Boland 1983) and to publish his paper "The Instrumentalism of Dewey and Friedman" (1984).[2] As noted, a wave of publications appeared in response to Boland's prior work on methodology, the Frazer-Boland essay, and Wible's 1984 paper. In responses to Wible, I especially turn to L-L (1985), Wible's reply to L-L (1985), Webb's much longer "Comment on Wible" (Webb 1987, 393–429), and Wible's "Reply to Webb" (Wible 1987, 430–440).

Although all of these authors persist in the false and unfounded view that Friedman is a neoclassical economist defending an indefensible position (first taken up in Chapter 3), they offer interesting positions and revealing interpretations to which I now turn.

Furthermore, I agree with the position I find in Wible's effort (Frazer 1988, 133–136; Wible 1984, 1049, 1058–1058, 1062; 1987), namely, any discernible philosophy of science found in Friedman's essay and in his economics would have to be based on the way Friedman did economics and on the implications of his indirect use of statistical methods. Most notably, I agree with his repeated use of the simple regression method to analyze a few interdependent data series at a time, and his proceeding indirectly to get at what is measurable, such as relating the ordinary and compensated demand curves to the terms of a price index, where direct measurement or identification is not attainable (say, as in the case of Marshall's demand schedule, Frazer 1994a, 15–16).

If we use the term "methods methodology" to fit into this context, I have no problem with such usage. However, Webb claims that Wible's effort to reduce Friedman's methodology to a special case of Dewey's instrumental philosophy is absurd.

THE WEBB AND WIBLE CONFLICT, USES OF TERMS, AND FRIEDMAN'S WORK

A part of the conflict between Webb and Wible lies in the two meanings Webb discerns in the term "instrumentalism." First, "the term 'instrumental view of science' is used in contemporary philosophy of science following Karl Popper's usage." According to Webb:

Karl Popper used the term "instrumentalism" in reference to a doctrine in which scientific theories are considered to be nothing more than convenient devices for the generation of empirical predictions, and that therefore the actual existence of theoretical entities (such as subatomic particles) is irrelevant. Whether institutionalists like it or not the use of "instrumentalism" (in Popper's sense) is firmly imbedded in the contemporary literature of the philosophy of science. (Webb 1987, 423 n.1)

Next, Webb uses the term in Popper's sense but notes that John Dewey's "instrumentalist philosophy" or just "instrumentalist philosophy" will be used as Dewey used the term.

This strange distinction in terms comes about for several interrelated reasons: (1) because Dewey's instrumental philosophy rejects the usage after Karl Popper, (2) because the AFEE institutionalists have philosophical roots in the instrumental philosophy of John Dewey (Webb 1987, 193; Wible 1984, 1049), (3) because Lawrence Boland identified Friedman's economics in instrumentalist terms (Boland 1979; Wible 1985, 986), (4) because Boland joined me on the *American Economic Review* piece "An Essay on the Foundations of Friedman's Methodology" (Frazer and Boland 1983).

Boland himself was very interested in philosophy of science arguments as opposed to the practice of economics, whereas a main tenet of the Frazer-Boland essay is that Friedman's philosophy of science should be discerned from his background and the writings on economics rather than from any interest of his in the formal writings of philosophers (including Karl Popper). In the *AER* piece we paid special attention to Friedman's "indirect method," as it related to uses of statistical methods and the mechanical apparatus found in economics. Although Friedman was closely tied to Wesley C. Mitchell via Columbia University and the National Bureau and to Karl Popper via meetings of the Mont Pelerin Society (Frazer 1988, 172–175, 180–182), he had only indirect links with the philosopher John Dewey via Mitchell and the Mont Pelerin connection to Popper.

Simply put, a main thrust of Friedman's work was that of bringing observation to bear on the mechanical structure of economics. Having a special interest in Mitchell's work on business cycles, an interest in Mitchell as an "empirical scientist" and an economic theorist (Frazer 1988, 107–136; Friedman 1952), and a remarkable background in mathematical statistics (Frazer 1988, 155–160), Friedman discerned early on that little of a fruitful nature could come from the efforts to identify static constructs in economics directly and to separate effects through the latter economics and the emerging fashion in econometrics directly. Hence, a Friedman variant of instrumentalism arises (Frazer 1984a)—a selection of mechanical features from economics that have the quality of instruments, combined with an "indirect approach" to an empirical economics.

Returning to Figure 4.1 and discussion the emphasis is on prediction—the indirect use of the apparatus and the uses of methods. However, the theory as explanation of observed behavior and as argument in support of policy A or policy B is not forsaken. The attention presently given to behavior does indeed require a release from the outdated psychology underlying neoclassical economics. Arguments for one policy over another call for some explanation. Even as Friedman's rule regarding monetary policy may be strictly stated (Frazer 1994a, 45; 1994b, 39–50), it makes no sense without the theory behind it (say, "policy B" in Figure 4.1), the discussion of policy A's implementation in the 1937–1938 recession (Frazer 1994b, 66–67), the concept of a more or less desired stock of money in relation to the actual stock (Frazer 1994a, 40–41), and numerous other arguments and counterarguments such as "pegging and chasing interest rates" (Frazer 1994a, 101–102).

To be sure, the entire body of the mechanical apparatus is expectation-oriented along highly specified and not simply arbitrary lines. The specifics extend to inflation rate forecasts, bull movements, consumer confidence, Gestalt psychology, motives for holding money when connected to the definition of money, episodic impacts, markets evaluation of returns, uncertainty, liquidity preference, liquidity shifts generally, the permanent income consumption function, interest rates, the Bundesbank effect, exchange rates, and the numerous instances of psychological time.[3]   The plausibility of the expectation orientation and its explanatory power are greatly enhanced by concepts such as "psychological time" (especially in regard to the effect of the interest rate, Frazer 1994a, 142), the slanting and discounting of best judgments, and the process for the dating of turning points in business conditions (Frazer 1994a, 235–238).   Indeed, psychological time phenomena are among the most likely repetitive prospects in economics.   Other, still expectation-oriented prospects concern behavior shared by parts (such as firms) and the economy as a whole, and the roles of bank credit, money balances, and the velocity of money (Frazer 1994b; Frazer and Guthrie 1995).

WIBLE, THE LIEBHAFSKYS AND LAGS IN INTERPRETING THE FAMOUS ESSAY

Wible attaches considerable importance to the papers by Boland plus Frazer and Boland (1979 and 1983, respectively), hedges this attachment somewhat, and introduces his own rather limited background in economics in replying to L-L.[4]   At the same time, however, he points to a clash of perspectives in his partial identification with Frazer and Boland and the defensive tone of L-L's comments (Wible 1985, 991).

I believe that Boland's [1979] essay and Frazer and Boland's [1983] later essay are the clearest interpretations of Friedman's positive economics and his economic research that he, Friedman, will ever endorse. They provide a coherent starting point when assessing Friedman. I accept their work as the best available substitute for direct statements on these issues by Friedman. (Wible 1985, 988)

Also,

L-L do not effectively refute the identification of Friedman's positive economics with instrumentalism. At this point in time only a direct, published disavowal by Friedman could destroy this identification. L-L virtually ignore instrumentalism as it is understood in contemporary philosophy of science, make no references to it, and simply dismiss Boland's contention that Friedman now accepts an instrumentalist characterization of his essay. If Boland's contention is true, then Friedman's original essay must be read somewhat differently. For example L-L state that "Friedman's reliance on the *a priori* constitutes a direct contradiction of Dewey's instrumentalism" (p. 979). Yet if L-L truly grasped the nature of Friedman's instrumentalism, they would realize that Friedman's earlier statements about the *a priori* can no longer be considered as representing his views. If Friedman now endorses instrumentalism, then he has essentially de-emphasized his concern for *a priori* considerations in science. (Wible 1985, 990)

Wible also asked, "Why did we have to wait three decades to find out that Friedman was an instrumentalist?" My answer to this includes several points: First, as already stated, we are talking about Friedman's variant of instrumentalism (Frazer 1984a). Although Friedman had had some association with Popper since 1947, he was not particularly concerned with the labored reading of the philosophy of science. Second, it took some time to evaluate the essay in terms of Friedman's background and experiences. Third, Friedman had a world vision of changing economics, as James Tobin suggested (Frazer 1988, 710), and, he had done some economics that would fit into his vision of a total body of economics as he moved into the stage of executing the research that was planned at the NBER.

And, fourth, successful revolutionaries in economics, as a rule, are not entirely unconscious of the need to peddle the revolution by one means or another. The economics itself aside, a means I see in Friedman's case is that of a "valid orthodoxy" (i.e., though revolutionary, the radical nature of the work is packaged with orthodoxy)[5]—that and crisis conditions that set a stage for some acceptance at a policy level (Frazer 1988, 21–25, 368 n.55).

In fact, the question Wible asks (1985, 988) can be raised in several other contexts. When Friedman and Schwartz's *Monetary Trends* (1982) was reviewed, why did reviewers express dismay at the "idiosyncratic" nature of Friedman's uses of statistical methods? They questioned the absence of modern econometric method (Frazer 1988, 540), although Friedman's distinct use of statistical method could be traced from Harold Hotelling and Friedman's early work at the National Bureau. Also, in the FS confrontation with HE in 1991, the issues from the early 1980s and even earlier resurfaced.

L-L provide good examples of the misreading of Friedman. Besides noting Wible's uses of the terms "short run" and "long run," they note the absence of any specific dating and then point out that in economics periods of time are defined analytically (LL 1985, 976). They specifically imply a neoclassically rooted economics—where plant and equipment are treated as a fixed cost (the short-run period) and labor as a variable cost in obtaining the total cost line and, consequently, the marginal costs associated with it (Frazer

1994a, 63–65), and where a so-called long-run envelope function may be associated with the series of short-run, average-cost curves obtained for different fixed values for plant and equipment (Courant 1936, 171–183; Frazer 1994a, 65–66).

In contradistinction to this view of time—and mathematically derived, static curves—time enters along five additional lines. First are trend lines (or more permanent, long-run) components in the time series, and the transitory (or short-run) states (Figure 1-3; Frazer 1994a, 23–27, figure 1-7, 40–49). Second, these distinctions are extended to the theory of the firm (Frazer 1994a, 66–68; Friedman 1976, chap. 12). Third is Friedman's early attention to a theory of economic change and to Mitchell's emphasis on process and dynamic change (Frazer 1988, 153–155; Friedman 1950). Fourth is the change in the structure underlying the formation of inflationary expectations in the mid-1960s (text pages x, 17, 46, 103, n.4; Frazer and Boland 1983, 138, n.14; Frazer 1994a, 46–47; Friedman and Schwartz 1982, 478, 558–573). And, fifth, episodic impacts on the time series occur and relate especially to "psychological time" (Frazer 1988, 731, 742; 1994a; FS 1982, 568–569).[6]

In addition to these roles for time and time based concepts, Wible points to time in the perspective of the philosopher, as I also do (Frazer 1988, 132–133). According to Wible:

> The short run refers to a period of time during which a specific statement is taken as being conjectural and hypothetical when experiments are being conducted and the evidence interpreted. The long run . . . refers to the state of opinion that prevails when this initial phase of experimentation and interpretation is over. The short run could be decades in length. The long run is decades if not centuries in length. (Wible 1985, 988)

L-L also offer a misreading of Friedman's "Marshallian Demand Curve" paper (1949). Traversing the common textbook distinction regarding the "ordinary" and "compensated" demand curves, they go into a tortured analysis of utility and real income (Henderson and Quandt 1971, 25; L-L 1985, 981–982) and miss the radical points of Friedman's view of the Marshallian demand curve. Following Roger Alford (1956), Friedman is offering an unusual interpretation of Marshall's work. First, his argument applies to the economy as a whole. There may be groups that share the impact of some episode (for example, a tax rate change). Next, backing away from *modus ponens* and something he cannot measure (namely, utility), Friedman moves on to a price index and to the terms of a price index to deal with something he can measure (namely, purchasing power losses or gains). Taking note of a price index, P, he readily sets up the prospect for a monetary analysis of inflation (Frazer 1994a, 13–19) in terms of the Cambridge equation of exchange.[7] Viewed in this way, Friedman is moving toward an analysis where groups (including households and firms) share impacts on the economy as a whole.[8]

POLICY CHOICES, THE MONT PELERIN SOCIETY, AND POPPER AND FRIEDMAN

Within the scope of policy alternatives introduced in Figure 4.1 and surrounding discussion, Friedman himself does not allow scope for "fundamental differences in basic values, differences about which men can ultimately only fight" (Friedman 1953a, 5). Here and especially here is where he aligns himself with Karl Popper and the Mont Pelerin Society (Frazer 1988, 172–180).[9]   Among Webb's comments on Popper where I find affinity between Popper and Friedman, with some qualifications, are the following:

Popper's intellectual temperament is more sympathetic to elitist policies and less confident that democratic institutions are resilient enough to solve all of society's problems[1]. Popper's biases lean toward laissez-faire tempered with compassion. He is most concerned with the danger of the grand dogmas, particularly what he calls "historicism" (the Marxian doctrine of the historical necessity of the progression of stages of society)[2]. This is not surprising. Popper's own life spans a period that includes participation in the vital intellectual life of Vienna between the wars, the rise of Hitler, and the Soviet colonization of Eastern Europe after the second world war. He is at best ambivalent about collective action and antipathetic toward central economic planning, although in principle he allows for piecemeal social engineering. Popper the social theorist should cause Popper the resolute advocate of criticism to blush: Popper's acceptance of neoclassical economics' status as a science is rather uncritical[3]. (Webb 1987, 401–402)

. . . .

[W]ithin limits, scientific conventionalism (in Popper's sense) helps add to scientific understanding by working out the implications of existing bodies of theory. If scientists really threw their theories in the intellectual garbage can every time a few empirical facts contradicted these theories, there would seldom be time to discover what things the theory "said." However, at the extreme of scientific conventionalism, science becomes religion and scientists become priests and apologists and the growth of scientific knowledge stagnates. It should be noted that neoclassical economics is particularly susceptible to such tactics[4]. (Webb 1987, 406)

The qualifications to these paragraphs follow the bracketed superscripts. [1]The term "democratic institutions," for example, can be viewed here as applying to the socialist governments in Britain over the post–World War II period before the appearance of Margaret Thatcher as prime minister (Frazer 1988, 539–630). Particularly in relation to this role for the market economy Friedman aligns himself with Popper's position as set forth in the 1966 volumes titled *The Open Society and Its Enemies* (Frazer 1988, 335–341). And, no elitist to be sure, Friedman rather saw Plato as too authoritarian in Popper's Plato/Socrates distinction.

[2]No strictly "laissez-faire" nineteenth-century view, Friedman's concept of economic freedom (Frazer 1988, 479–486) encompasses political freedom in

that "political freedom means the absence of coercion of a man by his fellow men." The main reason for the market's being—and its accoutrements such as the gold-specie flows mechanism in its day—is to disperse power.   In *Capitalism and Freedom*, Friedman says:

The fundamental threat to freedom is the power to coerce, be it in the hands of a monarch, a dictator, an oligarchy, or a momentary majority.   The preservation of freedom requires the elimination of such concentration of power to the fullest possible extent and the dispersal and distribution of whatever power cannot be eliminated. . . . By removing the organization of economic activity from the control of political authority, the market eliminates this source of coercive power.   It enables economic strength to be a check to political power rather than a reinforcement. (Friedman 1962a, 15)

[3]As stated in Chapter 3, Friedman was no neoclassical economist. Nevertheless, he saw the prospects for economics as a social science only in connection with market-economy arrangements.

[4]In a comparable passage to this paragraph, Friedman wrote:

Yet the continued use and acceptance of the hypothesis over a long period, and the failure of any coherent, self-consistent alternative to be developed and be widely accepted, is strong indirect testimony to its worth.   The evidence for a hypothesis always consists of its repeated failure to be contradicted, continues to accumulate so long as the hypothesis is used, and by its very nature is difficult to document at all comprehensively.   It tends to become part of the tradition and folklore of a science revealed in the tenacity with which hypotheses are held rather than in any textbook list of instances in which the hypothesis has failed to be contradicted. (Friedman 1953a, 23)

Now, Webb will respond to this last paragraph, "It is hard to imagine anything more contrary to the spirit of Dewey (or Popper) than Friedman's appeals to 'tenacity' and to 'tradition and folklore' " (Webb 1987, 413). But Webb misuses the point, as it relates to Friedman. The point centers about the distinction between "normal science" and revolutionary change (Frazer 1988, 711–723) where the former takes place within an existing framework, such as neoclassical economics.   It is a filling in of the gaps and "mopping up activity," whereas the canons of revolution call for a new orientation, which we find at Friedman's hands. The old paradigm, as it may be called, cannot change too fast or it never becomes well defined and illustrated. As to Friedman, himself, when it came to his own revolutionary work, he was actually even opposed to peer review (Frazer 1988, 707–708), saying it "favors established scientists and directions of research" (Friedman 1981, 99). Friedman goes on to note that the work of Einstein and economists such as Adam Smith and J. M. Keynes and of the majority of contemporary Nobel laureates in economics could not have taken place if it depended on "peer review" and on National Science Foundation funding. Indeed, Friedman's

1953 essay and all his major work at the National Bureau were outside the more strictly "peer review" oriented journals.

WEBB ON FRIEDMAN AS A METHODOLOGICAL INSTRUMENTALIST

Webb's section "Friedman as a Methodological Instrumentalist" (Webb 1987, 407–414) is skewed by the present view that Friedman is no Poppenian, methodological instrumentalist.[10] However, some of Webb's main points are confronted in the following discussion.

The False Image of Friedman as Methodological Instrumentalist

In an overview (Webb 1987, 407) Webb saw the original part of Friedman's 1953 essay as little more than what Paul Samuelson called the "F-Twist," that is, "the curious assertion that unrealistic theories are superior to realistic theories." Webb then notes that those who interpret Friedman's position as methodological instrumentalism (most likely he means Boland 1979) shift the attention to the "as if" doctrine, notably, as he quotes it, to the view that reality of assumptions is irrelevant if the theory generates successful empirical predictions and that true predictions are "as if" the assumptions were true (Webb 1987, 407). However, in my view and also in that of Boland, the "as if" methodology plays out as follows:

[I]t is essentially that the axioms (or the axioms themselves viewed as hypotheses) cannot be viewed as descriptions of reality. Essentially and along with simplicity and fruitfulness, a verified prediction is "as if" the predicted behavior followed from axioms (not "as if" the axioms were true). (Frazer 1994a, 72)

On the other hand, turning to Friedman, Webb says:

It is understandable that recent interpretations of Friedman's "as if" doctrine have been in terms of methodological instrumentalism, since other interpretations of his position are even less defensible. (If "unrealistic" is taken to mean "not exhaustively descriptive" then Friedman's assertion is trivial since—as has been frequently pointed out from John Stuart Mill on—no theory can or should aspire to descriptive completeness. If "unrealistic" is taken to mean "false," Friedman is advocating logical and methodological anarchy, since *any* false assumption has *some* true predictions [Nagel 1963]). (Webb 1987, 413)

Now several nontrivial problems arise here. First the axioms themselves are never exhaustive, and some flexibility must enter. For example, we move from a profit maximization case (Frazer 1994a, 63-68) with virtually static analysis (where the change in time approaches zero at the limit) to a share of markets case when notion is added and where the analytical system is open ended (and thus receptive to episodic impacts, psychological time, and so on).

Second, the theories of market structures (by way of Chamberlin, Robinson, and others), which Friedman chose to illustrate his case about axioms and abstraction (Friedman 1953a, 38), themselves become exhaustively descriptive of points on a segment of the demand curve (Frazer 1994a, 68–71).

Third, from the rife with the Cowles Commission (Friedman 1953a, 12–13 n.11; text, pages 120–212), we may readily move to Lawrence Klein's connections there, to the Klein–Goldberger model, to the "superbig" models where there appeared to be no limit on the amount of detail that could be introduced (Frazer 1988, 66–87; 1994a, 210–214; 1994b, 159–160 nn. 6 and 10, 184, 201 n.2).

Along these lines of almost "exhaustive description," it may appear that Friedman's attention to the "as if" method and his indirect approach were warranted. Moreover, along the foregoing lines, it should be clear that Friedman's essay was not just a partisan counterattack on Richard Lester and the institutionalists as Webb says.

Now in following Karl Popper's use of the term "methodological instrumentalism," Webb asks (1987, 395); "Is Friedman really a methodological instrumentalist[?]" Reviewing Webb (1987, 407–414), my answer is no. As earlier (Frazer 1984a), Friedman's instrumentalism is his own variant of instrumentalism to be discerned from what he actually does and from his background for doing it. We may use the term "methods methodology" to suggest the philosophy of science implied by the use of methods (and Friedman's indirect method in particular).[11]

Any philosophy of science in Friedman's work, as Wible argues (Frazer 1988, 133–36), must be discerned from Friedman's uses of statistical methods, the major parts of the mechanical apparatus found in economics, and Friedman's "as if" method (Frazer 1994a, 54, 71–73).

Neoclassical Economics

Even when Webb takes up the predictive adequacy of neoclassical economics, there is a great deal of alignment between Friedman's positions and Webb's. For example, Friedman refers to Henry Schultz's wrenching the data to make it fit the theory (also see Stigler 1994, 1200), while Webb says, "empirical work in neoclassical economics seldom involves *testing* . . . but rather applications of the theory" (Webb 1987, 410).

Further, returning to the review of the alignment between Popper and Friedman, Webb adds the following:

But seen as tactics in defense of traditional competitive theory (no matter what future facts might emerge), with the defense of competitive theory part of a larger polemical agenda advocating free market economic policies, everything Friedman does makes sense. (Webb 1987, 414)

As the preceeding discussion may suggest, Webb's position is not far from the mark. In the essay Friedman did indeed exclude differences in basic values, "differences about which men can ultimately only fight" (1953a, 5).

The Extended Friedman System

Friedman's uses of statistical methods are simple in that many variables are analyzed a few at a time, before proceeding directly to the multiple regression technique, and Friedman's uses are simple and indirect by comparison with the multiple regression method and variations of that method that lie at crucial stages on the "independence" of the right-hand-side variables in such equations. Next, the major parts of the mechanical apparatus in question start with the static constructions found in the Marshallian plane, Marshallian markets, and so on (Frazer 1994a, 13–27), where in the Friedman system, change in time approaches zero at the limit. These major parts also extend to ordinal analysis, demand and cost curves, productivity curves, the theory of relative prices, and theories of the perfect market and monopoly, (Frazer 1994a, 56–75). And they extend to the liquidity preference plane (Frazer 1994a, 33–40) and appear in the Keynesian plane (Frazer 1994b, 122–135). The theory of relative prices is extended internationally to a theory of relative price levels and fixed and floating exchange rates (Frazer 1994b, 119–161).

A dynamic three-part monetary feature is now added: First, price indexes enter via the connection to prices in the Marshallian markets. Second, the price indexes enter the simple Cambridge equation of exchange and connect as well to liquidity preference demand for money (Frazer 1994a, 15–19, 40–49). Third, a technological growth feature is added via NBER referencing of business cycles and the Simon Kuznets growth orientation for national income (Frazer 1994a, 23–27, 221–225).

From this package, we get Friedman's consumption function work and his money-growth rule; His utility analysis is not entirely just in the background of all this (Frazer 1994a, 155–177). Further, the preferred money aggregate should grow at the anticipated rate in output, with allowance for secular shifts in the velocity of money. This rule concerns sustainable growth.

Now to this essentially Friedman background, I add a few points that are totally compatible with it and extend the analysis in other respects to achieve what I call the Friedman system. Most conspicuous is the production function work that has it roots in Cobb and Douglas's 1934 *The Theory of Wages* (Frazer 1994a, 60–63). I also bring Evsey Domar's model into play as it bears on Kuznets, Keynesian variables, and Friedman's permanent income (Frazer 1994a, 144–146). General rules regarding the money stock, growth in stock and flow quantities, and great ratios appear (Frazer 1994a, 75–81, 213–214).

Less conspicuously, as compared to what Friedman himself actually did, I offer a more general analysis (where the learning by the agents occurs over shorter time spans), I extend the system of analysis to incorporate an industrial sector that connects J. M. Keynes's work to the more general system; and, taking up problems in the implementation of Friedman's monetarist work, I connect the Friedman system to central bank operations, bond-market behavior, and interest rates (Frazer 1994b). The overall result of these efforts is a more open-ended analytical system that dramatically extends analyses of expectations in potentially more fruitful and useful directions.

The "as if" method, which I revisit, facilitates the use of the mechanical apparatus I outline. It does so, in large part, by freeing the apparatus from its outdated nineteenth-century psychological roots and by facilitating dynamic analyses (motion, specific time frames, psychological time, market shares instead of indeterminate profit maximums, and so on).

As reference to Friedman's variant of instrumentalism suggests, Friedman is only loosely and ideologically aligned with Popper. Philosophers of science, such as Popper, tend to think of physics as the queen of sciences,[12] while Friedman is well aware that economics is not physics (FS 1991, 48–49). It is in this respect that—as we turn to Friedman's view of economics as empirical science—we encounter Friedman on economics as a difficult subject. In this respect, "evidence is far more difficult to interpret" than that from contrived experiments (Friedman 1953a, 10), and so we are left with the indirect way of proceeding.

The chains of reasoning required to introduce economics to the world that generates the data series can be long and indirect, as I note in the case of Friedman's liquidity preference and Marshallian demand views. Examples of proceeding indirectly include my use of the long-term bond rate as a surrogate for monetary policy; as well as my approaches to interest and inflation rates via U.S., U.K., and FRG data for selected decades (Frazer 1994b), to the relation between interest rates and capital spending, and to the bond market constraint on health care reform in the early years of Bill Clinton's presidency.

NOTES

1. In *Power and Ideas* I take up "normal and revolutionary" change as regards scientific revolutions (Frazer 1988, 711–715), turn to "neoclassical economics" (Frazer 1988, 715–723), and then show that Friedman economics meets the criteria for revolutionary change (Frazer 1988, 723–731).

2. In 1985 Wible said:

Lawrence Boland [1979] published his paper identifying Milton Friedman's positive economics as instrumentalism. Then in a later paper William Frazer and Boland [1983] related Friedman's essay to Karl Popper's work. Since Dewey also identified his views as instrumentalism, a comparison of the instrumentalisms of Dewey and Friedman appeared to be the obvious way to *begin* the task of comparing pragmatism and recent philosophy of science. (Wible 1985, 986)

3. All of these topics are well indexed in Frazer (1994a and 1994b) and in Frazer and Guthrie (1995).

4. Wible (1985, 984–985, 988–989) points to institutional, post-Keynesian, and neoclassical bodies of economics and addresses the Friedman issues with little if any awareness of Friedman as one of the two major revolutionaries in economics in the twentieth century.

Even as he ties his articles to the Boland and to the Frazer and Boland work, Wible says (1985, 988), "This should not be construed to mean that I accept the Boland-Frazer characterization of Friedman's views on utility and economic man as my own or as being philosophically adequate. This implication is not in my article."

5. Examples of what I call Friedman's "valid orthodoxy" include the following: (1) Friedman's "The Marshallian Demand Curve" (1949) is really not Marshall's view but Friedman's; (2) The Fisher equation enters but takes on its modern/contemporary significance from Friedman's work (Frazer 1994a, 40–52; Friedman 1968); (3) Friedman's linking of the Cambridge equation of exchange to Keynes's as well as to the Keynesian liquidity-preference construction; (4) the introduction of Walter Bagehot's *Lombard Street* (1873) in the Friedman-Schwartz discussion of the Federal Reserve as a lender of last resort (FS 1963, 395–399); (5) the alignment with Marshall in Friedman's emphasis on "Walrasian" as indicating mathematical elegance (Frazer 1988, 39, 117–118); (6) Friedman's use of his essay on Wesley Mitchell (Friedman 1950) to introduce dissertation topics that later surface in the Friedman-edited work of 1957 *Studies in the Quantity Theory of Money* (Frazer 1988, 180–181); (7) Friedman's invocation of Frank Knight as an authority (FS 1991, 39), even when he in fact departs from Frank Knight in numerous ways, including the prospects for economics as an empirical science (Frazer 1988, 116, 118, 306); (8) Friedman's decade-long avoidance of the challenge posed by Hendry and Ericsson.; (9) his consistent identification with Harold Hotelling on the regression fallacy; (10) his treatment of the liquidity preference analysis on both the so-called macro and firm levels (Frazer 1994a, 40–45, 65–67) while all the time avoiding confrontation over his view of microeconomics and macroeconomics as false distinctions.

6. Psychological time concerns the reaction to episodes where expectations regarding outcomes are formed by looking backward and forming a current view by analogy to some earlier episodic impact. The time concept is in terms of the historical episodes and not some fixed, distributed-lag, chronological view of time. A ready example is found in the case of the 1987 stock market crash where analogies were made to the 1929 stock market crash (Frazer 1988, 682–686, 690). My preferred example concerns the impact of interest rates on capital spending and the financing of planned capital outlays (Frazer 1994a, 142).

7. As readers may recall, The Cambridge equation may be written M = k (. . .) P Q, where M is the money stock, k (. . .) is the inverse of the velocity of money (i.e., inverse of Y/M), and nominal income (Y) is the product of the price index (P) and output in constant-dollar terms (i.e., Q = Y/P).

8. As Friedman proceeds with the theory of the firm, he is consistent in his analysis of Marshallian markets (Frazer 1994a, 66–67; Friedman 1976, chap. 12). In another instance of my Friedman-system view, I add production functions for the firm and the economy as a whole, notably (Frazer 1994a, 60–63),

$$q = f (n, k)$$
$$Q = f (L, K)$$

where lowercase letters represent firms and uppercase letters represent the economy as a whole. The letters q and Q are output, the letters n and L are labor, and the letters k and K are capital.

The idea is that labor's and capital's shares of income at the firm level are reflected in labor's and capital's shares for the economy as a whole.

9. In *Power and Ideas* (Frazer 1988, 173, 387 n.28) I cite two of Popper's books where Friedman finds views that reinforce his own (Popper 1965; 1966).

10. Webb views Popper as using the term "in reference to a doctrine in which scientific theories are considered to be nothing more than convenient devices for the generation of empirical predictions, and that therefore the actual existence of theoretical entities . . . is irrelevant" (Webb 1987, 422 n.1).

11. To recapture a few terms as we presently use them, "methodology" means philosophy of science (L-L 1985, 975) as a view of scientific decision making. "Methods" or "uses of methods" refers strictly to mathematical and statistical methods, to the techniques found there, to their uses, and to the mechanical apparatus Friedman draws upon in economics. As previously introduced, these uses may go along different lines (Figure 1.2). Following Webb (1987, 294 and 422 n.1), the term "instrumentalist view of science" is based on Karl Popper's usage. There, also, the term "methodological instrumentalism will be used in Popper's sense of instrumentalism."

12. Webb says, "Popper's philosophy is inspired by his admiration for sciences especially theoretical physics" (Webb 1987, 701).

Part III

Tenets of Monetarism, Institutionalists, and the New Classical School

Along the way to a more complete demarcation of the Friedman system of economic analysis, Part III draws distinctions between the Friedman system and three other bodies of work where confusion lies regarding the Friedman system and features of Friedman's economics upon which the present analytical system relies. As characteristic of Friedman's work, the analysis of money is present in all instances.

First, Chapter 9 lists and annotates tenets of the Friedman system. The term "monetarism" is defined, discussed, and assessed as to its origin. The common practice in attempting to provide the key features of "monetarism," as it were, has been to state the features in such a way as to encompass a sizable subset of economists. Since this approach has borne little fruit, I produce a set of tenets that focuses more on the work of Friedman and the Friedman system I offer. Not only do I point to undocumented statements regarding monetarism, but I note inharmonious positions even while reviewing the work of Karl Brunner and Allan Meltzer who, by most accounts, would unquestionably fit into the "monetarist" school.

Second, Part III deals with the terms "endogenous," "exogenous," and variations on them. In particular, I consider an AFEE/institutionalist view in Chapter 10, where the money stock is said to be endogenous, as opposed to the Friedman system view which has institutionalist roots of its own, as indicated by the Chicago I cell in Figure 1.2 and the Wesley Mitchell and Chicago-I cells in Figure 1.4. Of special prominence in Chapter 10, I offer Friedman-system/institutionalist hypotheses referred to as the central banks hypothesis (H_{CB}) and the theoretical works hypothesis (H_{TW}). In the Friedman-system view the government or the policymaking authority is responsible for the money stock. Following this route, attempts to impart refined statistical meaning to the definitions of "endogenous" and "exogenous" become problematic. Further, both the AFEE institutionalists I cite and Hendry and Ericsson, cited earlier, view the money stock as endogenous. Such views are in opposition to the Friedman system as well as Friedman/Schqarts positions (1991, 41–42).

Third, the new classical school (NCS)—which receives new visibility with Robert Lucas's receipt of the 1995 Nobel Prize in economics—has linkages to an inharmonious past at the University of Chicago. Dealing with this, I further delineate the Friedman–system view and the concept of rationality found in the NCS rational expectations.

Very much in contrast to the Friedman system, the NCS draws the distinction between risk and uncertainty whereby risk is actuarial (or classical) probability. In all of this, uncertainty is incomplete information rather than probability, and, in contrast to the Friedman system, it facilitates an increase in mathematical elegance, limits the prospect of learning by agents, and precludes a role for episodic impacts on the data series, psychological time, and so on.

Not only does the NCS facilitate enhanced elegance at the expense of relevance, I argue, it attributes knowledge of highly technical, abstract, ceteris paribus–based economics to the economic agents. It does all of this at a time and in regard to an economics that economists themselves would argue over. Even giving due allowance to Friedman's view whereby pool players can behave like they know the complicated mathematics behind their action, the NCS's economists ask too much of the agents, when, at the same time, they offer no insightful empirical hypotheses. Even so, the NCS gains significance by calling attention to the business conditions, stabilization policy, and expectations areas of study that gained visibility at the hands of Wesley Mitchell, J. M. Keynes, and Milton Friedman.

In Chapter 11's view of the NCS, the economy ends in a superrational state, with Walrasian equations and a very general quantity-theoretic equation where even stock market prices are lumped with those for the current output of goods and services. There is, to be sure, an inconsistency here, as taken up in the Appendix to Chapter 11, when analyses purport to focus upon the conditions illustrated in Figure 1.3.

Chapter 9

Tenets of Monetarism: A Friedman-System Variation

The addition of the term "monetarism" to the money/monetarist lexicon of economics is commonly associated with Karl Brunner (Laidler 1991, 639; Mayer 1978, 1 n.1; Meltzer in Wood and Woods, vol. III, 1990, 194; Stein 1986, 1).[1] In reference to the term, these economists cite Brunner's 1968 piece (reprinted in Wood and Woods [hereafter WW], vol. I, 1990, 368–396). Among them, Thomas Mayer goes on to assert that David Fand popularized the term in a September 1970 piece in *Banca Nazionale del Lavoro* (Fand 1970) and in *Kredit und Kapital* (Fand 1970, vol. 3).

However, the term appears in neither the Brunner article, nor in Fand's. And, as a Friedman student (Friedman 1962b, 3), Fand certainly has a Friedman orientation, with the exception of treating some fashions of the time.[2] Further, Lord Kaldor does not cite the Brunner piece in his July 1970 article "The New Monetarism," where he says, "The 'new monetarism' is a 'Friedman Revolution' more truly than Keynes was the sole fount of the 'Keynesian Revolution.' " Also, following Kaldor in the July issue of *Lloyds Bank Review*, a later exchange with Friedman appears in October 1970 under the monetarism label (reprinted in WW, vol. II, 1990, 29–34). Moreover, for 1970 *Lloyds Bank Review* was the twentieth most cited journal in economics, while *Banca Nazionale del Lavoro* and *Kredit und Kapital* were unranked journals (Laband and Piette 1994).

Friedman himself did not like the monetarist/monetarism labels for the work he engaged in. Although his early preference was "the quantity theory of money," and although I refer to "a Friedman system" of analysis as all-embracing, the term "monetarism" does reflect the ideological tensions and

---

This chapter is the basis for my "The Monetarist School of Economics," *Encyclopedia of Keynesian Economics* (1997).

passions of the debates that arise among economists on the topics of money and central banking. Most recent cases are the European Monetary System, the prospects for one money and one supercentral bank (whether a Bundesbank, EuroFed, or Bank of England model), and the idea of making the Bank of England a so-called independent central bank (Committee 1994; Frazer 1994b, 237 n.2).

Whatever these caveats about the use of the term "monetarism," it did gain widespread use in scholarly and other works in the second half of the 1970s and in discussions concerning Margaret Thatcher and her government in London (Frazer 1988, 525–630). To be sure, it captures the breadth and implications of reactions to Friedman's work (Frazer, 1988). Although one may look far back to capture "the politics of monetarism," as Macesich does (1984, 1–38), I presently see its beginnings in philosophically connected background essays, facts, and uses of statistical methods in a post–World War II context. Following a sketch and outline of this background, I present tenets of Friedman system monetarism. They differ from the numerous earlier efforts at listing the tenets of monetarism in two respects: First, the list appears with benefit of greater hindsight and, second, I can be more specific in offering the tenets by focusing on the work and background of one person and what I call "the Friedman system." Where the earlier efforts—such as Mayer's (1978, 1–3) and Laidler's (1982, 3–5)—attempt to encompass a large group of unidentified economists, they in effect end by pointing to the subjective and arbitrary nature of the characteristic features. By narrowing the search for tenets, I gain in being specific what may be lost by encompassing a large group.

ENCLAVES AND THE RISE OF MONETARISM

Monetarism, as dominated by Friedman, begins after World War II with Friedman's essays regarding economic theory and his facts and statistical methods. It has philosophical dimensions. The essays include the Wesley Mitchell essay (Friedman 1950) and Friedman's famous 1953 essay with the pre-publication title "The Relevance of Economic Analysis to Prediction and Policy" (Frazer 1988, 36, 112, 139). The philosophical dimensions arise from Friedman's background in mathematical statistics and his connections to Mitchell's National Bureau of Economic Research (NBER) and the Mont Pelerin Society (Frazer 1988, 143–160, 172–180). A Swiss national at the time, Karl Brunner entered the fray with a background in central-banking research and with Cowles Commission connections at the University of Chicago, following his fall term at Harvard in 1949.

Although there is much more, Friedman (1912–) had been at Chicago since 1946, when friction developed between the alternative approaches of Friedman's group and the Cowles Commission. The main post–World War II beginnings, then, are Friedman's Chicago and the NBER, the Mont Pelerin Society, and the Federal Reserve Bank of St. Louis, with its early ties to

Friedman (Frazer 1988, 138–144). Karl Brunner (1916–1989) and Allan Meltzer (hereafter BM) enter the discussion but along different lines. Brunner undertook a cooperative relation with Meltzer in the UCLA setting in the mid–1950s when Meltzer was a graduate student (BM 1993, 327–330; and Frazer 1973, 387–394).

Quick to recognize Friedman's connection to well established institutions (BM 1993, 331), Brunner proceeded to develop arrangements promoting his own values. These promotions came to include the highly productive tie to Allan Meltzer, the founding of two journals of economics, the Carnegie-Rochester Conference on Public Policy (cofounded with Meltzer), and the policy-review committee called the Shadow Open Market Committee (BM 1993, 332, 335, 352–353). Brunner was, to be sure, a visible figure and determined promoter.

Numerous individuals would become involved in the Friedman led onslaught. Initially, these included Arthur Burns and graduate students who in effect took dissertation topics from Friedman's essay on Wesley Mitchell (Frazer 1973, 153–155; Friedman 1950; 1956). Among the first students who went on to maintain a visible profile in the activities were Phillips Cagan (Frazer 1994b, 169, 180) and Richard Selden (1975; 1976; 1994). (Anna Schwartz, who had joined Friedman as an assistant, went on to obtain a Ph.D. at Columbia, under Friedman's sponsorship during his visiting year as Wesley Mitchell professor at Columbia, and to share authorship on Friedman's NBER/monetarist projects.)

Among others at Chicago, Friedman-connected students of some visibility were David Meiselman and Beryl Sprinkel. The former was associated with Friedman during the money-multiplier/Keynesian investment-multiplier debate of the late 1950s to mid–1960s (Frazer 1973, 95–107). The latter authored a book on the leading time rate of change in the money stock and stock market prices (1971, with an introduction by Friedman) and later played a prominent role in the Reagan presidency. Sprinkel served first in the monetarist oriented Treasury and then became Chairman of the Council of Economic Advisors (Frazer 1988, 634–635, 639, 660–664).

Friedman's view was holistic. It gained virtually worldwide attention, where market economies were concerned. Policy-, facts-, and theory-oriented, Friedman's view included philosophical foundations[3] and took on the sweeping nature of the total analytical system, which I have outlined (Frazer 1994a). As economic crises mounted in the 1970s, and as Friedman gained public/professional visibility in the United States, the United Kingdom, and elsewhere (Frazer 1988, 191–230), his influence extended to the United Kingdom in particular, where in the 1970s his ideas captured Margaret Thatcher's attention. Alan Walters, later prominent U.K. economist who supported to Friedman's monetarist positions, became an economic adviser to Thatcher (Frazer 1988, 575, 597–602, 628–629, 783, 779; Walters 1987). Another, who wrote on monetarism in the vortex of the late 1970s, as

Friedman gained in influence, was Tim Congdon (1978), and there were still others. James Tobin was not incorrect when he commented:

I believe that Friedman had a crusade that he was pushing all over the world, not just in the profession. He saw the big picture, and the big picture was right for him. (Klamer 1984, 106)

Friedman gained international recognition for his ideas at the time in what I call "The Big U-Turn" when there was no explanation of the inflation crises. On the policy-action side, the phrase "Big U-Turn" is a reference to the early moves by Margaret Thatcher and Ronald Reagan (Frazer 1988, chaps. 14, 15, and 16).[4]

By comparison, Brunner's (or BM's) was not an all-encompassing system with a view of transforming the world of economics. Although philosophically based and connected to the Cowles Commission at Chicago in ways different from Friedman's (BM 1993, 244, 328–329; Frazer 1973, 388–389, nn. 1and 2; Frazer 1988, 68–87, 289), Brunner's stance (including with Meltzer) was policy- and issues-oriented. BM proved more inclined than Friedman to take on the critics. Along the way, they helped in delineating monetarism, when confusion arose over whether to include Robert Lucas of Chicago and the Lucas-related new classical school under the monetarist label. This confusion was probably due less to the place of money in the NCS's work than to the facts that Lucas had been a student at Chicago, was a professor at Carnegie-Mellon University at the beginning of the NCS, and moved to Chicago as a professor during Friedman's last year there.[5]

Whereas Keynes and Friedman had dealt with behavior, shared a definition of money (Frazer 1994a, 47–49), and treated the demand for it as a source of instability in the economy, BM point out that NCS's concept of rational expectations (RE) places such strenuous information requirements on the economic agents "as to limit the practical relevance of the model" (BM 1993, 174). Rejecting the NCS in some detail (BM 1993, 173–182), BM go on to even harsher criticism of the real business cycles versions of the NCS's RE (BM 1993, 45–49, 59–62).[6] In these versions there are no monetary shocks to bring about transitory (or cyclical) change. They give instability in business conditions (or cycles) a "nonmonetary character." BM conclude, with respect to the real business cycle view, "that the choice of a monetary regime [say, an i-regime or M-regime] is irrelevant to the theory" (BM 1993, 63). I, however, view the monetary regime as essential to one or another of the approaches to policy while dealing with the Bank of England, the Federal Reserve, and the Deutsche Bundesbank (Frazer 1994b, 84–100, 163–240).

In departures from the view I express in the tenets that follow, Brunner shied away from treatments of expectations (Frazer 1973, 389 n.2), which were initially central to Keynes's and Friedman's economics. Other differences from the Friedman view are differences in the emphasis on capitalism as an economic system, and with respect to BM's emphasis on transaction costs. For Brunner the apparent "irreligiousness of capitalism . . . forms . . . an important virtue of the system" (BM 1993, 337). He favors the system because of belief in "individual opportunities to shape one's own life" (BM 1993, 327). Friedman would go along with this opportunities aspect, I am sure. Nevertheless, he turned to the micro basics and placed freedom as the highest goal in order to provide an added moral basis to the capitalist ethic (Frazer 1994a, 60–61; 1988, 509).

Even while asserting the importance of observation (BM 1993, 168, 175, 329), as Friedman would, BM place a heavy weight on transaction costs, which have traditionally fallen in the area of maximizing some welfare function (Niehans 1987, 678–679). There is formal analysis of the welfare optimization zone. Even so, BM see the study of transaction costs as a part of their contribution to the study of money (1993, 65–67, 70–74, 113, 137–138, 274; Frazer 1973, 439-447) in somewhat of an empirical positive economics context. Transaction costs are used by BM to explain the choice of media of exchange and some institutions that evolve to reduce uncertainty.

In the Keynes/Friedman definition of money, according to its functions, and in the elaborate restatement I offer (Frazer 1994a, 47–49), money serves as a medium of exchange, a standard of value, and a store of value. There are also motives for holding money under this definition. Holding it provides a means of dealing with an uncertain future, but BM (1993, 38–39) reverse this by taking up the cost of information to eliminate the uncertainty about the future. This elimination reduces the demand for money to be held as a precaution, even as low transaction costs (that is, costs of switching from money to another good) explain the choice of a commodity to serve as money. Though possibly important on their own merits, transaction costs would not and do not enter into Friedman's economics (or the Friedman system) as a major separable and significant feature governing observed behavior other than via an episode where tax-rate changes impact on the cost and thus the behavior. A symbolic function of Friedman's economics appears thus:

$$M/P = f(Y/P, \text{Wnh}/W; \ldots ; u) \tag{1}$$

Called a primary equation (Frazer 1988, 79, 539, 541; 1994b, 174–175), P is the price level, M/P is real money balances, Y/P is income in constant prices, Wnh/W is a ratio of nonhuman wealth to total wealth, the three dots (. . .) signify the expected returns on four classes of assets, and u is a portmanteau variable (and not simply an error term). The left-hand member of equation (1) and the first term on the right may be written (M/P)/(Y/P), which also represents M/Y (or the inverse of the income velocity ratio, Y/M). In this equation, transaction costs are in the portmanteau variable, viewed very differently from the role assigned to them by BM, and money retains the definition passed along by Keynes.

In 1976, Friedman's former student Richard Selden identified monetarism as consisting of two beliefs:

(1)   that "money matters"—i.e., that monetary changes exert a dominant influence on general business conditions; and (2) that monetary changes can be controlled by central banks. (Selden 1976, 254)

Continuing, Selden noted that twenty years earlier few economists held these beliefs, whereas by 1976 many economists shared them. However, the lists of tenets at the 1976 date are not very discriminating as to who would and would not be identified as monetarists.[7] I can be more specific, consistent with the view of an overall total analytical system and with the view that Milton Friedman was the head monetarist, that monetarism was his show.

TENETS OF THE FRIEDMAN SYSTEM

There have been numerous lists of the tenet s of monetarism—including Selden's (1976, 254), Mayer's (1978, 2), and Laidler's (1981, in WW 1990, vol. III, 227). What follows are the tenets, viewed in terms of the Friedman system, which is directed primarily toward economies with well developed money and financial markets. Though not limited strictly to the U.S., U.K., and F.R.G. economies, departures from such well developed markets may call for provisos regarding the following tenents.

1. *Friedman's law, in terms of the Friedman system:* Inflation in a developed markets oriented economy is a monetary phenomenon (Frazer 1988, 650–651; 1994b, 92, 239 n.8). For most of the 1867–1975 period for which FS analyzed U.S. and U.K. data, causation runs from the time rate of change in the money stock to business conditions (or income) with some feedback. However, in the presence of fiscal policy (viewed as a deficit) with monetary accommodation, Kaldor causation enters (Frazer, 1994b, 87–91), à la tenet 3 below. This causetion is from the time rate of change in income to that for the money stock $(\dot{Y} \rightarrow \dot{M})$. Nevertheless the inflation still follows from the monetary accommodation and not from fiscal policy itself as I indicate in considerable detail (Frazer 1994a, 97–101).   To be sure, a government budget constraint enters (tenet 3), so what we get in the detail of policy operations is simply more or less government (crowding out or enlarging the private sector).
    Furthermore, even as many pointed to oil shocks in the Keynesian years of the 1970s as explanations for inflations in the United States and the United Kingdom, the inflation rate series for the Federal Republic of Germany trended downward (Frazer 1994b, 44–49).   To be sure, the difference was that the Bundesbank did not accommodate the oil shocks, whereas the Federal Reserve and the Bank of England did (Frazer 1994b, 39–57). So, overall, the inflations in the United States and the United Kingdom appear as monetary phenomena (i.e., monetary accommodation in these cases).

2. *Friedman's monetary policy rule for noninflationary economic growth*: For relatively stable, noninflationary growth in income, the rule is that money stock growth takes place at the sustainable rate of growth in real output. This includes allowance for secular-trend changes in the velocity ratio (Frazer 1994a 45–46).[8] The inverse of velocity is the Cambridge k, as found in the cash-balance, quantity-theoretic expression

[M = k(. . .) Y], where the factor k is a variable factor k(. . .) in Keynes's 1923 work and in Friedman's work.[9] The matter of whether monetary policy is in fact disciplinary or accommodative of fiscal policy and inflationary spending generally is taken up in terms of tenet 8 (also later text pages 154–156).

3. *The government budget constraint (and the place of fiscal policy):* Given the preceding law and rule context and excluding international sources of funds, all fiscal policy as a deficit (surplus) can do on the domestic side is to drive the private sector out of (into) the total spending on the output of goods and services (Frazer 1994a, 130–135). Indeed, I offer and illustrate in terms of operations an analysis in which monetary policy and fiscal policy are substitutes (Frazer 1994a, 100–101, 130–135; 1994b, 87–94). For fiscal policy as a deficit to have fiscal stimulus it must be accommodated by monetary policy. If not accommodated, then the deficit and its financing simply shift funds and resources from the private to the government sector. A fiscal surplus and hence the shift of resources from the government to the private sector are possible, as illustrated by the case of the Thatcher government (Frazer 1994a, 132; 1994b, 179–184).

4. *Identification of the money demand function:* The central bank controls the nominal money stock while households control the real stock (Frazer, 1994a, 49–51), as in the left-hand side of equation (1). They do so through the demand for money viewed as velocity (or its inverse). Indeed, via this route Friedman dealt with the technical problem of identification (also, Allais 1966, 1137–1138, 1150–1151, 1154).

5. *An alternative system:* The Friedman system is an alternative to an interest-rate orientation with fiscal policy (à la Kaldor and the Bank of England) for controlling income and/or for stabilizing business conditions. Attempts to combine the alternative i- and M-systems are futile, even with reliance on heavy doses of the ceteris paribus assumption because the key variables are not in fact independent of one another and because monetary and fiscal policy appear as substitutes (Frazer 1994a, 97–101; 1994b, 87–93). Inflationary expectations enter into the long-bond rate to make it uncontrollable by the direct means of the central bank, and money-stock growth is not in fact independent of the inflation rate (tenet 1).

6. *Time frames and inflation:* Following practices set on a course by Wesley Mitchell's NBER, the Friedman system recognizes the dating of turning points in business conditions. Time series lead, coincide with, or lag these conditions. Trends are fitted in reference to averages of data points between peaks and troughs (Frazer 1988, 750; 1994a, 23–26), and deviations in the series from the trends are transitory or cyclical components of the series. Viewing these deviations in inflationary and decelerated inflation terms there may be an illusion (albeit rational in personalistic probability terms [Frazer 1988, 744]) among agents about the inflationary moves.

These moves are such that agents outside the bond-, stock-, and commodity-trading sectors do not fully sense them immediately and build them into anticipated changes along the Bayesian/personalistic-probability lines I indicate. The reason is simply that the outsiders are not specialized in taking risk for capital gains in the highly sensitive financial markets. Even so, Friedman observed (with Schwartz, FS 1982, 569–573) an overall change in the structure underlying the formation of inflationary expectations in the mid-1960s (Frazer 1994a, 46, 221, 227, 240). And, to be sure, we encounter this in the financial markets where the most representative and alert players appear among the bond traders (Frazer 1994a, 52 n.1, 68, 180; 1994b, 25, 129).

7. *The money illusion:* Expectations of inflation held by agents adjust to the fundamentals with less lag, in the mid-1960s, and hence a reduction in money illusion. The change in structure (tenet 6) held considerable importance for FS, in view of the search for a stable statistical relation, especially among money growth, income, and interest rates. This is because simple lead and lag relationships are complicated by the greater sensitivity of agents, and bond traders in particular, to the sources and prospects for inflation. This connects with the formation of personalistically weighted, inflationary expectations ($Pb[\dot{P}^e]\,\dot{P}^e$), where, as in the earlier cases, the dots over the price measure mean percent change in the inflation rate.[10]

8. *Long-bond rates, a surrogate for monetary policy:* In light of greater sensitivity in the formation of expectations (tenets 6 and 7), and in the presence of predominating data errors and affiliated data problems in relating to the short-run control over the money stock (M) and its velocity (V) (Frazer 1994b, 39–50), some interest rate phenomena are encapsulated in concepts such as "New York's revenge" and "the Bundesbank effect" (Frazer 1994a, 68, 113, 115, 180; 1994b, 7–8, 25, 98, 199). In this money-aggregates/errors/sensitivity context, I view the long-term bond rate as a surrogate for monetary policy viewed in terms of accommodation, neutrality, and discipline. Within that context, bond traders adjust prices of the bellwether bonds and the "trading books" gain importance in the short and medium terms in relation to the concept of a portfolio of securities.[11]

9. *Psychological time:* Agents respond to a current episode and look backward to prior analogous situations in forming views about the outcome of the impact from the current episode. In its presence time is not simply a chronological, lagged distribution of the recent past but a looking backward at analogous events which may occur in a more or less distant time interval. After it was introduced by the later Nobel Laureate Maurice Allais, Friedman added psychological time to the economic analysis. Indeed, I show its relevance in the analysis of the effects of the business conditions behavior of interest rates on industrial spending and finance (Frazer 1994a, 140–143, 74, 117, n.5, 151, n.9, 235, 244, n.8). See also Frazer (1994b, 17–19, 23, 175).

10. *Explanation of turning points in business conditions:* Turning points in business conditions come about in terms of psychological time (tenet 9), and a proposition from personalistic probability enters where opinions of forecasting agents regarding the turn coalesce. An accelerator (or "bandwagon" effect) enters the explanation as controversy over the dating diminishes and as the discounting of "best judgments" diminishes (Frazer 1994a, 232–238). Although Friedman himself offered the time rate of change in the money stock as leading business conditions and interest rates, as illustrated in Friedman (1968) and Frazer (1994a, 40–44), he did not see this as an explanation of turning points in business conditions, and, as indicated in tenet 6, the lag structure changed in the mid-1960s.

11. *A variant of Marshall's demand curve:* In Friedman's version of the Marshallian demand curve, the difference between ordinary and compensated curves is related to the terms of a price index (P), as it appears in $M = k\,(.\,.\,.)\,Y$, $Y = PQ$.[12] Plus, in this view, groups of agents in the markets and the economy as a whole respond

to outside events such as tax changes and money-demand/supply shocks along lines related to the analysis of money demand for the economy as a whole.[13]

12. *The information in a given time series:* In view of tenets 6, 7, 8, 9, and 11, the key time series may be viewed as containing trend and transitory (or cyclical) components. Both of these may be affected by the impact of events, to which I add Bayesian learning and shared responses.[14] Close corollaries to tenets 9 and 11 are (a) that analyses of expectations of a Bayesian learning sort come to the forefront and (b) that groups share with the whole reactions to inside and outside developments. In this latter sense, groups may differ in their outlooks (uncertainty and all) at a given time, even as they share responses to the inside and outside factors with different lags (Frazer 1994a, 234–236). It is axiomatic that markets for the most liquid assets will react with greater sensitivity than capital-goods and labor markets (Frazer 1994a, 76–79).

13. *The money stock as an umbrella:* Whatever the data problems (tenet 8), the control of the money stock by the government (or the central bank within it) to the greatest extent possible substitutes for an activist government role in numerous other respects. In the first instance, markets function best under the properly functioning umbrella. Power of the government is limited and dispersed in the private sector. The freedom for the units composing the society is enhanced. In the activist government instance, the role of government extends to direct intervention, simple majorities control minorities, governments intervene to regulate prices (and wages as a special price), incomes are redistributed (the "safety net" and poverty aside), and ultimately a command economy supplants a free market.[15]

14. *Stability in government policy:* Policy is a historical source of instability in the private sector to a great extent. Even so, a stable government policy facilitates adjustments in the private sector, particularly in wages and prices. By contrast, post-Keynesians envision a role for government with the capacity to stabilize an inherently unstable private sector (Frazer 1994a, 205). Invoking the political dimension, Fand (1970, 304–305) notes a preference of some economists for an activist as opposed to a less directly interventionist government.

15. *The indirect method:* In view of tenets 4 through 12 analytical difficulties are encountered by directly proceeding to analyze time series with fashionable multiple regression methods. A separation-of-effects problem arises (Frazer 1994a, 5, 46, 54, 81, 156, 164–165, 170–171, 203–204). In an early view of such problems with statistical methods, Friedman employed indirect methods and eschewed a tradition of looking for truth via detailed descriptive truth of axioms (i.e., via *modus ponens*).[16] He avoided statistical problems, such as encountered in identifying a Marshallian demand curve, by getting at things he could measure (tenets 4 and 11). The mechanical apparatus, or use of it, facilitated economic forecasting for policy purposes (*modus tollens*). Theories were to be tested against one another rather than via the naive model found in econometrics. Time series were explored by the use of the simple method—the analysis of data for a few variables at a time—before proceeding with more complicated analyses.

16. *Friedman criteria:* In science one looks for repetitive phenomena, and so Friedman proceeded. His criteria for a stable statistical relation are that it remain stable over a long period, under a variety of conditions and circumstances, that its

stability holds beyond the sample period; and that stability holds in at least two different but similar economies (Frazer 1994a, 46). The criteria call for knowledge of the experiments that generate the data and not simply reliance on the use of technique. They impose a large order. One proceeds with the view that repetitive and nonrepetitive changes appear in time series. The idea is to acknowledge both and separate the two to find the repetitive forces.

17. *Equilibrium/balance and growth:* Marshallian and other virtually static schedules (including in the liquidity preference demand for money) constitute statements of position as a change in time approaches zero (Frazer 1988, 696; 1994a, 19–23, 34, 52 n.1, 56–57), and the analysis of money, as in tenet 2, adds motion (Frazer 1994a, 40–47). There is allowance for technological change, to be sure, where logarithms enter as the language of growth and dynamic change in the stock and flow variables (Frazer 1994a, 23–27, 61–63). This change, in the monetary-rule/stability context gives rise to the great ratios (Frazer 1994a, 75–81)—the velocity ratio, the saving-to-income ratio, and labor and capital's shares of income—even as allowances enter for episodic impacts on the time series making up growth paths and ratios.

In the presence of the tie of Marshall's demand curve to the price index (Frazer 1994a, 15–22) and to the Cambridge equation (tenets 2 and 11)—and a virtually unattained stability in the paths and ratios—a stable state may only be envisioned. Even so, were it to be attained, the analysis ends with a system of many equations and unknowns that determine a set of prices composing a stable price average (Frazer 1988, 724). This system of equations appears in Friedman's view of Marshall and not Walras. Walras is identified with mathematical elegance and a much broader set of prices (Frazer 1994b, 112–117, nn.20–23).[17]

As judged by BM (1993), Brunner and BM would agree with six of the seventeen tenets, namely, tenets 1, 2, 3, 6, 14, and 15.

AN OVERVIEW OF THE FRIEDMAN SYSTEM

Beginning with the 1983 paper with Boland and *Power and Ideas* (Frazer and Boland 1983; Frazer 1988), I have recognized that Friedman offers a total analytical system of considerable breadth. In fact, in a sense I have used the breadth of his analyses and background of experiences to consider otherwise seemingly disconnected topics ranging over Jewish history, methodology, Arthur Burns and NBER connections, the Mont Pelerin Society, the monetary revolutions of the nineteenth century, Friedman's connection to Marshall's and Keynes's works, domestic and international perspectives, counterrevolution in Chile, changes at the policy implementation level in the United Kingdom and the United States in the early 1980s, canons of revolution in science, and uses of statistical methods. The major empirically connected theoretic problems I see with what Friedman actually wrote, said, and advanced to policy levels center about the following:

1. The change in the mid-1960s in the structure underlying the formation of inflationary expectations. This extends to Friedman's view of himself as an empirical

scientist, which tended to confine him in responses to his critics and supporters after the 1960s change in the structure underlying the formation of inflationary expectations.

2. Friedman's failure to deal with the implementation of monetary policy via central banks with different orientations, traditions, and practices. This oversight is considered in *The Central Banks: Analysis, and International and European Dimensions* (1994b).

3. Friedman's tendency to oversimplify in numerous instances, although the simplification contributed to his persuasive power in his most active years.

4. His complicated and yet highly simplified roles for time (psychological time, cycles, trends, and lagged relations mainly). These all bear on theoretic/empirical problem 1.

5. Friedman's uncompromising devotion to both the mechanical structure of economics and economics as empirical science, even as the structure part was essentially indeterminate in the face of the empirical science, and the presence of episodic changes and monetary influences of the government sector (hence the Friedman system reference to "open-ended closeness").

6. His anticipatory orientation at every turn in his theoretic contributions including his embrace of Keynes's definition of money, its functions, classes of money demand, and motives for holding money [Frazer 1994a, 47–51]), all without making explicit the almost entirely psychological/economic nature of the phenomena he dealt with.

7. His consideration of others as regards the extent of their sharing his statistical and mathematical acumen, economic goals, and ideology.

8. His failure to address the industrial/capital-spending sector (tenet 9), which played an important role in Keynes's *General Theory* (1936) and in the later Keynesian economics. Of course, the reason Friedman avoided this confrontation concerned the central place given to money-to-income causation ($\pm \Delta \dot{M} \rightarrow \pm \Delta \dot{Y}$) and the Cambridge connection in tenet 11 (namely, $M = k (\ . \ . \ . \ ) PQ$). Emphasizing the money-to-income causation Friedman in turn avoided stating the place of psychological time and the complexities of liquidity which I confront in the industrial/capital spending sector.

9. Friedman's tendency to avoid answering his critics unless virtually forced to do so, as in the case of the charge by Hendry and Ericsson (1983; 1984; 1985; 1991; FS 1991) and his tendency to work with a total analytical system (indirect method, uses of statistics, and all).

So I have extended and/or developed what Friedman actually said and wrote. Particularly I have done so as regards tenets 1, 3, 5, 6, 7, 8, 9, 10, 12, 15, and 17. *The Friedman System* outlines my view of a rounded and general version of Friedman's economics when seen in terms of his background and experiences and many of my own (including his association with Arthur Burns and the sharing of some of the same professors at Columbia

University, and separate educational experiences in mathematics and statistics as well as my work at two Federal Reserve Banks). This latter and the Keynes/Friedman monetary line of thought influenced my later efforts to study the Bank of England, the U.K. government of Margaret Thatcher, and the Bundesbank.

NOTES

1. To conserve space on references—where an enormous literature on monetarist matters and Friedman exists—I am drawing directly on the 1990 Wood and Woods four-volume collection of critical assessments of Friedman's work rather than citing the original sources given there (WW 1990). In a number of instances I also refer to the detailed analyses and references covered in *Crisis in Economic Theory* (Frazer 1973), *Power and Ideas* (Frazer 1988), *The Legacy* (Frazer 1994a), and *The Central Banks* (Frazer 1994b).

2. Most notable is the attention given to results and simulations achieved with the large models of the time (Fand 1970, 281-282 nn. 6 and 7, 305-307). Next, Fand, like the Chicago student George Macesich later (1984), looks further backward than I do and deals with "pre-Keynesian Monetarist theory" (Fand 1970, 277, n.1; 298-299). In this respect, Fand's article follows in some measure Friedman's tendency to invoke a valid orthodoxy (Frazer 1988, 119), even when he departs radically from it (Frazer 1988, 713-714; 1994a, 13-16). Also, referring to "modern quantity theory" (Fand 1970, 277 n.1), Fand includes writers such as Patinkin who are very much at odds with Friedman's approach (Frazer 1973, 394-398; Patinkin 1969, 48).

3. In the 1950 and 1953 essays—in his uses of statistical methods, in his rejection of econometric convention, and in his drawing on both Wesley Mitchell and Karl Popper—I find a philosophy of science. It is John Dewey pragmatism of a sort and has features of Popper's instrumentalism. To be sure, Friedman himself was more interested in doing economics than in writing about it. Nevertheless, there is a tie to Dewey, if only via Mitchell (Frazer 1992), and there is a connection to Popper, if only through casual reading, meetings in Switzerland, and what I have called Friedman's variant of instrumentalism (Frazer 1984, in WW 1990, vol. IV, 48-50). The variant is implied more by what Friedman does than by his philosophical writings. Indeed, Wible has maintained that Friedman substituted rather practical uses of statistical methods for more complicated elements of a complete philosophy of science (Frazer 1988, 133-135). Wible said, in reference to Friedman's indirect method, that it "serves as a vehicle for circumventing significant philosophical issues."

Hirsch and deMarchi devote an entire book to the Dewey/Friedman matter (HD 1990), as discussed in Chapter 3. As indicated there they make a common mistake; that is, they view Friedman as a neoclassical economist (see notes 6, 9, 13, 14, and 17).

4. I offer a "U-Turn" hypothesis (Frazer 1994b, 4-5, 109, n.5, 189-191).

5. On two types of monetarism, see Kevin Hoover (in WW 1990, vol. III, 527-551). On the NCS's rational expectations, see Chapter 11.

6. The BM position on NCS carries through to Laidler (1995). However, Laidler is more inclined than BM to make a connection to the Keynes definition of money (as in Frazer 1994a, 47-50). Also, as I state (Frazer 1994b, 112-115, nn.20-23)—and in contrast to Laidler (1994)—Friedman's economics is and has been "fundamentally incompatible with New-classical doctrine."

7. About the same time Mayer et al. were writing on monetarism (1978, 2), Mayer himself said, "Such listing [of tenets] is . . . quite arbitrary and the reader may want to add or delete items."

Some of the entries in Mayer's list reflect issues of the period, for example, "small rather than large econometric models," as in Frazer (1973, 287–311), which is very different from Friedman's use of simple regressions and the "indirect method" (Frazer 1988, 68–87). In other entries in Mayer's list, the statements are rather vague as to substance and so not discriminate amoung monetarist, Keynesian, and Mayer views.

8. Friedman himself limited the allowance for the velocity ratio to the secular trend because the effects of accelerated/decelerated money growth started immediately and accumulated, to exert powerful influence. However, central banks serve as lenders of last resort to noncentral banks and may also serve as lenders to reduce seasonal variation and/or to manage the short-term liquidity of the noncentral banks with the view to achieving target ranges for money growth, as in the case of the Bundesbank (Frazer 1994b, 95–107). The rule may be viewed as a guide to policy, even where not strictly imposed on the banking system from outside, although data and operations arise in this regard (tenet 8).

9. As with Keynes, this variation of the quantity theory equation symbolized a rejection or a redirection of neoclassical economics. It was the rejection of the separation of the theory of money and the theory of production, which are otherwise integrated in the Friedman system.

10. In the Friedman-system, bond-market-equation terms, $i_L = i(real) + Pb[\dot{P}^e]\dot{P}^e$. However, in general (or in a time-rate-of-change context) the dot over the variable signifies a time rate of change (x 100 = percent change), for example $(1/M)(\Delta M)/(\Delta t) = \Delta M/Y$ and $(\Delta M/M)$ x 100 = percent change in M, when Δt is considered to be one year (Frazer 1994a, 23–27). We may also note simply that $M = (1/M)(\Delta M)/(\Delta t)$. For the general rule for stock and flow variables via-à-vis interest rates and ratios, see Frazer (1994a, 76–81): "Change all stock and flow quantities at the same rate and the interest rate(s) and ratio(s) remain constant." Differential changes in stock and flow variables, such as accompany inflation, of course, imply changes in the rates of interest (returns, etc.) and the ratios.

In the Friedman system (as illustrated in Figure 1.3) all stock and flow quantities have this growth or time-rate-of-change property. Otherwise static arrangements are set in motion via this time-rate-of-change route.

11. In the long term, the errors diminish in importance. And, in any case, the success of the Bundesbank as a Friedman/monetarist institution is impressive (Frazer 1994b, 35–50, 95–107, 152–155, 224–231). The problem with viewing portfolio management (and supply-demand-quantity notions) as the immediate center of the impact of episodes lies in the area of the liquidity hedging hypothesis (Frazer 1994a, 150–151 n.6; 1994b, 107–108, 71, 107–108 n.2).

12. Friedman also connects the price index in the Cambridge equation to Eugen Slutsky's 1915 equation. Through this route he establishes a link between the monetary analysis and the theory of relative prices (Frazer 1994a, 9–23).

The extraordinary connection to Marshall was such that groups of agents (or behavioral units) at the Marshallian markets level could respond to the same shocking forces affecting money demand (actually the income velocity of money, or its inverse, k(. . .) = M/PQ, where PQ is income, Y).

Using Lagrangian and matrix algebra methods, I deduce a Slutsky equation (Frazer 1988b, 382–387) that appears thus:

$$(1.0) \qquad \frac{\partial q_1}{\partial p_1} \;=\; \left(\frac{\partial q_1}{\partial p_1} \right)_{u\,=\,\text{const.}} -\; q_1 \left(\frac{\partial q_1}{\partial y} \right)_{\text{prices}\,=\,\text{const.}}$$

where left-hand term represents the slope of the originary demand curve, and where the right-hand terms are, respectively, the slope of the compensated demand curve, and the change in income required to keep the individual on the same level of utility.

Also, in the equation, q_1 and p_1 are the quantity of the commody and its price respectively, and y is income to the household.

13. For Friedman's purpose, there was no distinction between microeconomics and macroeconomics. The twofold prospect is that the units the whole comprises share responses with the whole, and the theory of prices at Friedman's hands as viewed with hindsight by me addresses aspects of overall economic behavior (Frazer 1994a, 53–90).

14. In light of such behavior, Friedman's early background in mathematical statistics and connections to Wesley Clair Mitchell (Frazer 1988, 143–160), Friedman moved his analyses of statistical data along very different lines from those encountered in econometrics (Frazer in WW, 1990, vol. III, 464–473; 1988, 68–87, 735–760; FS 1991; Redman 1994, 77–86).

15. Ideology arises in the choice between the different systems (Congdon 1978, 77–78; Fand 1970, 304–305) and I offer Hotelling's line in relation to it (Frazer, 1994a, 82–89). There is also a connection to Redman's assertion (1994, 82) that Friedman "never tired of pointing out that hypothesis selection 'may suit the psychological needs of particular investigators,' i.e., estimation results simply reflect the prejudices of the investigator."

In the market-economy instance, money is of considerable importance (the indirect satisfaction of wants, the store of value, and all). Attention to its functions and central banks fueled controversy on the political right in the 1980s, as represented by Margaret Thatcher in the United Kingdom and Ronald Reagan in the United States. This politics extends to the historical origins and possible outcomes of a European Monetary Union (Frazer 1994b, 95–240).

16. Friedman moves to the *modus tollens* (reverse logic) connection. There the purpose of the theory is to predict. Error may be passed backward from the predictions to the axioms.

There is a connection between Popper and Friedman's variant of instrumentalism, where Friedman views the mechanical apparatus of economics as an instrument for prediction. The more visible theories offer alternative ways of achieving economic goals. Testing the predictions of one versus the other provides a method for resolving the conflict for those who share his social and political values.

Friedman's shift of emphasis offers further support for the view that Friedman was no neoclassicist. In fact, he was in this regard backing away from the so-called economic man emphasis found in the axioms of profit and utility maximization. At the same time, he was dissociating himself from arguments about small differences in products that led to an infinite number of different, non-Marshallian markets (Frazer 1994a, 68–73).

17. In traversing Friedman's, BM's, and NCS's economics, David Laidler comes to confront ambiguity in Friedman's occasional statements and connections to Walrasian equations (Laidler 1994), just as I did (Frazer 1988, 562–565). I resolve the ambiguity by giving the greatest emphasis to three features of Friedman's work: (1) the money/growth/logarithmic feature, (2) the fruitfulness-versus-elegance feature, and (3) the Savage/personalistic-probability foundations feature (Frazer 1988, 68–87, 116–

117). With the emphasis on these three positions, I have no problem crediting Friedman with the system of equations in the text.

Chapter 10

Endogenous/Exogenous Money Supply Theory

" Endogenous" and "exogenous" are terms that crept into use during the early phase of econometrics (Frazer 1988, 68–87).[1] Alvin Hansen observed (1951, 411–412) that econometric theories stress endogenous movements and that nonmathematical theories draw heavily on exogenous factors with respect to business conditions. This observation creates an apparent paradox, for Christopher Niggle who offers an institutionalist appraisal of endogenous money in the AFEE/institutionalist *Journal of Economic* Issues (Niggle 1991).

Confusion also exists because the term "autonomous" has been used at times to carry the same meaning as the terms "independent" and "exogenous" (Frazer 1973, 91–93, 102–107) and because Tobin introduced his argument about cause running from income to the money stock in reaction to Milton Friedman's leading time rate of change in the money stock (Frazer 1973, 126–129)—that is, causation running from the exogenous money stock to endogenous income, some would say. These autonomous, independent, exogenous, causation lines of controversy continue through literature on statistical testing (the Sims/Granger test, and so on), and the exogenous money concept is revisited by Friedman and Anna Schwartz (hereafter FS) in *Monetary Trends* (1982, 626–627; Frazer 1988, 544–546). At the time of its publication, David Hendry and Neil Ericsson (hereafter HE) observed that Friedman's approach involves his own uses of statistical methods and an exogenous emphasis in relation to business conditions (Frazer 1988, 735–760; FS 1991, 39–49; HE 1991, 8–38; Zarnowitz 1985). Also, in the early 1980s, the late Lord Kaldor in effect recasts the Tobin-Keynesian causation argument

---

This chapter was originally presented at economic meetings in January 1993, Anaheim, California.

along potentially more fruitful, institutional lines (1982; Frazer 1983, 261–284, 1994b, 87–93).

I attempt to shed some light on these matters, and I accept Niggle's ground rule that "the 'correct' theory is that which corresponds most closely to the actual behavior of the specific monetary-financial system under analysis" (Niggle 1991, 143). However, I avoid enormous complications and efforts at the likely unattainable consensus view by limiting discussion to Kaldor's recasting of the causation controversy and to the Friedman analytical system (Frazer 1988; 1994a; Frazer and Boland 1983).

A BRIEF RESTATEMENT OF LIQUIDITY PREFERENCE

There are several rationales for the shape of the curve which depicts liquidity preference, all of which have some basis in Keynes's work (see Chapter 5; also Frazer 1994a, 31–52). The ones I presently address, before turning to the Friedman system, are readily associated with Keynes, in the first instance, and Keynesians, in the second. The first of these may be obtained from known features of interest rates and bond prices and a limit on the speculator's choice to two assets (money balances and bonds). Also, there are differences of opinion at a given time and a pull of the interest rate (i) at a given time toward the normal (safe, or trend) rate of interest on the long-term (or 30-year) bond (Figure 5.4). At a reported rate above the trend rate, there is a likelihood of a rise in bond prices, and hence a preference for bonds over money balances and so on in order to take advantage of an anticipated capital gain.

The more Keynesian rationale retains the two-asset notion and also envisions the central banks as having the capacity to raise and lower interest rates, such that an increase in "the rate" (i) leads to a preference for bonds over money balances (M). Given income and expectations as constant, this interest rate increase implies a rise in the velocity of money (Y/M) in a case where the money stock (M_s) is partly extinguished in some way. Altering the matter somewhat, if M_s is constant, the rise in the rate induces a rise in the velocity and hence income (since M_s = const). It is this last feature of analysis that has provided the LM curve of the fashionable and infamous investment/saving- liquidity/money (IS-LM) construction.

The main point from a Keynesian perspective is that the interest rate and the velocity of money parallel one another in the construction of the liquidity preference curve, i.e., $\downarrow\uparrow$i and $\downarrow\uparrow$(Y/M) in the construction. In Kaldor's terms and those of two succeeding governors of the Bank of England,[2] the demand for the stock of money balances depends on interest rates and fiscal policy (a main determinant of Y, and quite explicitly so in the public-sector/borrowing-requirement, United Kingdom context). Following Kaldor's argument about causation, fiscal policy is the focus of the government's demand management policy. The expenditure of the borrowing requirement changes income. The central bank is expected to accommodate this borrowing by the government and to facilitate the expansion of any needed bank credit (viewed as bank loans at commercial banks mainly) at an accommodating bank rate. As bank credit expands, the money stock increases, and hence overall the causation from government spending to the money stock.

Now Friedman alters all of this (FS 1982, 16–72), as I do because I find no evidence of switching into bonds when interest rates rise during an expansion phase of business conditions, because a priori such switching concerns prospects for capital gains and losses, a wider range of assets, and because I embrace Friedman's and NBER time frames. In doing so, Friedman introduces these special time frames (transitory and trend components for the time series), as well as his own uses of statistical methods (Frazer 1988, 539–571, 735–760; FS 1991) as I emphasize.[3] Implicit in Friedman's approach is what Lord Kaldor called Friedman's "black box," because Friedman did not delve into the bank operations side of controlling the money stock as I do. As elaborated upon in Frazer (1994a, 66–67, 84–91), the "black box" includes Friedman's concept of "helicopter money," and, along with it, special notions of bank operations and others rooted in the 1937–1938 recession in the United States.

From the foregoing we get Friedman's causation (with feedback from income to the money stock), $\Delta \dot{M} \rightarrow \Delta \dot{Y} \rightarrow \Delta i$. First, the "helicopter" makes its regular run and drops currency notes (which are symbolic of the money stock). As this exogenous money, as it were, exceeds that desired by the households, spending by the households occurs (that is, $\Delta \dot{Y}$). The spending in excess of the growth in output (a trend path) contributes to inflation and ultimately expected inflation, P^e. In contrast to Keynes's view of the interest rate as a control variable (Keynes 1936, 141–142), interest rates rise via the probabilistically weighted expected inflation rate $i = i(real) + Pb[P^e]P^e$. Although Friedman found this to occur in response to accelerated money growth (the $\Delta \dot{M}$ impacting on income, $\dot{Y}$, with some lags), the structure underlying the formation of inflationary expectations could change and did so in the mid-1960s.[4] In addition, expectations about interest rates could be formed in accordance with the concept of "psychological time" as I have elaborated (1994a, 140–143).[5] Quite simply, to repeat, agents seek a trough rate of interest at which to lock in new financing in anticipation of an expansion phase of business spending and likely higher rates. In assessing whether a trough rate is present, agents look back to past troughs in business conditions. Hence looking back as psychological time.

Of course, in all of this, business conditions may be neutral, and simply follow a stable growth path. Such stable conditions would not be conducive to the transitory activity we depict.

Now, the institutional underpinnings of Friedman's causation consist of the following arrangements which exist in the United States: the bank reserve equation (Cagan 1965, 45–117; Frazer and Yohe 1966, 175–224); the presence of open market operations of a special sort (OMO),[6] which are rooted in the banking acts of 1933 and 1935 (Frazer and Yohe 1966, 164–165) and the

1937–1938 recession; and a distinction between the investment and bank-loan components of bank credit. The bank reserve equation (an accounting identity) may be symbolized thus:

$$R_0 = G + R + \text{residual}$$

(Here R_0 is reserves at depository intermediaries, G is gold and related monetary assets, R is central bank credit in the form of bank reserves, and there is a residual of secondary factors to balance out the bank-reserve identity in this accounting context.)

With the combination of OMO and the attention to the components of bank credit, the central bank control over the money stock does not depend upon any demand for loans (or failure of "agents" to take out bank loans, such as occurred in the United States in the 1930s [Frazer 1973, 220–244]). To be sure, there are changes in the context of the bank reserve equation for the central bank to monitor in putting R_0 in some targeted range. Further and in addition to households and firms, factors affecting the liquidity needs of banks must also be taken into account in targeting money aggregates. There is a complexity of control by the central bank that enters in the short run, which Friedman avoided (hence, the "black box," or unexplained part of bank operations) and which central banks persist in accepting as a primary part of their mission (namely, intervention in the money market to counter day-to-day shifts in speculative activity in that market.

Not avoiding the above complexities of control and related data/control problems leads to the monetary policy indicator and the surrogate I review later and offer for it (namely, the long-bond rate, i_L, Frazer 1994b, 39–50).

BANK OPERATIONS, ACADEMIC WORKS, AND TWO HYPOTHESES

There is much more (FS 1991, 41–44), but I continue with the central bank (H_{CB}) and theoretical works hypotheses:

H_{CB} *The central banks:* Traditions, operating procedures, and accounting controls influence the choice of economic theory on which government bases its central banking and financial markets policies.

H_{TW} *The theoretical works:* Underlying the academic/theoretic works on monetary policy such as Keynes's *General* Theory (1936) and FS's *Monetary* Trends (1982) are views of central banking arrangements, policy approaches, and the means of intervening in the money markets.

To address H_{CB} and H_{TW} I first offered what now appears as Table 10.1. There domestic operations at the Bank of England, with which Lords Keynes and Kaldor were most familiar, are juxtaposed with those at the Federal Reserve, with which Friedman was most familiar. For the Bank of

England the comparison indicates the linkage scheme I associate with the Keynes/Keynesian rationale for the liquidity preference curve. The public sector borrowing requirement (PSBR) (the budget deficit or funding policy with respect to it) drives the money and credit-creating process. The "bank rate" may be raised (or lowered) as the Bank intervenes in the sterling money market, but here one deals with an interest rate mechanism which has extremely tenuous links to control over the long-term bond rate, the structure of interest rates, bank reserves, and bank credit. There is no accounting identity comparable to the bank reserve equation. Virtually the only way for the Bank of England to conduct a monetary policy has been in terms of fiscal policy and interest rates.

This interest-rate view of policy appears in Keynes's *General Theory* (1936, 199–204, including the sentence on p. 200 cited by Niggle), and in Kaldor's work. Keynes himself was aware of the emergence in the United States of open market operations, but, even so, the concept of helicopter money was slow to come about and, in any case, Keynes draws attention to changes in the rate of interest as did the Keynesian James Tobin and those who advanced the IS-LM model.

Friedman's helicopter money approach is quite different. It proceeds as an alternative to interest rates and fiscal policy and connects directly to Cagan's work (1965), the bank reserve equation, and the 1937–1938 recession in the United States. Moreover, as actual reserves exceed desired reserves at depository intermediaries, bank credit expands, but it may do so via the investments part of bank credit rather than the bank-loan part. There is no need for the public to take the initiative to borrow at the commercial banks in response to low interest rates and in order for the money and credit aggregates to accelerate. As we may recall it was the failure of low interest rates to induce borrowing in the 1937–1938 period that dramatized the failure of monetary policy when viewed in Keynes/Bank of England terms (Frazer 1973, 220–224; 1994b, 66–67).

Of course, the Federal Reserve was not always cast in the hue I associate with Friedman's "helicopter money," and especially the prospect of increasing bank credit and the money stock without the direct link to borrowing by agents. The Federal Reserve's early discount rate arrangements for defending against liquidity crisis were not very different from those at the Bank of England. However, the Federal Reserve can follow the Keynes/Keynesian route, or the "helicopter money" route, except that we must recognize special statistical and other problems in connection with a money aggregates/velocity-of-money approach (Frazer 1994b, 39–50). The problems appear when I introduce the monetary indicator and its surrogate (Frazer 1994b, 39–50). The Federal Reserve may even attempt to follow an interest rate strategy in attaining noninflationary growth in the money stock (Frazer 1994b, 224–231).

Table 10.1
**The Central Bank and Theoretical Works Hypotheses: Operations at the
Bank of England and the U.S. Federal Reserve**

U.K.'s Bank of England	U.S. Federal Reserve
1. Banker to the government. This activity is the same as in the United States, with two exceptions. One is that the Bank of England is itself an operating bank. The other is that the Bank may transfer funds to the U.K. Treasury's account, which represents the assumption of some of the public sector borrowing requirement (PSBR) by the Bank.	1. Banker to the government. Treasury checks are drawn against accounts at the operating regional banks of the Federal Reserve System. Payments to the Treasury in taxes are transferred from private-sector accounts to the operating arms of the Federal Reserve.
2. The Bank assumes direct support of the U.K. Treasury's financing. It does so by taking responsibility for the PSBR and by assuming the financing for some, all, or an excess of the PSBR. Of significance here is the fact that the assumption of the financing is equivalent in its bank-reserve creating capacity to the open market operations (OMO) under item 3 for the Federal Reserve. In addition, as we addressed with respect to Keynesian (or Kaldor) causation, the counterpart to OMO in the United States is set in motion by the U.K. Treasury's PSBR and the Bank of England's funding policy.	2. No direct support of Treasury financing.
3. Dealings with discount houses in the London market by buying or selling commercial and Treasury bills at the bank rate. This activity is directed toward facilitating the clearance of the money market for commercial bills in the short run. Consequently, in contrast to item 3	3. Open market operations (OMO). Direct dealing is done with a select group of government securities dealers (London's equivalent to the discount houses under item 3), but with a major exception: no rate of interest such as a discount or bank rate is set. OMO

Table 10.1 (continued)

U.K.'s Bank of England	U.S. Federal Reserve

on the Fed's side, consideration of the permanent impact from these dealings on growth in the money and credit aggregates is ambiguous.

constitute the only major and permanent means for the Federal Reserve to expand the reserves of the noncentral bank, in part since the discount windows are only temporary means of obtaining reserves. This activity is set in motion via monetary policy (and not PSBR or deficit financing by the government, as under item 2 for the Bank of England).

However, as noted later, special problems arise in efforts at controlling the money stock, so I offer the following: (a) the Federal Reserve may follow an interest rate strategy at the operations level to achieve a money target (Frazer 1994b, 224–231), and (b) I offer later the long-bond rate (i_L) as an indicator of monetary accommodation, discipline, and so on.

4. Lending in the interbank market. Here and in close relation to item 3 above, the Bank of England sets the discount rate (or bank rate, or bank dealing rate, all without much difference as to meaning). A rate is set at which the Bank advances funds to the market. Whether the rate is below market rates determines the extent of the Bank's purchases of bills and extension of funds to discount houses. This depends also, of course, on matters surrounding the PSBR, under item 2.

4. Lending in the interbank market for bank reserves. This lending is said to take place through the Fed's discount windows. The discount rates are set at the initiative of the operating arms of the central governing board in Washington, D.C. Usually they are set in unison, so I speak of the discount rate (the price for borrowing reserves). It follows market interest rates upward and downward very closely and rarely appears as a means for controlling reserves. The so-called discount window is viewed as a temporary

Table 10.1 (continued)

U.K.'s Bank of England	U.S. Federal Reserve

source of bank reserves for the purpose of facilitating adjustments in reserves at noncentral bank, banking units. Moreover, the latter banks trade in reserves with one another on very short-term bases. The market is called the federal funds market.

5. Conducts open market operations in foreign exchange markets. This activity is the same as on the Federal Reserve side. In the years since 1971, when the United States closed the gold window (i.e., no longer offered gold at $35.00 per ounce in exchange for dollars held abroad and by foreign central banks) and moved toward floating exchange rates, the private-sector, foreign exchange operations have grown.

By the same token, private capital, which moves about the world freely, has grown in abundance. All of this is thought to have weakened any power central banks may have had to influence the rates (the prices, for example, at which one currency exchanges for another).

5. Conducts open market operations in foreign exchange markets. These may occur by the use of a pool of accumulated currencies or via outright purchase of a currency, as in the open market purchase of securities under item 3. In the latter case, the activity is more or less a substitute for OMO ordinarily viewed. It may be self-defeating as a means of supporting a currency since all the problems of expected inflation, which led to a weak currency at the start, may come about.

DEGREES OF ENDOGENEITY AND EXOGENEITY AND PURPOSE

Following the discussion of causation as taken up by Kaldor, the money stock is viewed as endogenous. It is so viewed because it is driven by the fiscal policy component of income (or the public sector spending of its borrowing requirement) and the accommodation of an expansion of bank loans by the central bank. On the other hand, Friedman's money stock is often viewed as exogenous, in part because of the time frames and the "helicopter" orientation.

Linking his discussion to the endogenous money supply theory and indeed drawing on Kaldor, Niggle (1991, 137–151) discusses "degree(s) of endogeneity," while in relation to econometric efforts, HE discuss weak, strong, super, and strict exogeneity and cite the institutional structure of money markets in the United Kingdom (HE 1991, 21, 27–30). The argument appears very close to Kaldor's when HE say: "The money stock appears to be endogenously determined by the decisions of the private sector since the Bank of England in effect acts as lender of the first resort by standing ready to rediscount first-class bills at the going Bank rate."

In any case, if we start to deal with degrees of endogeneity and exogeneity, then we must be dealing with all the institutional detail. For a single variable such as the money stock, if it is x degrees (or percent) endogenous then it must be 1 - x degrees (or percent) exogenous. Appearing to end the matter, FS say, "Everything depends on the purpose" (FS 1991, 42). They continue by referring to the post–World War I period in the United States and the secular trend in money demand:

We do not believe it would be equally appropriate to . . . (refer to the money stock as exogenous) for week-to-week or month-to-month movements for which, in HE's words, "the money stock appears endogenously determined by the decisions of the private sector." (HE 1991, 27)

My own inclination is to avoid the matter of degrees entirely by accepting a purely institutional approach. In the Friedman-system terms, the approach is that the policymaking authority (the central bank, the treasury, the chief executive, in other words, "the government sector") is imposing a monetary policy upon the economy. The policymaking authority remains responsible; the buck stops there (Frazer 1994a, 104–105) and, to be sure, there are no known statistical means to meet any operations requirements for separating and assigning degrees of endogeneity and exogeneity. However, in purely institutional terms the approach may in fact operate along Kaldor's fiscal-policy/interest-rate lines or along the Friedman system line, depending on traditions and practices (as in H_{CB}), ideological orientation (for example, as to Kaldor's or Friedman's approach),[7] and possible statistical problems to which I turn.

THE MONETARY INDICATOR

Viewing the money stock as it may bear on inflation (deflation) or the attainment of a zero inflation goal, I review the monetary indicator, which is closely related to Friedman's rule (Frazer 1988, 412, 549). The rule is that the central bank should seek to achieve the same growth rate in monetary-trend terms that it expects for real income (Y/P, or output, Q, Y = PQ), after making allowances for changes in the income velocity ratio (Y/M) in the context of the trends. Without immediate regard for FS's time frames, the indicator and the relevant definitions in terms of it are

$$\Delta \dot{M}(Y/M) \times 100 \; > \; 0 \; \text{(accommodation)}$$

$$-\Delta \dot{M}(Y/M) \times 100 \; > \; 0 \; \text{(discipline)}$$

Using the symbol $\widetilde{M}$ for the indicator, $\Delta\widetilde{M}$ is monetary accommodation, $-\Delta\widetilde{M}$ is monetary discipline, and monetary neutrality is attained when the indicator approximates a zero value for a sustained period.[8] The velocity ratio (Y/M) enters the indicator as a measure of the work performed (withdrawn) by increments (decrements) in the money growth rate. In the case of monetary accommodation $(\widetilde{M} > 0)$ we expect inflation, and in the case of monetary discipline $(\widetilde{M} < 0)$ we expect the taming of inflation.

This is sound analysis and even connects to a Keynes/Friedman view of the Cambridge cash balance approach to the quantity/theoretic expression M = k(. . .) PQ. There, of course, income is the product of a price level and production (Y = PQ) and k(. . .) is the inverse of the velocity ratio. However, H_{CB} may intervene as a source of difficulty in the actual use of the indicator and statistical problems appear. Most notably, income data are quarterly and appear with some lag, and errors that prohibit a refined use of the data enter. Further, changes occur in the composition of the money stock data, whether accounts draw interest or not, and in the detection of currency drains, where dollars may appear as circulating media in the underground and foreign economies. Where refinement is sought, as to acceleration and deceleration $(\pm\Delta\dot{M})$, the errors may even dominate the data.

So I offer the long-term bond rate (i_L) as a surrogate for the policy indicator on the grounds that after some smoothing of circumstances bond traders can form inflationary/deflationary (accommodative/disciplinary) outlooks that surpass the ability of economists to measure whether monetary policy is accommodative, disciplinary, or neutral (Frazer 1994b, 39–50). Rising bond prices lower the long-bond rate $(-\Delta i_L)$ and reflect monetary discipline, lowering bond prices raises the long-bond rate (Δi_L) and it depicts monetary accommodation; and so on.

To support this approach to monetary accommodation and discipline, I show inflation and interest-rate data for the United Kingdom and the United States for the 1970s and 1980s (Frazer 1994b, 39–50). The trends for the 1970s are upward, and for the 1980s the trends shows monetary discipline, as

Margaret Thatcher's government and the Reagan administration sought to tame inflation by monetary means (Frazer 1988, 572–690). Indeed, for most of the two decades (1994a; 1994b), even the effects of the departures from the trends appear in the data.

As I have indicated, there are inadequacies in the United Kingdom's control arrangements for implementing a Friedman-type policy (Frazer 1988, 573-630; 1994b, 237 n.2). Consequently, the Bank of England missed policy targets to such an embarrassing extent that it reverted to reporting policy in short-term, interest-rate terms, which of course, does not necessarily mean the policy changed in fact but simply that the reporting to the public changed. Whatever the case, the policy in money-aggregates terms was endogenous in the 1970s (in the Kaldor sense of reacting to fiscal policy and accommodating price increases). Although disciplinary in the 1980s for the most part, the money policy remained fiscal policy and credit-driven as the United Kingdom moved toward budget surpluses as a means of achieving a disciplinary policy.

In the United States the policy was accommodative in the 1970s (Frazer 1988, 231–274), as indicated, and it turned along lines similar to that in the United Kingdom in the 1980s. However, problems of control were encountered early in the 1980s in the United States but for different reasons (Frazer 1988, 648–668; 1994b, 179–184). Considering both the United Kingdom and the United States and viewing the respective governments as the responsible policy units, the 1970s reflected one sort of policy experiment in both countries and the 1980s another sort for a time. The respective governments (or policy regimes) clearly appear as the exogenous shocks which moved the monetary indicator and the inflation rates as well as other time series. I would say that monetary policy in M-orientation terms dominated in the efforts to control inflation in the 1980s. For the United States this could readily be called exogenous. For the United Kingdom the policy was also politically driven, although in policy implementation terms the monetary part of the policy depended on the move toward budget surpluses.

Although this may not be directly connected to Alan Greenspan at the U.S.'s Federal Reserve in the 1990s, we encounter him in fact as arguing for the move toward a balanced budget as a means of reducing interest rates via a reduction of the expected inflation component in the interest rate (Frazer 1994b, 8–9, 57–58 n.2, 75–76, 79, 89, 106).

To be sure, in both the Kaldor-U.K. instance and the Friedman-U.S.-U.K. instance, the specific technical meaning econometricians attempted to give the terms "exogenous" and "endogenous" are inadequate for policy-related purposes. Rather, I have questions about the following: limiting the boundaries to the domestic or international economies, attempting to deal strictly with a variable as a time series exclusive of episodic impacts, and juxtaposing very different policy orientations. Moreover, these are as different as assigning 0 or 1 to a "dummy variable" in a multiple regression equation, except that no analytical or policy problem is dealt with in any fruitful way by assigning 0 or 1 to a dummy variable. The analytical problem is that the most important forces at work in the movements of the major economic time series (GNP or GDP, prices, production, employment, and so on) are relegated to subordinate roles by the use of the technique.

Observing the big-picture forces of the 1867–1975 decades, FS went on to say simply, "Everything depends on purpose" (FS 1991, 42). Mentioning the quantity of money, they said: "For the United States after World War I, we believe it is appropriate to regard the money stock as exogenous (for example, determined by the monetary authorities) in an economic analysis of long-run money demand." Of the private sector they said, "We do not believe it would be equally appropriate to do so for week-to-week or month-to-month movements."

FS go on to review the exogenous-endogenous matter for the period before and after World War I (1991, 42–43). For the decades before World War I they point to the international gold standard as controlling the money stock and see the domestic stock of money as endogenous to the international standard. For the period after World War I they point to the Federal Reserve as a political institution (and not as independent of Congress and the president) and they say the money stock is best regarded as endogenous, as would be the case I attribute to the United Kingdom during Margaret Thatcher's period (1994b, 179-184). This perspective is what I point to in viewing the trends in inflation-rate and interest-rate data (Frazer 1994b, 37–50) as being dominated by political regime shifts.

Moreover, in all that is said above about the interest rate, its control, and its use as a surrogate, it should not be surprising that the Federal Reserve's Chairman Alan Greenspan embraced early on a monetarist approach (Frazer 1988, 256–257, 263, 686, 790 n.13), entered the Federal Reserve as a Reagan appointee, combined his money-aggregate leanings with bond-market sophistication (Frazer 1994b, 8–9, 57–58 n.2, 75–76, 79, 89, 106), gained reappointment as chairman under Bill Clinton, steered President Clinton toward a stable economy policy, and in fact presented the president with a relatively stable economy at the time of the 1996 elections. Elements of this feat reappear in Chapter 12, where we confront President Clinton during his first year in office.

ANALYTICAL PROBLEMS

Nine analytical problems encountered in Niggle's AFEE/institutionalist consensus view follow. They are juxtaposed with aspects of analysis that have been reviewed above.

1. Monetary policy is not explicitly defined. And on one occasion Niggle writes of changes running from monetary policy to the money supply (1991, 143), as if somehow monetary policy were separate from the money aggregate. In contrast, I point to an indicator of policy to show the direction of movement in it, whether accommodative and so on.

2. Political boundaries are not set for the purpose of the control unit. In contrast, I introduce the prospect of the control unit as being international, as under the international gold standard, or domestic, as under the pre-Thatcher and Thatcher political regimes.

3. Niggle's discussion of the endogenously determined money supply (1991, 137–138) is inadequately discriminatory as to what in fact is the case. In general, whether Kaldor causation or Friedman "helicopter money," the interaction of depository intermediaries and bank credit is involved.

4. Depository intermediaries interact with their "loan customers," but no attention is given to the importance of expanding bank credit without dependence on the initiative of "agents" to take out bank loans under the Keynesian/i-regime theory.

5. Niggle draws on both British and American literature, as if the U.S. and the U.K. central banks were identical, in terms of operations and practices. He does so even as he introduces Lord Kaldor and focuses on United States control arrangements and operations. By contrast, I differentiate between Bank of England and Federal Reserve operations and introduce central bank and theoretical works hypotheses.

6. Next, Niggle offers descriptions of institutional and historical details. However, he fails to point to phenomena that may be repetitive (for example, as to the source of inflation).

7. Further, Niggle relies on the simplest of ideas (1991, 147), such as that of credit supply and credit demand, in treating interest rates. He does so without regard to the time frames, the expectation of inflation as a primary determinant of interest rates, and whether the supply and demand sides can be distinguished. Niggle's treatment goes back to the pre-Keynes loanable-funds theory of interest rates (Frazer 1994a, 208–209) which Keynes most justly attacked.

8. Niggle views commercial banks as engaging in innovations in the form of liabilities and asset management techniques that allow banks to increase their lending for a given amount of reserves (1991, 146). "As a result," he says, "the money supply becomes increasingly endogenously determined." The difficulty I see here, however, is that the political entity (or the Federal Reserve) may be expected to monitor these developments in determining the link between reserves and the money stock. Moreover, in Friedman's time frames and in reference to the monetary indicator, the central bank also may be charged with the equally difficult task of targeting money growth (or its range), after allowing for secular shifts in the income velocity of money (Y/M).[9] All of this complexity does not alter the central bank's responsibility. There is still the matter of holding the political entity responsible and thus viewing the policy as politically driven (for example, as exogenous) as I do in the discussion of FS's 1991 paper.

9. Finally, despite the extent of complexity—as I indicate in relation to Niggle's discussion of innovation—there is still the need for simplification in assigning responsibility and in making theoretic statements.

NOTES

1. A most straightforward and highly restrictive definition of "exogenous" as it related to time series had appeared by the 1960s (Christ 1966, 155-157). The exogenous variable in a regression equation was also equated with autonomous and independent variables and said to be uncorrelated with the error term in the equation and independent of other variables in the test (or regression) equation (Frazer 1973, 102-107). Others still viewed it as originating outside the usual economic calculus (the Vietnam War or change in the tax structure) or as a control variable (such as that for bank reserves).

2. They are Sir (later Lord) Gordon Richardson (Frazer 1988, 557-558), and Leigh-Pemberton (1987).

3. Friedman proceeds "indirectly" in his testing of theory. In doing so, he avoids efforts to identify curves of the static sort we associate with a Keynesian orientation. For examples and discussion of the "indirect approach," see Frazer (1988, 82-84, 134-135, 542, 560-561, 776), Frazer and Boland (1983, 135-139), and Frazer (1994a).

On the Friedman system and the identification problem see Frazer (1994a, 49-51; 1994b, 21, 226, 239 n.10).

4. This change whereby the bond-market participants could process information about monetary policy more contemporaneously with policy changes has been called "New York's revenge" (Frazer 1988, 447, 545, 653, 669; 1994a, 68, 180; 1994b, 129).

5. In the context of upward and downward movements in interest rates, psychological time enters when the "agents" form expectations by looking back at earlier phases of business conditions that are comparable to the current state. The time dimension is in relation to the earlier phases (or episodes) and not simply a fixed time dimension in calendar terms. Also, it is not simply a lower (or higher) rate that matters as to its effect on expenditure plans, but rather an assessment of the current state in relation to the comparable past states.

6. On OMO of a special sort, see Frazer (1994b, 100 n.10, 110, 169). The effects via the bank reserve equation and the omission of any direct tie to interest rates and fiscal policy make them special. At the household level of control over real money balances we encounter the excess (or the reverse of a short supply) of the actual money stock in relation to the desired money stock.

7. In the classification of ideological orientation as it relates to the economic topics, Kaldor and Friedman positions, and so on, I introduce Hotelling's line (Frazer 1994a, 82-85).

8. The indicator is in fact based on Friedman's rule (Frazer 1994b, 47-50). It was intended to guide policy for the achievement of a zero or lower inflation-rate goal. A variation of it is that the money stock should grow at the same rate as real output, but with allowances for secular-trend shifts in the turnover of money balances (Frazer 1988, 412, 549; 1994b, 38). The shifts in velocity were thought to occur in response to episodic matters, such as a distinct change in the payments mechanism. As a guide to policy, the central banks were not expected to make allowances for the shorter-run changes in the velocity ratio, because the effects of acceleration (deceleration) in the money stock were thought to start immediately and accumulate for a long period. However, I do not view the concepts "accommodative" and so on, as guides to policy (that is, in normative terms). Rather, I am simply dealing with effects and the way the world works.

9. Admittedly the central bank is left with no easy task. Even so, one can view it as a part of the responsibility that goes with discretionary policy as opposed to rules (see discussion in note 8; Frazer 1973, 349–381).

Chapter 11

The New Classical School and Rational Expectations

D ating from the appearance of Robert Lucas's 1969 paper with Leonard Rapping, the New Classical School (NCS) is not so new any longer. However, the NCS's "rational expectations" work has drawn renewed attention since Robert Lucas's receipt of the 1995 Nobel Prize in economics, so I deal once again with the school overall.

Hereafter referring to the NCS's rational expectations (RE), I abstract a caricature from the details found in the NCS publications. I do this because— in contrast to Keynes and to a lesser extent Friedman, where somewhat unified bodies of work can be closely identified with the principal figures—so many were involved along the way, and because the principal figures have written so much of a highly technical nature from which I abstract (Fisher 1980; Lucas 1981; Lucas and Sargent 1981; Sargent 1987). Following John Muth, the NCS offered a highly stringent view of rationality, which I call "super rationality," namely, that agents form expectations on the basis of the best economics available, including profit and utility maximization (Frazer 1994a, 53–75), except that now the concepts are given the time frames illustrated in Figure 1.3. In these, the cyclical part of Figure 1.3 is claimed to be a state of incomplete information among agents and the trend is seen as a state of rationality (for example, NCS rationality).

Besides Walrasian equations and the conditions they imply, NCS's "best economics" includes the separation of the theories of money and output and knowledge of the actuarial probability distributions for the expected outcomes. Muth's paper on which the probability part aspect of the NCS's work drew was titled "Rational Expectations and the Theory of Price Movements," which appeared in 1961, over a decade before it sparked interest. Muth dwelt on

---

This chapter is the outgrowth of a paper presented at the December 1977 meeting of the association for Evolutionary Economics in New York (Frazer 1978, 343–372).

prices and a rather general view of rationality. According to it, "rationality" is the formation of expectations in such a way as to be "essentially the same as the predictions of the relevant economic theory." However, Muth himself does not claim complete rationality in every respect. He says the assumptions can be modified, and "systematic biases, incomplete and incorrect information, poor memory, etc., can be examined with analytical methods based on rationality" (1961, 330).

The NCS's significant impact, with the leadership of later Nobel laureate Robert Lucas, was its attempt to reorientate almost the entire body of economics in one bold stroke. "The Friedman system" does so, too, at least as it has evolved, but it proceeds in radically different ways from the NCS's. Most notably, it drops any distinction between uncertainty as incomplete information and risk as actuarial probability. The transitory state of irrationality in NCS terms vanishes, and "the bond trader" enters as an agent that processes information in a timely way. This bond trader processes information of a theoretic, empirical, institutional, and episodic sort, and in contrast to much economic theory (for example, Tobin 1958; text pages 85–89), capital funds are placed at risk on the basis of expected outcomes. Other groups may be specialized and take risks in a different way. In any case, the Friedman system views agent rationality as personalistic, such that behavior over the states of business conditions is rational in personalistic terms. Furthermore, in such a context, where motion and time rates of change in stock and flow variables enter, one encounters the Friedman variant of instrumentalism (Frazer 1984a). In that variant Friedman and I depart from strong reliance on economic man axioms and I view firms as more or less maintaining market shares once time and motion enter, as opposed to profit maximization with time fixed (Frazer 1994a, 63–68).[1]

Although not primarily rooted in the University of Chicago, the NCS did draw on an inharmonious past at Chicago when combining the distinction between risk and uncertainty, and that between cycles and trends. In the long-run or secular-trend state, the NCS's analytical part ends with Walrasian equations (Appendix to Chapter 11) and, I will argue, a major inconsistency.

From NCS positions, an interesting proposition follows: A stabilization policy of the government is not required, because in the anticipation of a policy-achieved stable/secular-trend state, agents will be rational, and, as a consequence, stability will come about from the agents' acting rational in NCS terms, all without the government policy. There is a corollary: The only way the government's control mechanism can have its effects is by tricking the agents—generating what amounts to information they do not have. This is viewed in terms of the Frank Knight distinction between risk as classical probability and uncertainty as incomplete information. That is, the transitory state (or cyclical component of Figure 1.3) is a period of incomplete information and the matter of nationality is restricted in this state. By contrast, during this transitory state (Frazer 1994a, 63–75), the Friedman system recognizes market shares and rationality in personalistic-probability terms where uncertainty encompasses both risk and incomplete information.

In a rather extreme contrast to the NCS corollary, the Friedman system proceeds thus: episodic impacts on time series data are a prominent part of reality, central banks from the time of Walter Bagehot's *Lombard Street* (1873) have been thought of in relation to liquidity crises, governments and their constituencies offer no prospect for abdication of the role, and agent reactions to the episodes and to the central bank's position are rational.

More specifically, as to origins and exclusive of the connections to John Muth and to Knight and Friedman's "Wesley Mitchell–connected" work, the NCS is associated with an early paper by Lucas and Leonard Rapping (1969) and with early and related work by Robert Barro and by Barro and Hershell Grossman (including Barro and Grossman 1971; Barro 1977; 1981; Barro 1984). If there is any common connection these people appear to have had in the NCS's formative years, it is centered about Carnegie-Mellon University. John Muth was affiliated with the institution when he wrote his 1961 paper and Lucas collaborated with Rapping. Lucas's 1969 paper with Rapping was written at Carnegie-Mellon. Thomas Sargent taught there in 1968–1969 after receiving a Ph.D. from Harvard, before moving to the University of Minnesota, where he encountered Neil Wallace. Leonard Rapping, a Chicago Ph.D., spent the 1960s at Carnegie-Mellon before making a mental break with his past at Chicago and with the NCS.

Barro's textbook reflects some of the characteristics of the NCS. First, however, it presents a view with no meaningful attention to alternative theories and hypotheses, which is contrary to Friedman's approach, in which there are always competing theories. To get its overall result there is a good bit of distortion and one-sided referencing of statistical results. The overall result is the neoclassical dichotomy, where the theories of money and production are separated.

$$M = (Q/V)_{\text{constant}} \ P$$

where change (or accelerated growth) in the money stock (M) goes entirely into the price level (P) and the numerator and denominator of the production-velocity ratio are constant (and, consequently, Q/V = const). Although there is incongruity in holding output constant and treating paths for the money stock (M) and the price index (P) in the long run, this is what occurs in Barro's textbook, and it does so even without a careful regard for empirical work as in FS (1982, 588–620). In other words, the text deals with growth in money balances as found in Friedman's work but without the dynamics and time rates of change found there and exclusive of results for analyses of long waves in business conditions (Frazer 1994a, 121–125). The dynamics found in Friedman and thus in the Friedman system include the monetary theory as a statement of motion, the cycle/trend distinction, the parallel growth in money and output that yields greater price-level stability, the interaction between the real goods and monetary sectors, and the treatment of the volatile Cambridge k (the reciprocal of the income-velocity ratio, Y/M). To be sure, the Friedman system is not pre-Keynes with the Cambridge k as a constant.

The inharmonious past at Chicago, which the NCS drew on, was that of Knight and Friedman. In viewing economics, Knight backed away from the prospect of its becoming an empirical science. He simply saw it in terms of ethics or a proper code of behavior, and the risk part extended to insurance or actuarial risk. On the other hand, Friedman moved in an empirical direction. Uncertainty was something in the mind of the agent, and the analysis of uncertainty was linked with the demand for money, as it was for Keynes.

Even for Friedman, the agent may not act rationally in the cyclical context, because he/she has not figured out what was going on, but two things come about: (1) FS report on changes in the structure underlying the formation of inflationary expectations (Frazer 1994a, 227–228; FS 1982, 478, 558–573), and (2) I introduce the notion of a system of analysis that imposes pre-mid-1960s behavior and post-1960s-behavior. Hence, far from drawing on the actuarial/incomplete knowledge distinction, Friedman offered the seeds for a learning prospect. As addressed by me, it goes along the line I have attributed to Bayesian learning and psychological time (Frazer 1994a, 73–75; 142–143). In addition, Friedman introduced episodic change as a part of the time series analysis as well as the cycle-trend distinction, as I relate to time series and turning points in business conditions (Frazer 1994a, 232–241).

However, again two things happen. First, the controversial subject of filtering the time series arises (Frazer 1988, 755–757; Frazer 1994a, 74). It comes about as early as Friedman's work with Simon Kuznets (1945, 331) but does not begin to achieve high visibility in professional circles until the early reviews of FS's *Monetary Trends* (Frazer 1988, 543–544; Goodhart 1982; Mayer 1982) and until HE present papers on FS's *Monetary Trends* before the Bank of England's panel of academic economists in October 1983 (Frazer 1988, 736–741; HE 1983; HE 1991). Second, I view filtering the time series as a way of separating transitory and trend components in data series as well as a way of confronting episodic impacts on the time series which exist (Frazer 1994a, 88, 227–228; HE 1991, 33). Looking at the conventional econometric/economics means of separating the components of time series data, I see a separation-of-effects problem (Frazer 1994a, 29, 50–52; 1994b, 55–57) and suggest other possibilities (1994a, 232–245).

Additional matters implied previously extend even further to a consideration of the worth of the "superrationality" concept found in NCS's national expectations, and particularly as it relates to what I identify as "the naive economic model" as far as analyses of time series are concerned. I identify such a model and return to the practical twofold data analysis problem which I first introduced in reference to Friedman's primal equation, to the purpose of the economics (Frazer 1994a, xvi, 29, 54), and to episodes and time series.[2]

Also, the question raised earlier in the discussion of Lawrence Klein and the great ratios still lingers (Frazer 1994a, 75–81). Klein looked for "flat out" stability in the ratios. On the other hand, I saw the prospect of stability in the ratios only in terms of a phenomenon, after the adjustment for episodes impacting on the time series.

Further, in all the attention to money and finance plus the integration with the analysis of money and the real goods sectors, money is the link between the past and the future. In a world where money and finance play a fundamental role, money, finance, and liquidity overall determine the state of business in the real goods sector. It is not the reverse, except in the collectivist state. There, government spending and intervention may determine production with monetary accommodation as where market power creates inflation rather than monetary matters (Frazer 1994a, 130–135, 204–205). Power theories of inflation enter and, consequently, the controls that accompany them.

The NCS views agents as forming expectations on the basis of the best economics, the actuarial probability, and so on, and implies a lot about static constructs and methods of analyzing data, to which I return. I have anticipated the difficulty of this in several ways: by questioning the prospects for the identification of the static schedules by direct means (Frazer 1994a, 49–51, 71), by introducing the separation-of-effects problem (Frazer 1994a, 29, 50–52), and by stating the closely related twofold data analysis problem.

THE ANALYSIS OF THE TIME SERIES

A main route in the analysis of time series in the 1960s and 1970s has been adding variables to the right-hand side of a regression equation and extending this process to the big models (Frazer 1994a, 210–213; 1994b, 159–160 n. 5, 6, and 10). In the rather straightforward form in which we have considered this, the static constructs, such as Marshall's demand curve, are believed to be potentially identifiable (or at least the slope parameter estimable in the neighborhood of the crucial point is potentially identifiable). In addition, variables and equations may be added, and there false presumptions enter, namely: that effects (the stable and estimable parameters) can be separated by known direct means, and that bounds may be set on the true regression coefficients as variables are added to the right-hand side of regression equations.

Friedman's approach and that most consistently set forth in the Friedman system has been an alternative to this, although Friedman did not rule out the prospect of combining his indirect approach with simultaneous equations models. A main distinguishing feature of Friedman's approach, as I have presented it (for example, Figure 1.3), is the role of episodes and the time frames—the very short run, the transitory component (or the cycle, $|Y-Y_p|$, and the permanent component of the time series. Those distinctions have also appeared in considerations of economic policy with reference to stabilization and faster or slower economic growth (trends). Friedman has said that it is a matter of the purpose you have in mind when you wish to extract information from the series. The policy emphasis on stable and noninflationary growth would appear to impose a special purpose. I proceed with a general orientation, the naive and general economic models, and Friedman's orientation which I adapt to the Friedman system.

A General Orientation

A general orientation in economic theory in data analysis, as in other scientific study, is that there is a twofold property: there is order in nature, as distinct from chance occurrence or random forces; and this order awaits discovery. This orientation was expressed by the Anatole France (1844–1924) and Albert Einstein (1879–1955), respectively:

> Chance is perhaps the pseudonym of God when He did not want to sign—*Le Jardin d'Epicure*, 1984

> I shall never believe that God plays dice with the world—Philipp Frank, *Einstein, His Life and Times*, 1947

Thus, I look for order, regularity, and/or a stable relation in the study of the real world, but I also encounter ideas in which some occurrences are commonly viewed as just chance events when in fact we simply have incomplete information and/or are unable to recognize the information and errors in the time series of data. One common idea regarding chance events appeared with considerable visibility in a London newspaper, *The Guardian*, when HE first attacked FS's uses of statistical methods. On December 15, 1983, it offered the following as regards HE's attack and the chance idea of a "random walk," which has often been associated with readily recognizable episodic changes:

> It is a very long time since there have been any bomb-shells from Oxford University quite like the one which Professor David Hendry has just dropped on Professor Milton Friedman. The emperor of international monetarism is roundly declared to have no clothes on.

Continuing, Christopher Huhne reported, "Hendry and Ericsson's work gives us a good idea of just how unpredictable—indeed, dangerous—the monetarist 'relationships' are." According to Huhne:

> Professor Hendry likens velocity to the walk home of a drunken man: he's heading roughly in the right direction but one can never predict whether his next step will be backwards, forwards, or sideways. It is a "random walk." What this means for policy-makers, and market watchers, is that a given money supply target could finance

vastly different levels of transactions and inflation and in a wholly unpredictable manner.

Another important finding of Hendry and Ericsson's work is that the money supply is clearly not independent of events in the rest of the economy, yet the Friedmanite claim of independence ("exogeneity") is vital if he is to saddle governments and central banks with the responsibility for controlling it.

Another idea of chance alone in the analysis of economics is that found with respect to the error term for the estimate from a regression equation, for example, $\ln Y = a + b \ln M$, where $\ln Y$ is conditional on $\ln M$. The reference is to value $\ln Y$ from a given $\ln M$, but with deviation from $\ln Y$ due to chance alone as symbolized by an error term, ε. That is, one wishes to depict derivations that are viewable as the normal probability distribution. This probability distribution is based on assumptions underlying forecast error, $\ln Y - \overline{\ln Y}$. The assumptions are that (1) the different conditional distributions of $\ln Y$ at given values of $\ln M$ are all of the same shape and are all normal distributions and (2) these distributions have the same variability (that is, the standard deviation, $S_{\ln Y\text{-}\ln M}$, is the same in all distributions), which is to say I have homoschedasticity (the same variability in the distribution of error as $\ln M$ increases, as illustrated in Figure 7.2b).

The Naive Economic Model

In the mid-1970s, as the NCS's RE was gaining attention, an MIT Ph.D. economist at the Federal Reserve Bank of New York was asked what was meant by rational expectations. She responded with a simple example of the strict regression equation, big model method, presently referred to as the naive economic model. However, defining rationality in reference to the "true" model made her illustration more interesting, by defining rationality in reference to the real world. Arak's definition in brief. Let the real world (or "true model") of the price level determination be

$$P_t = \alpha_0 + \alpha_1 X_t + \alpha_2 Z_t + \varepsilon \qquad (1)$$

then the expectations for the price level are rational when they are in conformity with the "true model,"

$$P^e = \alpha_0 + \alpha_1 X_1 + \alpha_2 Z_t \qquad (2)$$

The conformity of equation (2) with (1) is indicated by the equality of the parameters ($a_0 = a_0$, $a_1 = a_1 = a_1$, and $a_2 = a_2$). Presumably the variables operating through ε are offsetting and unsystematic.

In the illustration, the "rational" way of forming expectations concerns two steps: First, ascertain the actual pricing mechanism for the economy and then form an expectation ("likely outcome") for the price level (P) from the first step, as in the Arak definition. "Moreover," Arak notes, "each factor [for example, X_t, Z_t] would receive exactly the same weight in forming the expectation as that factor has in determining the actual outcome."

Two properties are used in testing for "rationality" of expectations in the Arak context:

1. The expectation is no more likely to be too low than to be too high. (This property is called "unbiasedness".)

2. The expectation depends upon other variables in exactly the same way as does the actual outcome for that variable.

Using the notation in the Arak definition, a test using the first property would rely upon the following relation obtained with classical least squares regression analysis:

$$P = \alpha_0 + \alpha_1 P^e + \varepsilon$$

The test is whether P^e is an unbiased estimator of P. It is such if $\alpha_0 = 0$, $\alpha_1 = 1$, and P should equal P^e plus an error term which averages 0.

An example of a precise test of "rationality" using the second property eludes us as a practical matter. It requires that the forecasting entity know the structure of the economy as represented by the coefficients of an ideal structural equations model of the type mentioned on earlier occasions. In this ideal case, the coefficients are used in such a way that certain determinants, such as X_t and Z_t in equation (1), translate into an actual inflation rate, $(1/P)(dP/dt)$. The coefficients would be compared to the coefficients which relate the same information, such as X_t and Z_t, to the expectations (P^e in the example).

Of course, we know this big-model method and thus the testing prospects for rationality of the implied sort fall short of the mid-1960s claims and hopes for the methods (Frazer 1973, 287–311), but the example makes some points and illustrates a way of thinking in economics that has proved less than fruitful. Recognizing such an outcome, the point is that a true representation of the real world is likely unattainable via the econometric fashion of the 1960s, 1970s, and even the 1980s (Frazer 1994b, 160 n.10; Friedman and Schwartz 1991; Volcker and Gyohten 1992, 146–147, 154, 161). Even if seen as an abstraction and not simply a microscopic search for more detail, the failure of the approach over the decades since the mid-1960s, when it was ushered in with much fanfare, suggests that we do not have with respect to it even a fruitful way of thinking aside from any econometric estimates (as first introduced in Figure 2.1). A second point is that the method actually represents a common way of thinking in economics generally which calls unrealistically for a separation of effects (say, of X and Z in the examples) which can be terribly misleading as variables are added and even dangerous for the initiated victims and even uninitiated students. We should learn from the failure, view it as such until better evidence is forthcoming, and move along new lines of thinking. The Friedman system is one of these. It offers a personalistic approach to rationality, recognizes the prospect of an interrelation of numerous phenomena in the central banking context that take on the characteristics of economic psychology, emphasizes an alternative way to approach the search for repetitive phenomena, and points a way between the half truths that history never repeats itself and that history always repeats itself. To be sure, the analytical system I offer stresses the potential fruitfulness of the roles for psychological time and episodic changes, even as it encompasses central banking and retains the major portions of the mechanical apparatus found in economics with a positive venue.

Modeling the Real World: The "Naive" and "General Models"

The Arak example of modeling is essentially that of the structural equations models as pioneered by Lawrence Klein, but with a difference. Notably, the whole orientation of the model is converted from contemporary and lagged values of variables to an expectations orientation and to a period going beyond the sampling of the data. This would be essentially what was so bold about Muth's 1961 article and the even more dramatic NCS orientation, as I view it.

The NCS orientation is important, not so much because of any fruitful hypothesis that depends upon it, but because in one bold stroke it shifts the attention to the possible role of the economic theory in making predictions and forecasts. It leaves in the lurch, at one extreme, years of teaching and a mass of literature based on static constructions, the ceteris paribus centerpiece, and statistical problems, and, at the other, it takes this all forward and further compounds its shortcomings by having the static optimization hold over time (as in metastatics) and by adding market clearing conditions à la Walras and the actuarial probability as a part of agent rationality.[3]

Indeed, these rather strenuous assumptions call to mind Friedman's 1953 discussions of the role of axioms and controversy about the "as if" method set on course by him (Boland 1979, 513; Frazer 1988, 131-132; Frazer 1994a, 71-73; Friedman 1953a, 16-20; Samuelson 1963, 232). As reviewed earlier (text, page 45) Friedman raises questions about the purpose of the work. He questions the need for detailed descriptive accuracy of the assumptions, implies the emphasis placed on the detailed descriptive accuracy of the "homogeneous product" axiom found in the theory of the perfect market (Frazer 1994a, 68-71; Friedman 1953a, 34-35), and makes positive remarks about the significance and role of assumptions. Questions are raised about the purpose and usefulness of the theory and about the use of axioms as a means of classifying a theory and getting at its key elements.

So we ask whether the NCS's approach is useful as a guide to making and understanding monetary policy. Although we note "a policy dilemma," attributed to Sargeant and Wallace later, we find Robert Lucas wishing to place distance between the NCS and an emphasis on the monetary matters Friedman set on course (Klamer 1984, 29-37).

In response, I conclude that truth, and the problems of treating time, uncertainty, and money properly, do not reside in the NCS orientation. In the policy context without influences on expectations, we encounter a feedback relation,

$$M = M^*_t + h(Y_{t-1} - Y^*_{t-1}) \tag{3}$$

In it M is the control variable, M* is an equilibrium time path, Y_{t-1} is national income, Y^*_{t-1} is the equilibrium time path (or "desired" path for income), $Y_{t-1} - Y^*_{t-1}$ is transitory income, and h is a factor (say, h < 0 for stabilization policy traditionally viewed in the abstract), although we know of no such policy that has been employed in the United States. In any case, in the hypothetical relation, we have the idea, even beyond the Keynesian period, that stabilization could be achieved through monetary policy in money-aggregate terms if officials responded in the opposite direction to the transitory component of income. The presumption is that this policy could be established and pursued without influencing the expectations ("the forecasts") of the behavioral units (including large industrial concerns and active participants in the financial markets).

This foregoing concept of policy without the influences on expectations is completely wiped out by the introduction of NCS's RE. The NCS achieves this obliteration of the countercyclical notion, as it were, by substituting one aspect of "purity" for another—for example, by substituting the concept of expectations in the manner of actuarial probability (strong rationality) for simple repetition and feedback. The substitution gives rise to what Sargeant and Wallace called "a policy dilemma." Notably: *If monetary policy is in fact a repetitive, countercyclical policy—as noted in equation (3), h < 0—then, in the presence of NCS's RE, the economic agents can form rational expectations about the policy and the policy is no longer needed. The central bank can just as well follow a constant money-growth path. The activist policy in fact would work only so long as agents were "tricked" by it to the extent that they had incomplete information.*

The potential difficulty in making an analysis and in simply abandoning central bank stabilization policy is that the cycle denoted $Y_{t-1} - Y^*_{t-1}$ may not be simply endogenous and repetitive, as depicted by a sine curve. Rather, a variety of even overlapping events could happen: episodes may impact on the time series; some lags in learning of agents may enter; even more likely, various focal groups may simply specialize in risk and information gathering, for example, as to bond traders, manufacturers of distinct product lines, and households; the structure underlying the formation of inflationary expectations may shift as reported by FS for the mid-1960s; and in fact a sizable portion of the agents may not have the capacity for superrational expectations, as it were. These potential developments open up the prospect for the central bank to search out and react to the happenings so as to offset their destabilizing influence.

Indeed Friedman's rule, as encountered earlier, would only allow the Federal Reserve to offset secular shifts in the income velocity of money in the secular-trend context, when in fact central banks tend to place a strong weight on reactions to events in the short run and to induced liquidity crises. There may be dangers in this, stemming in part from lags in the accuracy of information regarding the public's shifts in and out of liquidity and from the lag in information arriving at the policy level regarding such important variables as income and the money stock. Even so, I offer a more general approach.

That approach recognizes that central bankers will continue to confront short-run happenings and adopts the hope that they may learn from past errors and even gain the recognition given to the Reagan appointee Alan Greenspan in his relatively successful tenure at the Federal Reserve, extending beyond the first term of the Clinton White House (text page 32). This Friedman system model is more general and useful than the model in which agents hold actuarially sound probabilities with respect to outcomes and otherwise anticipate the future in NCS/RE terms.

The more general model is more general because it depicts agents more as potential learners and as Bayesian decision makers (say, as forming views about prospects and as revising them on the basis of new information). The Bayesian concept encompasses both actuarial probability and incomplete information as probability. It accommodates evolutionary change and has several key ingredients. For one, time is unidirectional in certain respects; put simply, there are some nonrepetitive, evolutionary changes that occur over time, such that the universe is continuously changing in some respects. In other respects, man himself changes in that he learns over time. The state of his knowledge is never the same; there is an unfolding sequence. The statement of Bayes's theorem is relevant, plus we have more of a clinical view of rationality (Frazer 1994a, 73–75). It emphasizes the mind of the beholder, psychological time, and adjustments to episodes, and so on, rather than rationality in terms of expectations based on the largely static "sampling from the same universe" constructs.[4]

The decision making by "agents" may be a continuous process and learning related to the decision may take place as new information is obtained. Sampling (data, new information) may be from a changing universe as it goes on continuously. In other words, the degree of belief in the outcome of the event and hence the expectation of the event (for example, the probabilistically weighted outcome) depend on both prior judgment and observation, such that the degree of belief and expectation may change with new information. This learning from data and experience contrasts with the role of the classical probability found in the NCS's RE and in the reliance on least squares regression analysis.

Consistent with sequential decision making, there are Bayesian statistical methods for estimating parameters in structural equations models. However, these have not been and likely will not be satisfactorily worked out for large models. Mostly we are interested in just the distinctions among transitory change, trends, and episodic change, including sequential variation (Frazer 1978; Mullineaux 1977). The old least squares method can still be used for estimation, as it was by Friedman. Among such uses taken up thus far are the following: setting the "true bound" on the regression coefficient, (2) allowing for episodes and time frames, (3) filtering data, and, in general, (4) having knowledge of the experiment that generates the data. The latter I associate in particular with the 1920s and 1930s, the "Keynesian era" and the "U-Turn," changes in the structure underlying the formation of inflationary expectations, and the interwar and post–World War II periods.

In all of this I again turn to Friedman, who, at the time he made the statements that follow, was actually responding to questions about the highly formal work of Lucas of the NCS. Friedman said:

> What he [Lucas] is saying is that if the objective circumstances to which people have to adapt do change, their reactions will change. They will adjust their behavior to the objective circumstances they face. Now those objective circumstances may consist of government policies. They may consist of other things, for example, he would say, an econometrician evaluates the way in which a farmer behaves in relation to the weather. There is a major change in the whole pattern of weather. Something happens; there is an earthquake or something changes. His former equations would no longer be relevant. (Frazer and Sawyer 1984)

Continuing on the example of a Lucas principle, Friedman said:

> What he's essentially saying is that you have to be sure that you have not assumed as given certain variables that are very important in determining people's behavior. When the basic variables change, you're going to have to change the rest of them. Now, there's no reason in principle why econometric calculations may not be able to meet the Lucas point, if they had the right variables in there. (Frazer and Sawyer 1984)

However, in these remarks I see far more of Friedman than of Robert Lucas and NCS's RE. In fact, these ideas fit much better into the Friedman system than into NCS's RE.

Categories of Information

As I have recognized, the analysis of data must have a purpose, which I have related to stabilization (including as affected by episodes) and economic growth. Along such lines, the terms "endogenous" and "exogenous" arise, as they did in the last Chapter. Although, they have been defined and illustrated and taken up in relation to episodes; I now reintroduce them in reference to categories of information and recall again observations by Harvard's Alvin Hansen in the early 1950s.

As we recall, Hansen noted: "Many 'literary' (or non-mathematical) theories draw heavily upon exogenous factors for an explanation of both the cumulative process and the turning points. Econometric theories, on the other hand, have stressed endogenous movements." Hansen further saw the interacting multiplier and accelerator model (Frazer 1994a, 227–232) as combining "the exogenous factor—autonomous investment with the endogenous factor—the multiplier and the accelerator."

Since Hansen wrote I have come much further with the principal strands of thinking, but still diversity exists, and there is no highly ordered repetition (or cycle) that would appear as a sine curve, nor is there a perfect theory of the cycle. If there were, no problems would arise from separating categories of data as to cyclical, secular, and so on. As it is, we know from the observation of certain phenomena and the dating of turning points (Figure 1.3; Frazer 1994a, 25–26, 232–238) that cycles are irregular in amplitude and timing, that trends appear discernible, and that episodes such as political and ideological shifts and pronouncements by public officials of more or less credibility play havoc with the behavior of certain classes of series.

In the policy sphere we want not only to test theories against one another (Frazer 1994a, 3–28) but to address separate questions about stability and responses to shocks impacting on the time series and even long swings in them. Friedman, more than other data analysts, introduced these classes of information, as we have noted. In doing so, he offered a "primary equation"

$$M/P = f(Y/P, w; \ldots ; u) \qquad (4)$$

With respect to it, the terms M/P and Y/P call attention to money demand, $(Y/P)/(M/P)$; w is a liquidity factor representing holdings of liquid wealth, the dots signify "expected" rates of return on four classes of assets; and so on. We call the equation "primary" because it pertains to monetary policy, which moves other key time series about, and to liquidity shifts and monetary phenomena which we associate with the interacting monetary and real goods sides of the market economy. Said differently, a primary equation is one which can be dealt with separately from other equations, plus it is an equation that comes first and from which other relationships in the economy follow.

THE NCS: AN OVERVIEW

The "NCS" was not so new after decades of gestation and criticism, except that it was further recognized when the Nobel committee awarded Robert Lucas the 1995 Nobel Prize in economics. As was partly the true of Friedman's policy-oriented economics, the NCS gained its early momentum in the wake of the failures of Keynesian economics—(1) its inability to confront issues of the day, most notably the inflationary recession phenomenon, and (2) the inability of economics generally to deal with expectations phenomena and episodes which appear so relevant to them. Though drawing on parts of work made prominent by Friedman, such as the cycle-trend distinction, it is more unlike than like Friedman's economics, particularly in relation to probability and the treatment of time series and monetary matters.

The New Classical School represents a reaction to conditions and past failures, as I have stated, like Keynes's original work and later Friedman's. But rather than moving along as empirical economics with relevance to policy questions, which was so central to Friedman's economics, the NCS's economics turned inward in response to the failures of the past. Consequently the NCS paid great attention to technique as such.

Later I discuss the features that characterize the NCS's economics as essentially technical. They are static optimization, even over time when episodes are common. Indeed, we encounter the price theoretic statics, the actuarial probability, the Walrasian equilibrium, and the separation of production from the analysis of money. To be sure, there are the superrationality thesis we have alluded to and a neutrality-of-money thesis. The latter contends that money does not matter in relation to real output. Rather it enters only as a numeraire, and, in contrast to Keynes's and Friedman's definition of money (Frazer 1994a, 47–50), the store of value function does not enter and liquidity shifts do not occur.

In the superrationality context several things happen: (1) the classical postulates of utility and profit maximization are present (agents are consistent and successful optimizers); (2) in terms of probability the agents are capable of forming expectations such that the probability distributions about outcomes are identical to the objective probability distributions; (3) the decisions by agents are intertemporal in that they encompass time periods, including those in which there is continuous market clearing in terms of Walrasian equations and in which the classical postulates (profit and utility maximization) hold; and (4) business cycles are present and still generated but those are left outside the rational processes and dealt with through "uncertainty" via the Knight distinction (Hoover 1984; Klamer 1984, 13–25; Lucas and Rapping 1969). Indeed, Knight distinction facilitated the second, third, and fourth parts mentioned. The probability distributions under part (2) can be depicted in terms of actuarial probability.

Barro's textbook reflects some of the characteristics of the NCS as we have stated. Referring to the classical dichotomy expression $M = (Q/Y)_{const}P$, the entire Barro volume may be viewed as a proof of it. Along the way to getting there, he gave special attention to market clearing conditions. In short, all markets clear as represented in a set of Walrasian equations. These conditions are very static, come about in the long run, and stress the neutrality thesis (Barro 1984, 123–140, 422–423, 477), plus money balances are held only for transactions demand. For Barro, doubling money balances doubles the price level but leaves real variables unchanged—that is, d ln M/d ln Y = 1 where Q/V = constant. All of this dramatically contrasts with the Friedman/Schwartz tenet that money matters play the major role in decades-long historical savings and not simply in the more ordinary trade, credit, or business cycle (Frazer 1994a, 219–225; FS 1982, 588–620). In stating the relevance of money to the long waves, FS held that Hamlet, the prince of Denmark, had been left out of the long-swing drama by the prior analysts.

Differences between positions taken in Barrow's text, on the one hand, and those found in Friedman's economics and the Friedman system, on the other abound:

1. True enough, agents treated separately may control the dollar quantity of money they hold (Barro 1984, 58). But the matter dealt with by Friedman actually addressed equation (4) and the identification problem (text, pages 55–57). The nominal quantity of money is controlled by the monetary authority, and agents collectively determine the real stock of money (M/P) shown in equation (4). The central bank control is referred to quite simply as "helicopter money." But the central bank operations and means of control underlying this label are in fact quite complicated (Frazer 1994a, 94–102; 1994b, 81–105, 224–231). For the public's part, its control over the real stock centers about groups in which individuals share in the desire to hold more, less, or the existing stock of money balances. An excess of actual nominal balances over those desired by the groups gives rise to an increase in the velocity (or turnover) of the money stock and hence spending as prices rise to bring about the real stock, M/P. A less than desired stock implies reduced velocity and spending, and so on.

2. We get the real rate of interest as found in Fisher and in connection with Friedman's consumption function (Barro 1984, 70–71, 172, 259; Frazer 1994a, 166–174), and the Friedman system statement on text pages 82–85, namely, $i = i(real) + Pb[\dot{P}^e] \dot{P}^e$. However, in Friedman's economics the absolute amount of an increase in future consumption accompanies an increase in the real rate of interest, defined as the rate at which real goods today exchange for real goods one year hence or in the previous Friedman system statement. Faster income growth and the consumption depending on it require a larger saving-to-income ratio. This real rate is, to be sure, not controlled by the central bank, while in Barro the real rate is a controlled variable with no explanation as to how it is controlled.

3. Barro introduces the great constant S/Y and says his results are comparable to Friedman's (Barro 1984, 91–93), but when he talks of permanent income it is a constant level rather than the growth path illustrated in Figure 3.1 that occurs in other instances (Frazer 1994a, 166–170; 1994b, 17–19, 23–29). For the growth paths and their ratio and rate counterparts, the rule is that when stock and flow quantities, such as the money stock and income, change at the same rate, the ratio(s) and interest rate(s) remain at constant levels. However, in actuality even the permanent magnitudes, such as those for the money stock, income, the great ratios, and the rates of return and interest, may vary, particularly in response to episodes such as technology-induced change in the payments mechanism or a dramatic reversal in economic policy generally such as we encountered with the Thatcher government in Britain and the Reagan presidency in the United States (Frazer 1988, 524–690). When the growth paths in the

time series for the stock and flow quantities start to diverge, the ratios and rates also depart from the more permanent time paths. An example occurs in the mid-1960s, when the structure underlying the formation of inflationary expectations changed (Frazer 1994b, 68–77).

4. In discussing surveys of the demand-for-money literature, Barro (1984, 113) will cite David Laidler without recognizing Laidler's treatment as radically different from Friedman's (Frazer and Boland 1983, 135 n.12). Although David Laidler held a Ph.D. from the University of Chicago, he had not been a student at that university under Friedman or earlier. Laidler's textbook *The Demand for Money* (1977) was Keynesian (Frazer 1988, 560–561, 776, n.69).

5. Barro says (1984, 159–162) that agents form expectations of the inflation rate $(\dot{P}_t)^e$ that equal the inflation rate $(\dot{P}_t)$ and that the agents will not make systematic mistakes, for example, errors, $(P^e - P)^2$, are not moving in the same direction. Results from analyses of data, however, indicate that agents will under- or overforecast fairly consistently. Even in the case of the stock market, where the random walk hypothesis has been thought to provide a good approximation, Franco Modigliani adds (Klamer 1984, 124), "but [it is good approximation only] with the understanding that it [the random walk] is consistent with fairly long-lasting disequilibrium." Therefore, "In the short run you can get trapped into a situation in which no gain can be made, even though it is not one of fundamental equilibrium."

The Monetary Rule Prospect and The RE Policy Dilemma

In reviewing Robert Lucas's discussion with Arjo Klamer (1984, 29–57) on the RE debates he contributed to throughout the 1970s and on into the early 1980s, one is struck by Lucas's frankness and positions. I state these revelations because of their relevance to the role of money and the earlier monetary rule prospect. Lucas's positions in the Klamer interview are as follows:

1. That he set about putting together an enormously formal, analytical structure with very limited background as to methods. This and the fact that he received a Ph.D. in economics from Chicago may explain why the "classical" component of economics came to play such a large role.

2. That he saw RE as an idea exclusive of money and business cycles. The relation of RE to money he saw as bearing on chance—his and Thomas Sargeant's interest.

3. That he appears as a persuasive person, on the one hand, but as taking NCS's RE lightly, on the other. He seems to stress experimentation—"People [economists] . . . thinking about what's puzzling them or taking more scientific points of view" (Klamer 1984, 29–57).

These matters aside—the formal structure, the "experimentation," the notion of RE exclusive of money analysis—a main thesis that emerges from

NCS is the RE policy dilemma. As posed by Sargeant and Wallace (1976a; 1976b), key words are "systematic" and "countercyclical." One question is whether stabilization policy can be effective in a world where expectations are formed rationally in NCS/RE terms. Another is whether the NCS/RE model is useful in the conduct of policy or in the understanding of the policy that emerges. Still another is whether the Federal Reserve and even other central banks which operate in sizable money and capital markets can follow an interest rate strategy to achieve noninflationary money-growth conditions as I suggest (Frazer 1994b, 224–231).

An example of rationality and ineffective stabilization policy is straightforward in the context of the pure (I said "naive") rational expectations model. If monetary policy is simply countercyclical ("systematic") and conducted in the "feedback" context surrounding equation (3), then the public can learn about it and form a rational view of the future. In this case, the policy has no effect because the expectation ("forecast") of stability leads to plans that are based on stability and hence to stability. Townsend (1978) speaks of a "self-fulfilling equilibrium" where feedback is an inappropriate basis for policy.

The policy dilemma is whether to pursue an "active" or passive monetary policy. In the NCS's RE framework, unanticipated changes in policy may have desired effects, but anticipated movements do not. In the formation of rational expectations a systematic stabilization policy is discounted in advance.

For the NCS rationalist only "surprises" in policy work, whereas in text we point to stability and confidence in the monetary authority. In effect, in the NCS case, the behavioral units must be "fooled" and "tricked" to make the economic policy work. No doubt the government has miscalculated at times, extended itself beyond its capabilities, and thereby contributed to economic instability. At other times, authorities have clearly manipulated the system for political ends. In such instances, many would see a strong argument for a simple policy rule, but no central bank or government has moved toward one.

Whether an "activist" policy is defensible may depend on how one views instability to begin with. Historically there have been two views with some possible relevance. According to one, instability is generated internally to the economic model (one may say, within the mechanical workings of the economy). The accelerator principle referred to earlier (Frazer 1994a, 230–233) is illustrative of this sort of instability, but in larger measure there is the idea that "shocks" that impinge on one variable also impinge on others in the system of equations. Thus, in the first view, change occurs without altering the structure. But, in the second view, the economic system (or structure of equations) is being buffeted about by outside occurrences. This is the view whereby the participants in markets are not just reacting to forecast information (with fixed structure) but to news events and to other new information bearing on the future for the economy. Changes may even come about, for example, a crisis in policy combines with a backlog of new and old ideas for dealing with it, as in the Reagan presidency.

The episodic view does not necessarily rule out making structural adjustments in equations, but it does alter the claims for the usefulness of structural and multiple regression equations generally and especially for their power to separate the effects of episodes and technological change. Indeed, analyses of data series seem mostly to support a personalistic-probability/learning/episodes view. Recognizing the combination of the dangers of unwarranted political manipulation of the public by the government and some lags in the cumulative effects of policy lasting a long time, there is a role for an "active" policy in this view. Its rationale would go as follows: An unfavorable and possibly unforeseen event occurs (for example, the stock market crush of 1987, the United States intervenes in the Persian Gulf region in 1990, or the president and the 104th Congress fail to arrive at a balanced budget plan). The events have the potential for causing the behavioral units to take a more uncertain view of the future and thus reduces total spending. The central bank could counter this not by reacting to a target variable, as in the case of "feedback," but by reacting to the episode with an announced, countering change in policy. Such was reported in comparing the stock market crashes of 1929 and 1987 (Frazer 1988, 682–690).

One could say that in time, given enough episodes, the public could forecast stability, even in a world of unanticipated shocks. This prospect for "transition" to a "superrational" public is not immediately present although we have applauded Alan Greenspan (text pages 35, 171, 182 n.4).

NCS: The Critics

Kevin Hoover dealt with ascertain aspects of the NCS (Hoover 1994a), and the relation between NCS and the methods of Lawrence Klein's big models has led Klein to offer some criticisms (1983, 98–120), as have others. Klein claimed that ordinary citizens do not follow the steps of reasoning found in his models, nor do they reach the same conclusions. Taking his cue, the Nobel laureate Franco Modigliani said (in Klamer 1984, 124), "I am hesitant to accept those complicated calculations in maximization problems, except when they reflect a long repetitive process." Robert Solow, a more recent laureate, took critical note (in Klamer 1984, 138–145) of Knight's distinction between risk and uncertainty, and the intersections of supply and demand curves, where all of the most important markets are supposed to clear "nearly all the time." Citing the NCS's belief in "perpetual Walrasian equilibrium," Solow said, the school's strong propositions arise "from the hypothesis of market clearing" rather than from the hypothesis of rational expectations. Echoing Alan Blinder (Klamer 1984, 160), Solow saw the NCS's appeal to students as their being able to learn some "sophisticated techniques" other people do not know. As Blinder put it: "Many younger economists didn't give a damn about the substance . . . it was an elevation of technique over substance."

Also, in the Klamer interviews, we come to Leonard Rapping (Lucas and Rapping 1969), who was among the first to embark on the course we refer to as Lucas-Sargeant rational expectations. Rapping's later comments, as reported by Klamer, show how far he departed from the course that elevated so much technique—static optimization over time, static stochastic processes over time, Walrasian equilibrium, actuarial probabilities, and so on. He pointed to psychological possibilities, which of course had gained even earlier visibility at the hands of George Katona (Morgan 1987a; 1987b). Rapping even says, "Psychology begins to dominate the movement of many variables, such as the exchange rate or the interest rate. Keynes knew this. He was insightful [except, as I note, Keynes (1936, 141–142) ruled out the dependence of the interest rate on inflationary expectations]." And then, he said, "This opens up the possibility of an interaction between people's thought processes and material reality."

And, finally, as if elaborating on Solow's and Blinder's position, Rapping stated:

The second reason why Lucas's approach . . . became very popular among younger people is because it opens up possibilities for the further use of the mathematical technique. . . . But you can become so enraptured with technique that you lose sight of the underlying processes. You ask the wrong questions as you get enraptured by mathematics and mechanical issues; you start to ignore important behavioral processes. This is not an argument against technical training, just against excessive reliance on it. (Rapping in Klamer 1984, 229–231)

SUMMARY

The role of expectations and anticipations with more or less certainty gains in importance in economics along several paths. A main route follows Keynes, Friedman, the role of liquidity, the definition of money, the role of money, uncertainty, speculation, and asset structures. The principal figures here entered into economic study with special interest in probability (or in Friedman's case, mathematical statistics and probability). Some question Keynes's exact position, as to classical or subjective probability, although Braithwaite sees Keynes as an important transition figure, and Friedman sees no other probability but that in the mind of the beholder, although he is less explicit than we encounter in the Friedman system. Even so, Friedman moved the economics passed along by Marshall and the Keynesians along the lines of subjective probability.

This economics with probability as uncertainty gained impetus in the wake of the failure of Keynesian economics in the 1960s and 1970s, which also gave high visibility to the NCS. Possibly in part because of this, and some common ties to Chicago and business cycles, some critics confused Friedman's economics with that of the NCS (Frazer 1988, 262–263; Klein 1983, chap. 6). Nevertheless,—and counter to this misconception—Friedman elevated the fruitful hypothesis over the elegance of technique.

By contrast to Friedman and the Friedman system, the NCS links up with the Frank Knight distinction between risk as actuarial probability and uncertainty as incomplete information and relates the latter to the cyclical part of change in the time series, which I have pointed out in Figure 1.2. Also, the NCS offers static stochastic processes and often static optimization over time.[5] By contrast to the NCS, and especially, in the Friedman system, learning may occur (a Bayesian process enters, as does "psychological time") and episodic change occurs. Liquidity, money balances, and monetary analysis are inextricably entwined in Friedman's economics with uncertainty and the interplay of the real goods and financial markets, where as the NCS disputed this relationship, even while drawing on Friedman's empirical studies for support.

Still further criticisms of the NCS's economics include the following: (1) It relies on markets clearing all the time through price adjustments, without much attention to the resulting environment, which may make a difference; (2) postulating that agents form expectations on the basis of very static constructs and actuarial probabilities is technically neat and nice, but it elevates "techniques"; and (3) Lawrence Klein, the structural equations model builder, said agents do not reach conclusions in the same way as model operators in forming expectations. However, whatever these criticisms, the bond traders we introduce (text, pages 46, 137, 162) as main players in determining bond prices (and hence interest rates) do the ultimate test on the views they hold. Most notably, they actually put large amounts of capital at risk in the market positions they take, and succeed or fail in doing so, whereas I suspect that no identifiable member of the NCS ever put to such a test the static and metastatic apparatus found in the NCS's economics.

Harking back to structural equations methods, such as found in the famous Klein–Goldberger model, Arak offered a definition of "rational expectations", which both contrasts with the NCS's RE and helped illuminate it. In particular, she defined the true model as the real world, the process, and all actually there, although she did so with the implied method of a regression equation and sampling from an unchanging universe. Rationality then followed when agents formed expectations in the same way that prices, and so on, are generated in the real world, via regression equations and all.

At such a juncture, two analytical problems arise. First, the NCS's rationality lies more in the agent's perceptions of economic technique (static constructs, separation of effects, and all) than in the way the world works. And, second, episodic changes do not appear and a learning process for the agents is precluded by the attention to actuarial probabilities rather than Bayesian processes. The structural model à la Arak leads to the addition of variables and equations to a structural equations model. The search goes toward the achievement of flat out stability à la Klein by adding detail and seeking entirely endogenously determined variables. In contrast, economics where bond traders and other agents enter and where episodic change and learning processes leads to efforts directed toward the separation of one class of changes (nonrepetitive) from another.

Going beyond the NCS's emphasis on technique and even the model Arak suggests, Rapping pointed to the unqualified importance of psychological possibilities. He noted the relevance of the interaction between people's thought processes and material reality, the prospect of uncertainty with respect to factors impacting on behavior (shared common experiences, say, as opposed to the von Neumann-Morgenstern approach to games); and the presence of psychological elements in interest rates and exchange rates. Such positions give perspective, to be sure, but the difficulty with them is that they are much more evident in the Friedman system view via Keynes and Friedman than that of the NCS, the NCS's predominant feature is the presence of technique.

Efforts to both emphasize the NCS and disengage its approach from the monetary emphasis may have appeal for just psychological study alone, exclusive of money. However, the emphasis given to the role of liquidity and the study of monetary policy, money, uncertainty, speculation, interest rates, and exchange rates goes beyond that on the part of the NCS.

NOTES

1. "Metastatics" refers to the extension of static-state extreme-value mathematics to a period of time. The static-state axioms may be retained and time added; only motion and episodic impacts are excluded to retain the conditions of the static state.

2. See note 1.

3. The data analysis problem is twofold: For one, it requires finding a stable statistical relation (a repetitive prospect); it also means separating the repetitive from the nonrepetitive happenings which are also reflected in the time series.

4. Going back to the concept of Bayesian learning and the processing of new information by the behavioral units, I take from Keynes and Friedman the prospect that the behavioral units process information of an episodic sort as well as that which may be repetitive. For Keynes there was a prospect of volatile ("autonomous") capital spending due to the volatility of expectations in the very short run (Frazer 1994a, 135–140); for Friedman there was the leading time rate of change in the money aggregate, "psychological time," and a change in the mid-1960s in the structure underlying the formation of inflationary expectations. He had seen the latter as occurring in the long run, prior to the mid-1960s, and for both Keynes and Friedman there were closely related features of the liquidity preference demand for money. As with the causation controversy (Frazer 1994b, 79–94), the money policy as treated by Friedman appeared exogenous.

Returning to the Bayesian concept, I take it that "episodes" and possibly prior episodic impacts provide a major source of the information the behavioral units process. They must be judged of course to be of sufficient potential to make a difference—for example, to cause the agents to reappraise the economic outlook and/or to contribute to more or less certainty about it in such a way as to make a difference.

Taking this route, I see monetary shifts on the part of the public that appear in the demand for money and liquidity generally. Factors giving rise to these shifts, moreover bombard a number of time series (for example, the bond prices and hence interest rates, the inflation rates, and exchange rates) and extend effects to other series where liquidity and uncertainty may be less immediately on stage. I see the effects as increasing the amount and the nature of information contained in the time series, as calling for a concept of rationality which is compatible with the idea of processing the new information (Frazer 1994a, 73–75); as complicating the matter of the separation of the effects of some variable (for example, time series) on others; and as complicating the notion of using economic policy to stabilize such key time series as employment, production, and purchasing power.

A list of episodes from 1970 through the early 1990s would include the following: (1) those for monetary accommodation and monetary discipline which I relate to the regime shifts that occurred with Margaret Thatcher and Ronald Reagan; (2) the efforts of "direct" control over prices in the 1970s, first by Richard Nixon and then by Jimmy Carter; (3) Richard Nixon's decision to close the gold window in 1971; (4) oil cartel pricing, which first appeared in 1973; (5) the Iranian crisis of 1979 and the Iraqi invasion of Kuwait in 1990; (6) Margaret Thatcher's privatizing of British industries in the second half of the 1980s; (7) pronouncements by a U.S. Treasury secretary to the effect that the government would allow the dollar to decline (say, in lieu of further declines in the U.S. inflation rate); (8) the matter of whether the Gramm-Rudman Act of 1985 would force cuts in spending by the federal government; (9) Reagan's and Greenspan's assurance at the time of the 1987 stock market crash that the Federal Reserve would not repeat the mistakes of the past; and (10) news about the balancing of the U.S. federal budget at the time of Newt Gingrich's 104th Congress, President Clinton's reappointment of Alan Greenspan, and later reelection of Clinton.

All of these episodes call attention to two sets of difficulties—one, the separation of the information contained in a given series (for example, the episodic, transitory, and trend parts); and, two, the difficulties of separating the effects of one set of time series from others by direct means, such as we take up in considering relative price levels ($P_{US}/P_{rest\ of\ world}$), dollar/pound exchange rate, the interest rate (i) and fiscal or funding policy, in the following symbol of a multiple regression equation:

$$\text{GNP or GDP} = a_0 + a_1\ P_{US}/P_{rest\ of\ world} + a_2\$/£ \\ + a_3\ i + a_4\ (\text{funding policy}) + \ldots$$

All this, along with considering the true bounds on the regression coefficient (the "Leamer problem"). As stated earlier, the Leamer problem arises when variables are added to the regression equation. To be sure, it's extremely difficult to set the bounds illustrated in Figure 7.3 on separate regression coefficients when variables are added. At some point, one may be unable to set bounds at all.

5. See note 1.

Appendix to Chapter 11

Walrasian, Quantity-Theoretic, and Friedman/Marshallian Equations

Writing approximately sixteen years before Marshall published his *Principles*, Walras offered a system of equations and unknowns called general equilibrium (Walras, 1954). From a mathematical point of view he was relying upon the theoretic concept whereby a system of equations had a solution if there were as many nonredundant equations as unknowns. Today the notion of the existence of a solution is a bit more complicated, and the equation system has been related to the quantity theory of money (Frazer and Yohe 1966, 88–93). From the economics point of view there is the notion of balance in the various markets and in the demand for money.

Milton Friedman's analysis of trends and long swings in economic conditions, as shown in *Monetary Trends* and my own analyses in *The Legacy of Keynes and Friedman* (1994a) for the 1970s and 1980s would not lead us to expect much by way of balance in the markets and the demand for money. However, general equilibrium, as set forth by Walras and extended by others, is an important concept in the quantity theory discussion. Several views exist: that in the very long run this tranquil Walrasian state may be reached (say, the result of a world where monetary policy and money demand matters work harmoniously) and that those who seek mathematical elegance and detail, as opposed to empirical relevance, as a goal of economic study are in essence Walrasians.

Friedman expresses this latter view. First, he accepted the common interpretation of Marshall and his crosses as partial equilibrium (say, equilibrium in a single Marshallian market), but he saw Marshall as having his own system of equations and unknowns which are extended to the markets for the current outputs of goods and services known as GDP and GNP respectively. Second, he added another distinction, that Marshall was searching for a fruitful empirical hypothesis, as opposed to mathematical elegance.

A general equilibrium system à la Walras may be expressed as follows. Let S denote the supply function and D the demand function; and then we may denote the supply-demand equality for each item and the general equilibrium for all goods and services in the economy thus:

$$S_1 (p_1, p_2, \ldots, p_n, A, M) = D_1 (p_1, p_2, \ldots, p_n, A, M)$$

$$S_2 (p_1, p_2, \ldots, p_n, A, M) = D_2 (p_1, p_2, \ldots, p_n, A, M)$$

$$\vdots$$

$$S_n (p_1, p_2, \ldots, p_n, A, M) = D_n (p_1, p_2, \ldots, p_n, A, M).$$

where p_1, p_2, . . . , p_n are the respective prices of the n items, including money as one item, and where A, in combination with the average stock of money (M), is an index of the nonhuman wealth of the economy.

The system could be expanded by including other variables and parameters (for taste, expectations, and so on). Given the values for the parameters A and M and the prices in the present instance, the system contains as many unknowns (the quantities) as equations, and presumably a solution exists.

However, a complication arises. One of the n items is money, and the price of a single unit of money is one dollar. Thus one of the prices in the system must be the number 1. In such a case, one would have a redundant equation, and, though this need not prohibit a solution, earlier economists were concerned that it might. Consequently, they excluded the equation for the demand for money in their statement of general equilibrium and spoke of simply a numeraire or unit of account, but, to account for the demand for money, an identity (albeit one that can be extracted from the Walrasian system of nonidentical equations) was used. The identity was named Walras's law. It may be denoted as follows:

$$\sum_{i-1} p_i q_i (S) = \sum_{i-1} p_i q_i (D)$$

where the left-hand member is the sum of all of the products for the respective prices [p_i (i = 1, 2, . . . , n)] and the corresponding quantities supplied [$q_i^{(S)}$ (i = 1, 2, . . . , n)], and the right-hand member is the sum of all the products for the prices [p_i(i = 1, 2, . . . , n)] and the corresponding quantities demanded [$q_i^{(D)}$ (i = 1, 2, . . . , n)]. To further, emphasize the matter these product quantities extend beyond the current output of goods and services and even include stocks where existing issues of stock are traded.

The use of Walras's law to refute the notion that money is simply a numeraire to be excluded from the determinant system of equations is straightforward. Those demanding commodities are prepared to exchange an amount of money (for example, currency and demand deposits) or some other commodities of equal value, and those supplying goods are prepared to accept in exchange their equivalent value in money (for example, currency and demand deposits) or other commodities. Note, in particular, that the exchange does not necessarily require the use of money in the specific sense of currency and demand deposits. It may involve units of items other than currency and demand deposits, and the item chosen is independent of the item called money, although all values are expressed in terms of the unit of account (say, the dollar, the mark, or the pound). In fact, Walras's law tells us that the supply of and demand for any single item omitted from the n items must be equal, not just the supply of and demand for units of currency and demand deposits. That is, if the value of the goods supplied is equal to the value demanded for all but the first item, as we may assume from a system of n - 1 items and n - 1 equations, then for the first item

$$p_1 q_1^{(S)} = p_1 q_1^{(D)}$$

or

$$p_1 q_1^{(S)} - p_1 q_1^{(D)} = 0$$

$$p_1 (q_1^{(S)} - q_1^{(D)}) = 0$$

and

$$q_1^{(S)} = q_1^{(D)}$$

It makes no difference which equation we choose to drop from the initial system of n equations and n unknowns. The first was simply a convenient choice.

It follows from the requirement imposed by Walras's law, and the solution to the n - 1 system of equations that the quantity and price of the first item are also determined by supply and demand conditions. Since $q_1^{(S)} = q_1^{(D)}$, the n prices and n quantities are determined. The redundant equation, therefore, is harmless and causes no difficulty in our initial statement of general economic equilibrium.

As implied by the initial equilibrium equations, the solution is n specific prices on n specific quantities, given the quantity of money, M. Since the n prices relating to each other and their absolute values make up the price level, the equations must also determine the price level, and presumably this is determined whether prices are high or low (inflated or deflated), given M. There must be one price level at equilibrium, and others will produce disequilibrium. But this is also implied by the equation of exchange where the concern is with the respective prices on all transactions (T), or it is implied by the crash balance approach to the quantity theory where the concern is primarily with current output alone. In the former case, for example,

$$M = (T/V)P \qquad (1)$$

where T (= const) is the constant dollar value of all transactions, V (= const) is the velocity of money balances with respect to the total of transactions, and P is the average of prices on all transactions (including those on the stock market). In the case of current output,

$$M = (Q/V_y)P \qquad (2)$$

where Q (= const) is current output, V_y (= const) is the income velocity of money, and P is the average of prices on current output. In both instances, the higher the price level the greater the amount of money balances needed for effecting expenditures in a mathematically elegant sense. However, differences in equations (1) and (2) take on importance when growth trends and the stock market prices are introduced (included in equation [1] but not [2]), and when equation (2) is altered and written along the lines of J. M. Keynes version of the Cambridge equation (text pages 57, 64 nn. 6 and 7, 80), M = k(. . .) PQ. This is because stock market prices are tied to economic growth and stock prices grow along with income (Y = PQ) and assets over the long run, whereas bond prices (in this secular-trend and income-growth context) and the index of prices (P_y) for the current output of goods and services are constant when the money stock (M) and real output (Q) grow at the same rate, at least when allowances are made for changes in the income-velocity ratio (V_y) or its inverse (the Cambridge k).

This assertion about stock-market prices is true in the a priori case (Frazer 1994a, 23, 76), where the value of a fixed amount of equities (allowance for stock splits and all) is quoted in terms of stock-price indexes and tied to smooth, sustainable income growth. We may say that equity value is equal to the income from the capital stock when the income is divided by the interest rate, or for wealth (W) and the current income (Y) in general, W = Y/i (Frazer 1994a, 75–79). This income-growth-oriented case would appear in the long-run facts too, if allowances were made for special bonuses, crashes, and transitory changes.

So, the difference between equations (1) and (2) and the Cambridge equation (text pages 57, 64 nn. 5 and 6) as it relates to the price of equities is significant, where the analysis is oriented along growth lines for the stock and flow quantities. In the growth-oriented Friedman system (Frazer 1994a, figures 1–7, 5–6, 5–8, 6–6), equilibrium balance in trend-line terms does not end with Walrasian equations. Rather Friedman suggests and I adopt a more limited set of Marshallian equations that depict the current output of goods and services.

Part IV

From the Bond Market to Development Economics

Although the assets serving as money enter in all instances, Part IV deals with the extremes of a spectrum of monetary phenomena. This spectrum is bounded by the bond market at one extreme, where matters of liquidity and capital gains (or losses) come to the forefront, and it is bounded by development economics at the other extreme, where we encounter developing countries with essentially no money and bond markets.

As variously emphasized already, the traders in the bond market will form and act on expectations regarding bond prices (and hence interest rates) within very short time frames (text pages 10, 18, especially H_{BT}, Figure 6.1, Figure 6.5, where I emphasize the term $Pb[P^e] P^e$, in the equation $i = i(real) + Pb[P^e] P^e$, pages 14, 73, 76, 149 n.10). Indeed, within this short time frame, bond traders are processing new information about monetary and related prospects for inflation and the probability of their realization (for example, $Pb[P^e] P^e$). Such monetary and related matters (most notably regarding federal budgets and thus the federal debt) may affect movements into and out of liquidity (Figure 6.5) and hence may ultimately affect numerous variables.

Such new information is generally of an episodic sort and imposes quite generally upon the time-series counterparts to the economic variables. We return in Chapter 12 to this episodic/outside influence which introduces a source of analytical difficulty in the interpretation of empirical evidence in economics. The analytical difficulty reminds me of the presence of institutional matters in numerous interpretations that also bear on theories and operations. Consider, for example, Table 5.1 (text page 79), the indirect method (pages 107–109), H_{BT} (page 84), H_{LH} (page 84), the monetary indicator (pages 162–164), Table 10.1 (pages 157–159), H_{CB} (page 156), and H_{TW} (page 156).

The added difficulty encountered in Chapter 12 reminds me of Friedman's view that the economic evidence "is frequently complex and always indirect and incomplete" (text page 46). "Its collection is often arduous, and its interpretation generally requires subtle analysis and involved chains of reasoning." The particular episode I treat in Chapter 12 is that of the Clinton administration's efforts at health care reform in 1993 and 1994, where I turn to the bond market's behavior as a powerful constraint on that. In fact, what I call here "the bond market constraint," actually was also a separate policy Bill Clinton embraced which was at odds with the attainment of health care reform as it was embraced by the Clinton White House during the early years of his first term.

The Chapter 12 presentation of the bond market constraint on the president's premier program during the first two years in office is part of the more general analysis of budget deficits and the goal of Chairman Alan Greenspan and the president of maintaining low interest rates (text, pages 32, 179, 186, 190 n.4). In fact, Chapter 12 is quite harmonious with Greenspan's consistent articulation of the thesis of achieving and maintaining low interest rates by sending verbal and other messages to the bond market regarding a balanced budget and noninflationary actions in general as the means of maintaining low inflationary prospects (Frazer 1994b, 8–9, 57–58 n.2, 75–76, 79, 106).

I could have turned to the Gingrich-led, 104th Congress and even to the president's offering his own proposal to balance the federal budget. In this matter, as in the health care case, the bond traders in the thirty-year, long-bond market process information as to the likely impact on future inflation and hence on day-to-day and month-to-month changes in bond prices. The background prospect for lower (higher) bond prices (and thus higher [lower] long-bond rates, in the manner of the bond-market equation) is quite circuitous in that it actually connects to whether the central bank may be forced to accommodate government financing via open market operations and hence inflate the currency (Frazer 1994b, 8–9, 39–47).

I am fully aware that many concrete arguments can be given for the general public's opposition to the president's 1992–1993 health care plan and for the legislative branch's failure to support it. I would not underestimate these reasons for the plan's failure, although from a truth/significance point of view I argue that these concrete reasons for failure were very secondary to the more hidden prospects inherent in moving toward a balanced budget and the maintenance of low interest rates via the inflationary-prospect term, $Pb[P^e]$ $\dot{P}^e$. In other words, throughout the 104th Congress the budget deficits and inflationary prospects in terms of monetary accommodation were the most crucial agenda items and colored much else. Not only did the debate over deficits aid the Fed's chairman's efforts, but the reappointed Greenspan provided the U.S. president with a reasonably favorable economy during election year 1996. To be sure, we encounter here the matter of the pervasiveness of monetary phenomena and the reason why the search for truth and significance in economics encounters a need for the indirect approach.

At the other extreme, but still proceeding indirectly, the need to put in place a set of underlying institutions and infrastructure for developing economies comes into play. Even though it is not readily admitted, the institutions and infrastructure ultimately called for over the long haul by nonsubsidized development imply movements along market economy lines. As capital development proceeds, markets for the financial instruments behind the real-goods capital outlays must arise. Money and banking systems must assure confidence in a medium of exchange and the stability of long-term contracts denominated in terms of the currency unit.

In the light of these needs, we take an overview of development economics in Chapter 13. There is an amazing absence of monetary considerations at all among economists engaged in the field of economic development.

Chapter 12

The Bond Market Constraint on Health Care Reform

C andidate for president William Jefferson ("Bill") Clinton placed health care reform high among his legislative priorities during the 1992 campaign for president in the United States, at a time of sluggish economic recovery. Likely reasons for the sluggish recovery include: the need to contain inflation as a means of providing reassurance about the future of the economy for financial markets; the preoccupation of bond-market activists with large federal budget deficits as the potential for the reacceleration of inflation; and the views of the monetarist/Ayn Rand philosopher at the Federal Reserve who had come to see deficit reduction (and the elimination of monetary-accommodation prospects for large deficits) as the key to achieving lower interest rates on the bellwether long-term bonds (Frazer 1994b, xiv, 8–9, 57–58, 75–76, 79, 89, 94, 106, 224), as Clinton pollster and political strategist Dick Morris would appreciate (1997, 10–11, 29, 32, 158–189, 267, 270). To complicate the matters, there also had been a decline in saving as a share of gross domestic product in the United States from the mid-1960s to the early 1990s (Browne and Gleason 1996), so one may ask where the extra saving would come from to support greater deficit spending by the government.

Moreover, even as media interests may relate monetary policy to short-term interest rates, a Bundesbank effect arises (Frazer 1994b, 8, 9, 98, 199). By that an increase (decrease) of short-term rates may signal deflationary (inflationary) policy, such that long-bond rates move in the opposite direction. Also, for the United States, this phenomenon may be viewed as a part of the more general New York's revenge (Frazer 1994b, 124; 1994a, 68, 180). It is that the financial center's bond traders processes information (especially that

---

This chapter was initially presented at the 1995 meetings of Allied Social Science Associations, Washington, D.C., January 6–8, 1995.

which originates in the nation's political center) and its inflationary (deflationary) potential in setting the long-bond price (and thus "the" interest rate).

Now, against this background—and the U.S.'s national debt and entitlements matters (including health care)—President-Elect Clinton confronted his own campaign rhetoric, the advice from the main cadre of his advisers, and the less-familiar advice from the more unsettling Alan Greenspan.[1]

Greenspan's advice was that the broadest and most sweeping of national health care reform packages had to be sold to the bond market and the general voting public as a deficit-reduction or budget-neutral measure (Woodward 1994, 86). The problem with respect to the promotion of the Clinton package à la Greenspan, however, was one of providing arguments that would convince the bond market of its deficit-reduction prospects. As long as the latter could not be achieved, congressional and other political opponents to the Clinton package were reinforced by an inconsistency in the President's efforts and by important allies (for example, those in the bond market who channel private saving into expenditure programs). The bond-market outcome is well capsulated in Bob Woodward's quotation of Clinton:

"You mean to tell me that the success of the program and my reelection hinges on a bunch of . . . bond traders?" (Woodward 1994, 84)

The twofold purpose of this chapter is to indicate the route by which Alan Greenspan and hence bond traders placed constraint on the health care reform package and thereby in effect, to enlarge on the substance of the quotation attributed to Clinton. However, to repeat, the president was actually working at cross purposes once he adopted the Greenspan strategy and persisted with the health care reform package the White House put forward. Even so, at the end of his first term it was more likely the economy that contributed to his reelection than any success along the lines of earlier White House plans, again as Clinton strategist Dick Morris would appreciate. As the President faced reelection he frequently asked the electorate whether they were better off economically than they were four years earlier. Even as it turns out, a large proportion of what had been personal saving in the mid-1960s had already been diverted to medical expenditures by the early 1990s (Brown and Gleason 1996, 15-27).[2]

PRESIDENT CLINTON'S HEALTH CARE REFORM PROPOSAL

The health care plan took various turns in the 103rd congress where no health-care reform bills passed. To identify the Clinton plan specifically, I draw on the President's Report and the text of the Health Security Act (Clinton 1993; Staff 1993).

The president's plan was extremely bold under three sets of circumstances: It was nonneutral as bond-market activists view it; it included budget deficits (with some temporary respite only through fiscal year ending in 1996)[3]; it would promote growth in the government's existing Medicare and Medicaid programs;

and there was already a decline in the saving rate by the American public (Brown and Gleason 1996; Reischauer 1994).

The connection between the major sets of circumstances and the constraints on reform is the movement since Margaret Thatcher and Ronald Reagan toward noninflationary, market-driven economies. As a part of this, the financial markets sector is positioned to prevail ultimately where private-sector financial resources are thrown into opposition to central bank policies over prospects for inflation.

In summary, the major problem confronting the passage of the Clinton package was the vision bond-market activists held of the projected growth of federal debt. Simply put, at some point the financing of debt increases would likely have to come from the inflationary accommodation of the debt by the Federal Reserve (hence a monetary accommodation of fiscal policy, text pages 143, 162–164).

As to the Clinton proposal overall, it offered a lot and promised even more through savings. Besides offering a Health Security card (which extended a comprehensive package of health care benefits to all legal residents), it would have purportedly strengthened Medicare and provided new coverage for prescription drugs and greater access to quality care.

The savings were to have accumulated as follows: (1) health alliances to achieve more buying power; (2) mandates for insurers to cover high-risk people at enforced premium caps; (3) criminalized health fraud; (4) reduced "defensive medicine" (meaning more preventive care); (5) added efforts to discourage "frivolous" malpractice lawsuits (by limiting lawyers' fees); and (6) governmental control of the prices on prescription drugs.

Among these, items (2), (5), and (6) are simply what economists recognize as direct price controls. Since the U.S. experience with them has not been good, even in wartime (Frazer 1988, 191–200), direct controls for the most part remain ineffective in containing price increases and possibly simply hide inflation in some instances. The health alliances offered some promise of reducing costs, as did criminalizing health fraud, but these measures were possible without the overall package. Preventive care is clearly good, but there is a time preference problem—dollars spent in the present are harder to come by than dollar outlays in the future (Frazer 1994a, 170–174).

As to additional revenue, the health-care package added costs to employers and individuals. Quite clearly, cost-push pressures are placed on prices (Frazer 1994a, 195–206). Whatever the other problems surrounding Clinton's reform proposal (for example, bureaucracy and patient choice), the expanded package of benefits was unlikely to be covered by the savings noted. Even with a detailed study that the Congressional Budget Office could make (Christenson 1993), the bond-market activists would surely perceive that the costs of Clinton's plan would exceed any claim to budget neutrality.

THE EVOLUTION OF THE RELEVANT ECONOMIC THEORY

In 1936 a banking view of the interest rate prevailed.[4] In Keynes's work it appeared in regard to the liquidity preference demand for money, where variations of it seemed possible (Frazer and Yohe 1966, 64–73). Even more about liquidity preference came to appear (Frazer 1973, 72-94). In retrospect and in connection with more recent treatment, two approaches to liquidity preference stand out (Frazer 1994a, 29–52) in regard to bank operations (Frazer 1994b), one essentially Keynesian, the other a "Friedman system" view (Frazer 1984a, 31–52).[5]

In Friedman system terms, developments of some significance arose. Most notably, once structural change in the formation of inflational expectations had occurred in the mie-1960s, (Frazer 1994b, 69–73; Friedman and Schwartz 1982, 569–573), information on inflationary prospects gets processed almost immediately by the most sensitive and active of the bond market participants. I call them bond traders (Frazer 1994a, 52 n.1; 1994b, 21–26).

Connecting all this to Alan Greenspan and the Clinton plan (Frazer 1994b, xiv, 8–9, 57–58 n.2, 75–76, 70, 89, 106, 224–231), interest rates, money velocity, and money stock are important. However, Greenspan used short-term interest rates not as the policy indicator, but as an aid to the imperfect forecasting of what the money stock may be at the current time (also along with an estimate of its velocity). This comes about when in fact the stock and its turnover together will not be known with much accuracy until perhaps as much as six months after Federal Reserve actions and inactions.

THE CONSTRAINTS

The constraints on deficit spending in the context of deficit-spending crisis, which first appeared in dramatic proportion in 1987 (Frazer 1988, 682–690), are monetary policy and bond traders' perceptions of what it is and what may occur in the future. Present in regard to monetary policy is the underlying prospect that monetary policy could accommodate deficits à la the Bank of England and Lord Kaldor (Frazer 1994b, 87–94). It is via this route that bond traders process information bearing on the inflationary (deflationary) prospects for government projects and legislative actions and inactions. In the congressional context, the continuing budget crises merged with calls for deficit reduction and even a balanced budget amendment to the Constitution (Frazer 1988, 575, 585, 680, 690, 773 n.14).

Particularly since Friedman' work, we have as relevant pieces of analysis the following: first, Friedman's rule (text, page 142); second, the closely related indicator of monetary policy (text, pages 162–164); third, the zero inflation rate goal (also allied with low long-bond rates, text, pages 13–14, 73–75, 158); and, fourth, the long-bond rate as a surrogate for the current and anticipated values for the monetary policy indicators (text, pages 144, 162–164, Frazer 1994b, 39–51).

Although the indicator reflects the same information as the surrogate (i_L)—apart from being a policy measure itself—the information contained in the surrogate is more concentrated and immediately available. The time series for the indicator stated later is more fundamental, but the information contained in it is more dispersed as to the indicator's component parts.

Briefly, the normative rule for noninflationary policy is that the money stock should grow at the same secular-trend growth rate (or sustainable M) as that of constant-dollar production (Q), after allowances for secular changes in the income velocity ratio (V = $\dot{Y}$/ M).[6] Friedman limited such allowances for velocity to the secular trend because he saw the effects of monetary policy changes as powerful, as starting immediately, and as cumulative, and hence he saw short-run policy manipulations as a potential cause of greater rather than less instability in business conditions. Where the rule holds for a time, it also provides the outcome anticipated by the bond traders.

Yet whatever the case, in drawing on the normative rule to get an indicator of monetary policy, one turns to positive (not normative) economics. In this regard, two policy-connected matters stand out—policy makers have shown little inclination to forgo a short-run, activist role, and the structure underlying the formation of inflationary expectations changes in the mid-1960s, as FS reported (1982, 569–573).[7] As such, the effects of policy actions, inactions, and potential prospects became more immediate, especially in the highly sensitive long-term bond market. In this regard, an indicator of monetary policy appears thus: Δ M (Y/M) x 100, with < 0 for monetary discipline, > 0 for monetary accommodation, ≈ 0 for monetary neutrality.

All this occurs with respect to prices (wages as a special price) and federal budget deficits. In addition, anticipations by economic agents generally of inflation/deflation are built into the indicator through the velocity ratio, which is higher (lower) in the presence of anticipated inflation (deflation).

However, along this route the quality and timing of the availability of the data do not accommodate us, as reviewed elsewhere (Frazer 1994b, 41), so I offer the long-term bond rate as a surrogate: $-\Delta i_L$ is an indication of discipline, $+\Delta i_L$ is an indication of accommodations, and $\pm\Delta i_L$ ≈ 0 is an indication of neutrality.

To focus on the monetary policy and bond market constraint on health care reform, I restate the preceding in the context of a well known identity, MV = PQ, where V is P(Q/M), or Y/M. It is a measure of the work the money stock performs as well as the work of additions to the stock (or even additions to the stock's time rate of change, in the dynamic case). Also, Y = PQ, and Q is production in constant dollars. Drawing on the identity and giving it this dynamic orientation (in connection with the preceding indicators), M(Y/M) = PQ. As long as Friedman's rule is adhered to, in the secular time frame, the price level is constant and the growth in the money stock and production are the same, as in the rule context.

Recognizing the mid-1960s change in the structure underlying the formation of inflationary expectations and the more rapid processing of information about the inflationary potentials of programs, the dynamic orientation of the identity may still hold. It does so as the lag in time approaches zero at the limit, without the longer lags Friedman initially posited for the impacts of the monetary variable on interest rates (and hence on other variables via the interest rates).

Now, if we introduce into the analysis a deficit-enhancing program, such as that implied by the initial health care reform measure, and if monetary policy is not to be accommodative of the added deficit financing, then only one thing is possible in the last equation context: It is that the production comprising current output (Q) be reallocated by some measure or combination of measures, including the crowding out of the nonmedical sector by the deficit financing of the health care reform.[8] Tax and transfer measures of government are also possible, but the necessary taxes were largely ruled out. Next, reallocations are possible via the imposition of some combination of mandated costs to firms and workers and direct controls over prices.

If monetary policy is accommodative to the deficit, then a higher price level (itself a tax of sorts) results. Reverting to the surrogate for the policy indicator, the long-bond rate rises as an indication of monetary accommodation.

To pass the muster implied by a zero-inflation goal and a neutral monetary policy, tax and transfer measures were the most obvious for achieving the Clinton goals for health care. Setting these aside, the health-care reform package must be perceived in analytical terms as "budget-neutral" or better. It was by this route that the various opponents of Clinton's health care reform gained a powerful allies from the long-term bond market and from Alan Greenspan who was advocating a low-interest rate, depicit reduction package for the president and to congress.

Finally, adopting the logic of the "Bundesbank effect" (say, raising the short rate prior to the event of renewed inflation and further increments of it), we may turn to Greenspan's twofold view in the mid-1990s. First, he employed an interest rate strategy for hitting noninflationary money-growth rates. Second, he hoped to move the short-term rate more along the lines of a leading rate with respect to inflation. By this route, one gets narrower swings in the inflation rate and in the long-bond rate in the same direction. As the rates swing within narrower bounds, one also brings the market rate closer to the real (or noninflationary) rate of interest. There is the possible remaining effect of achieving the money growth that goes with a real rate of interest (Frazer 1994b, 224–231).

Greenspan's move was toward monetary neutrality (text pages 171, 172, 202, 203. Returning to health care reform, the money and bond market constraints restricted reform to "budget-neutral" or deficit-reducing reforms. The actual delivery of these could be seen by the bond traders who process old and new information and, at the same time, determine bond prices through their actions and inactions. Direct interventions to impose costs and control prices were possible, but these measures also were likely to be detected as imposing some hidden inflationary costs on the economic system.

NOTES

1. This conclusion follows from Bob Woodward (1994, 69-70, 84-85, 94) and from an independent reading of the print media. It is also reinforced by the later accounts of Clinton political strategist Dick Morris (1997, 10-11, 29, 32, 158-189, 267, 270).

2. Taking up the matter of a decline in the U.S. personal saving rate from 8 percent in the mid-1970s to under 4 percent in the mid-1990s, Brown and Gleason say (1996) that the missing saving indeed went to medical care—that an already rising expenditure on medical services absorbed a larger fraction of income.

Recalling the saving-investment equality from Keynes's and Keynesian mechanics (Frazer 1994a, 122-130, 144-146), Browne and Gleason argue (1996, 16) "that the real issue is not saving per se but how to boost productivity growth and rising standards of living." They close thus:

The Saving problem is not about thrift versus profligacy, good versus bad; rather it is a competition between two 'goods'—more and better medical care, on the one hand, and more investment, on the other. (Brown and Gleason 1996, 27)

3. Actions taken in 1993 provided some respite from the growth in deficits through 1996, but this respite is viewed by Reischauer (1994) as only temporary. In any case, the 1993 actions are thought to have contributed to the low long-bond average of 5.94 percent for October of 1993.

4. The latter appears in Skidelsky's review of Keynes (1992, 561), albeit in a rather loose form. However, Keynes's view of the central bank control over the rate of interest also appears (Skidelsky 1992, 326, 500, 562). In contrast to the bond-trader/"Friedman system" view I offer, Skidelsky injects what he calls open market operations, whereby a purchase of bonds shifts the price-quantity demand curve outward to raise bond prices and lower interest rates. Even so, this injects a general notion of open market operations that was rather foreign to the 1920s and even the 1930s. This view of controlling the interest rate smacks very much of Bank of England entry into the London discount market, where it sets an interest rate to acquire or sell debt instruments.

5. "The Friedman system" view circumvents interest rate control and focuses more directly on accounting arrangements regarding reserves and money and credit aggregates. As I turn to Greenspan with it, discount-rate changes may be used to send messages to bond traders and even to help in targeting a real rate of interest and the money stock growth that goes with it. However, the "bond trader" prospects I come to regarding monetary expectations encompass large changes in bond prices (and thus interest rates) without a smaller or larger quantity of bonds coming on or off the market in any time frame that may matter to the operation.

6. In all instances the dot over the variable (as in $\dot{M}$, $\dot{Y}$, and $\dot{Q}$) signifies time rate of change (or quite simply growth rate). See text page 149 n.10.

7. For a different tack on the same phenomenon, see Frazer (1994b, 68-73).

8. This is simply the old government budget constraint (Frazer 1994a, 130-135).

Chapter 13

Development Economics and Money

G erald Meier's edited work (1994) presents an overview of development economics. He notes that "surveys of the present state of development economics . . . still stake a claim to an independent existence for the subject." Drawing on Bliss, Meier defines "development economics" as consisting in part of "refinements of general economics to deal with questions which arise in the context of development" and in part of "certain special ideas which have proven useful in studying developing countries" (Meier 1994, 245). On the whole there are developed countries (DCs) and less developed countries (LDCs). Britain would be an example of a DC, examples of the LDCs would be India, under British control during the first quarter of the twentieth century, and, in more extreme cases, Bangladesh and Sri Lanka.

The main question posed in Meier's book is, How do we move from a country like India in 1900 or Bangladesh and Sri Lanka to the policy goal (the category DC)? Abstracting from a few skirmishes and meaningless platitudes like "the new growth theory," "rigorous refinements of imperfect competition," and "neoclassical resurgence," such as appear in Meier's final chapter, the economics appears rather straightforward in most respects. It is that of a very basic growth equation where growth depends on technological change and capital accumulation (for example, investment, in one respect, and saving out of income, in the other). The technological change is embodied in the human and nonhuman capital, where both are partly rooted in the culture of the countries at issue. Meier (1994, 18), referring to J. S. Mill, notes the instillation of new ideas and the breakup of habits of thought. Among the authors represented in the

This chapter originally appeared as a book review. Reprinted by permission of Transaction Publishers. "Review of *From Classical Economics to Development Economics, Studies in Comparative International Development*, 30, 2 (Summer 1995).

Meier collection there appears to be no squeamishness about imposing the goal of development on LDCs (Meier 1994, 220, 229, 233, 237, 239, 250).

Development economics starts with Adam Smith and David Hume (who in turn had roots of their own) in Meier's Chapter 2. There is international trade such as Smith observed along the Clyde River in Scotland, and, to use the text's term, there is the "progressive state." It is growth in production per head (Meier 1994, 6), and it is connected to "the desirable social and personal characteristics" of the capitalist-sector population. The story of the success of Britain and free trade has been told many times. But then there are the British empire and colonial government. The collection continues along such lines in a piece by Lal (Meier 1994, 28–50) and in another (pages 51–67) where Barber takes up classical works in economics and underdevelopment in India.

Along these lines, Rostow offers a useful chapter (Meier 1994, 144–172), confronts writers on India, China, and Africa; and then reflects on development. According to Rostow, the single most important way to bring about development is by demonstration that is limited by the foreign government. Rostow says, the major influence in the long run "was the Western capacity to seize and hold power, to occupy and impose humiliating conditions in places far from home." There is an ambivalence in the later escape from colonialism, but still the effect of demonstration appears lasting.

Economic development comes more to the forefront after World War II, where the experience is said to be different (Sundrum in Meier 1994, 104–120). Sundrum concludes: "Rapid technological progress depends . . . on high rates of investment." If we ask why some countries grow faster than others and take an overall view of the Meier collection, the following provide answers: (1) the saving-to-income ratio (also investment-to-income ratio as on text pages 103 n.3, 199, 205 n.2, 207), (2) the institutions called for by the market economy, and (3) the freedom of market-oriented, entrepreneurial agents. The first depends on traditions, practices, and the tax code. The second and third go hand in hand, and monetary arrangements enter (pages 100–103).

Looking at the post–World War II period, government comes to play different roles in economic development (Meier 1994, 3, 206, 229, 233, 237, 239). Reynolds (in Meier 1994, 229) offers this summary:

First came a strong revolt against neoclassical liberalism, and the general adoption of an "economic planning" approach to the subject. Later, beginning around 1970, there was growing disillusionment with planning and government intervention in the economy accompanied by gradual reversion to more traditional growth prescriptions. During the late 1980s this movement was accelerated by the collapse of communism in Eastern Europe and the Soviet Union, and by the fumbling efforts in those countries to re-create a market economy.

The role of government as such I have termed, in reference to Thatcher's Britain and European matters, "the Big U-Turn" (text pages 140, 148 n.4, 150 n.15, 229 n.3; Frazer 1988; 1994b, 39, 77–79, 109–164, 179–191).

Ishikawa also addresses "structural adjustment" (SA) (Meier 1994, 205–225) in relation to the move toward markets and away from the command economy. We appear at times to move toward imposing the markets orientation on a host society, whether the society likes the imposition or not, but, since Thatcher's move toward a market economy, the moves are more voluntary. In any case, Ishikawa's investigations of Asian countries leads him to conclude with three common factors that determine the success of SA programs.

(1) The most successful tend to be those in which per capita incomes are already in the middle-income country range and in which the market economy and administrative systems are fairly well developed.

(2) Feasibility tends to be greatest in economies that are rich in natural resources and small in population.

(3) A decisive role is often played by institutions and policies and the underlying political culture of the economy.

Continuing on this U-Turn theme, Drake offers a contribution on the role of money (in Meier 1994, 94–103); I have emphasized in the Thatcher government and European cases (Frazer 1994b, 163–240), a markets/monetary-oriented economy reaches an apex under particular market/monetary arrangements. Although these rely on the definition of money and the place of liquidity found in J. M. Keynes's work, they find the minimum government-interventionist role along Deutsche Bundesbank and Friedman lines (Frazer 1994a; 1994b).

With a development orientation, Drake treats some aspects of the evolution of money. He correctly gives importance to Keynes's store of value function of money and in turn to capital accumulation. Agent access to liquidity encourages capital accumulation (also savings). On the other hand, reaching back to the colonial days when colonies may have had surpluses on the trade accounts, Drake notes that the colonies initially received coins or notes from the trade-deficit power in the evolutionary process and that these could enter as reserves or as a hoard of cash in the colony. Where colonists may prefer to hoard money (as where it did not enter bank reserves) rather than invest real resources or consume, a loan of real resources is said to arise and to be an interest-free loan to the colonial power. Drawing on Ingram, Drake says: "In other words, the progressive accumulation of a stock of modern money represented a cumulative balance-of-payments surplus in which the net increase in the money stock had its counterpart in a net real transfer of goods, services, or property rights to foreign interests." But this strikes me as just anticolonial rhetoric. It may be quite correct under the conditions posited, but does it have the meaning given? I doubt it.

To illustrate the Drake's point and the counterpoint, think of the colony as having a trade surplus (hence +s on its trade account; à la Frazer 1994b, 135–137, as in Figure 13.1). Now, Drake's point is to rule out categories 2 and 3 on the simplified balance of payments statement for the LDC country, and to posit, as it were, that currency notes and coins go into private boards that are off the record (category 3 alternative). So Drake concludes that the colonial power receives the surplus of real goods from the LDC and that this surplus is in effect an interest free loan to the colonial power.

The analytical/ideological problems with Drake's analysis are, first, that only the real goods matter, as in the socialist position, and, second, other things could not in fact happen in categories 2 and 3 of Figure 13.1. Had the surplus on the trade account taken the form of an inflow of monetary reserves, a banking sector would be called for in the LDC. Had the LDC imported securities (a net outflow of funds), as via the capital accounts, then the colonial power would have made interest and/or dividend payments to the LDC.

Going off the record (category 3 alternative), quite possibly as Drake posits, selected LDC agents could hoard the colonial power's note and coin issue. If they did so, then thereby they receive liquidity which provides security and convenience to LDC agents. However—quite contrary to any benefits the LDC may have received—we have at Drake's bottom line, a hidden socialist or Keynesian positions.

Figure 13.1
Simplified Balance of Payments Statement for LDC

	Credit (+)	Debit (-)
1. Trade	$+s$	

2. Capital
    Short-term
    Long-term
		above the line balance (net)

3. Monetary reserves
    (gold, paper gold,
    international reserves
    generally, as case may
    be)
            or
		below the line balance (net)

3. (alternative) cash hoards
    by selected agents (no
    banking system)*
	$-s$	

*To balance the net $+s$ on the trade account, the offsetting below-the-line balance takes the form of cash hoards by selected LDC agents.

In fact, hard currency countries, such as Britain in the nineteenth century, extend the benefits of a hard (or sound) currency to the trade surplus colony. The interest-free loan argument has even been used against the United States in its period of post–World War II trade deficits, even as it exported gold to the rest of the world (Frazer 1994b, 119–141). At the bottom of Drake's position we have simply socialist or Keynesian rhetoric that only real goods matter.

In the period since the Big U-Turn, Germany has come to extend the benefits of a hard currency to other members of the European Monetary System (Frazer 1994b). The services bestowed on those countries themselves have value in a markets/monetary world, as may be well illustrated by the EMS.

In his final chapter, Meier gives no attention to monetary matters, despite the EMS experience that economic integration calls for monetary integration, and that monetary integration calls for political integration (Frazer 1994b, 165). Rather, Meier speaks of "neoclassical resurgence" in economic thought, where he finds promise for future research. However, no neoclassicist (text, pages 40–42, 62–63, 148 n.3; Frazer 1992), Milton Friedman offers the most revolutionary, complete markets/money system found in economics (Frazer 1994a). Further, it is growth- and trends-oriented.

Part V

Behavior and Economics

art V is an overall sketch of "the Friedman system." I present it as an
analytical system with emphasis on behavior and economics. A feature of
the system is that it does not call for the rejection of major parts of the
mechanical apparatus found in economics from Alfred Marshall onward. Those
parts include the Marshallian demand curve as restated by Friedman (1949), the
liquidity preference demand block (Figure 5.1), the Keynesian aggregate-
supply/aggregate-demand block with the simple consumption function (Frazer
1994a, 122–135, 165–181), and the marginal-efficiency-of-capital-schedule
concept (Frazer 1994a, 143). Rather than rejection, these static, cross-sectional,
mostly ceteris paribus–based constructions are approached as a zero state of time
at the limit (Limit of $\Delta t \to 0$). Beyond that the constructions are in motion, and
components of the time series corresponding to the variables in the constructions
include trends, transitory conditions, and impacts of episodes. The episodes may
impact either or both components of the time series data. This addition of
motion to the static states is what Professor Shogo Doi has referred to as "open-
ended closeness" (text pages xi, 80–81, 146, 203–204).

Although we cannot say with great confidence what portions of a given
time series, such as the long-bond rate and capital outlays, are trend, (free of
episodic impacts), episodic, or just plain error, I am inclined to venture the guess
that overall and on the average over 75 percent of the variation in the quarterly
aggregate, index, groop-behavior time series and their trend values is due to
episodic (policy-pronouncement, political-shift, tax-change, budget-balancing,
inflationary-prospective) impacts on the key time series of the sort encountered in
Friedman's economics and the Friedman system over the post–World War II
years. Of course, a part of the problem of quantifying the proportions of the
classes of variation in the series is definitional and a part is making a
meaningful/useful connection between definitions and the world we proport to
observe. This first part especially enters as regards the short-term stabilization

roles of central banks and their responsibilities for liquidity and the stock of money. Complications in quantifying the proportions especially arise, for example, where the Federal Reserve acted to neutralize the potential impact of episodes such as relate, say, to the 1987 stock market crash in the United States (Frazer 1988, 682–690), or where major European Central banks unsuccessfully acted to maintain the fixed exchange rates for EMS countries in September 1992 (Frazer 1994b, 132–135). In any case, the time series broadly viewed as to overall and group behavior are not independent of these complicating matters, so if the conservative 75-percent guess was in fact significant, then much of the economics surrounding the traditional use of the fashionable constructions remains irrelevant. As a move toward remedying this I offer the Friedman system as an open-ended closed ($\Delta t \to 0$ at the limit) analytical system with emphasis on its behavioral nature, where the study of economic behavior contains a substantial psychological component and ties to the social sciences generally. Most specifically, in the investment demand case I review (Frazer 1984a, 140–143):

"[P]sychological time" is present and agents form expectations by looking at past "transitory states" and turning points, where rates of interest and returns on real capital vary with the states. This is such that the agents anticipate patterns of rates in the light of past patterns. The effort then for "locking in" a low rate on the capital financing of new expenditures becomes one of making a judgment about the trough in rates or the present rates in relation to future rates by looking back at past states of business conditions.

Moreover, as I indicate in the present text and in the ranking of assets according to their liquidity (Frazer 1994a, 78; text pages 97–100), episodic impacts on a day-to-day or month-to-month basis will appear first in the assets traded in the most liquid of markets and only later in accelerated and decelerated additions to capital. There are two reasons for this. First, by definition there is greater liquidity in the markets for the most liquid of assets. Quite simply, they provide the easiest way to make short-term adjustments to short- or long-run prospects. Second, the agents operating in the most liquid of the markets gain most from specializing in knowledge within a very compressed time frame, whereas those operating in the manufacturing sector, for example, are not primarily specialized in the impact of day-to-day or month-to-month changes in financial markets.

Although I conclude that the ratio of behavioral research and writing to specialization in narrow sub-disciplines should be greater, I am in all of this fully in agreement with Milton Friedman, that in science the search is for repetition and that in the monetary matters the search should facilitate prediction for policy purposes.

"You can't get a scientific understanding of a unique event" and so on. However, even as episodic change enters (as in response to episodes), I take note of "psychological time" that frequently entails a reflection upon past episodes (a prior period of price controls, a stock market crash, a prior period of inflation, and so on). A hint of repetition enters—agents form expectations by looking back at some earlier occurrence and by making an analogy between the past occurrence and the more contemporaneous one. (Frazer 1994a, 241)

Most notably, hints of the interdisciplinary nature of the analytical system have appeared in Chapter 1 of my 1994a work and in the section 9.3 titled, "An Explanation of Turning Points [in Business Conditions] in Terms of Expectations." The work in question mainly concerns economics, history, social psychology, political science, and sociology.

As to the factual, theoretic, institutional features of my contribution to the Friedman system, I offer the following list of interrelated features:

1. The liquidity structure of firms: Although partly empirical, the liquidity-of-firms phase of my work had an anticipatory orientation regarding Keynes's link between the long-bond rate (i_L) as a controlled variable and capital spending (I). For Keynes, in one instance, uncertainty as regards the future could prove pervasive, but the main source of economic instability entered through the short-cycle volatility of long-term, expectations-connected capital spending, and, in another instance, expectations remained constant in Keynes's short run, such that the central bank could control capital spending and hence stabilize income through direct control over the rate of interest. Now, the analytical/central bank control problem Keynes addressed here does not go away, but—when we see the expectations matter Keynes faced, move to link the behavioral groups (Frazer 1994a, 13–23), and turn to the long-bond rate as a surrogate for complicated measurement problems—we move in a potentially more fruitful direction than that provided by other routes.

My work on the liquidity of firms revealed patterns of financing which were connected to planned capital spending. Liquidity could be increased in recession and early recovery phases so that funds were readily available for capital spending as interest rates rose in the expansion phase of business conditions. In other words, the Keynes/Keynesian schedule for the marginal efficiency of capital (also treated as rate of return on capital) appeared at odds with observations and fixed lag models and led me to question the hypothesized banking-view effects of interest rates on capital spending by firms. Also, the empirical data regarding this anticipatory financing by large firms stood at odds with key theoretical papers by William Baumol and James Tobin (Frazer 1967, 218–256). In Tobin's conception, the transactions demand for money balances varied inversely with the excess of the rate of interest over the cost of switching into and out of interest-bearing assets (also, text pages 79–81).

2. Liquidity and expected returns: Turning quite early to Keynes on liquidity as illustrated in Figure 6.5, I produced the expected-returns/liquidity thesis using Lagrangrian mathematics (Frazer and Yohe 1966, 354–359, 368–373, Frazer 1967, 192–202). I connected it to the empirical work referred to in the first feature.

3. The liquidity preference demand for money: Via this route I focus on the velocity of money and the rate of interest and then I illustrate in simple statistical terms the change in the structure underlying the formation of inflationary expectations in the mid-1960s (Figure 7.3), which Friedman and Schwartz had reported with considerable disappointment (FS 1982, 478, 558–573). In fact, I had earlier linked expected inflation to both the rate of interest and the velocity of money (Frazer 1982), such that causation was not running from interest rate changes to the velocity of money.

However, of special importance to the demand for money orientation was Friedman's explicitly connecting the rate of interest and the velocity of money (Y/M) to the liquidity preference block (Figure 5.1) and to cycles and trend components in the data series.

4.   Monetary policy as monetary discipline, accommodation, and neutrality (Frazer 1994b, 39–50): In these instances and by comparison with Keynes in feature (1) the orientation of central banking changes from the direct control over the long-bond rate to the use of the long-bond rate as a surrogate for monetary discipline, monetary accommodation, and so on. In this way I circumvent the difficulties central banks may encounter in conducting policy in the short term in money and credit aggregate terms and depart from Keynes's orientation as regards the long-bond rate as the control variable.

5.   Friedman's "black box": Lord Kaldor was not amiss when he referred to Friedman's concept of "helicopter money" as Friedman's "black box" (Frazer 1994a, 98). With actual money balances more or less than desired money balances, it set the stage for the reorientation under item (3), plus it remained for me to "fill in" for the "black box," which in fact concerned the central bank's conduct of policy. In contrast to the interest-rate orientation as viewed in the context of the United States 1937–1938 recession (Frazer 1994b, 66–67), the money-growth orientation permits central banks to take a more dynamic outlook and to take the initiative to achieve stability rather than simply to react to seasonal crises and variations illustrated by equation (3) on page 178 and text pages 186–187. Along such lines, I took up the task of "filling in" the "black box" and of relating the theoretic matters to central bank operations (Frazer 1994a, 97–101; especially 1994b, 85–107).

Although Friedman no doubt considered his rather stringent statements of statistical results to be empirical science, I do not see that we can ignore the experimental (and thereby the operations and surrounding circumstances) that generate the data in arriving at understandings about the statistical results and the political positions of the analysts that often accompany the statistical results. This particularly would appear to be the case in policy-oriented economics, even empirical economics.

6.   The identification problem, the time frames, and psychological time: Friedman's restatement of the quantity theory of money in such a way as to confront the identification problem, as brought out in my discussions with Friedman (Frazer 1988, 210; 1994a, 49–51, 71; 1994b, 21, 226; Frazer and Sawyer 1984), is of analytical importance to what I offer. Also, there is in the early appearance in the U.S. research the dating of turning points in business conditions à la the NBER. This appearance gains in importance when I note the growth orientation of the trend components in the data series for stock and flow quantities and adapt psychological time to the dating of turning points and to the role of interest rates in regard to capital spending and to other situations (Frazer 1994a, 32, 116, 117, n.5, 142–143, 166–167, 168).

7.   The cycle/growth orientation. While Friedman employed the cycle/growth orientation quite early, it appears partly ignored by critics, even as late as the reviews of Friedman and Schwartz's *Monetary Trends* (text page 44). Enlarging on Friedman's work, as I did, this orientation facilitated and/or permitted three things: (1) the explicit statements I made about time in combining J. M. Keynes's interest and Friedman's (Frazer 1994a, 130, 140–142); (2) the introduction of the Cobb/Douglas production

function as a part of the Friedman system because of the indirect way it proceeded to get at data interpretation and the great ratios; and (3) the introduction of Evsey Domar's model as a means of recasting Keynesian variables in such a way as to achieve compatibility with the Friedman system. All of these moves facilitated an extension of the discussion of the great ratios found in the foregoing works. These ratios include the velocity of money, the saving-to-income ratio, plus labors and capital's shares of income (Frazer 1994a, 63, 75–82, 144, 213–214).

8. The indirect method and the separation of effects: The indirect method as regards the mechanical apparatus and the uses of statistical methods is a way of proceeding that circumvents analytical and empirical problems inherent in economic theory and that proceeds directly by relating a left-hand-side variable to right-hand side variables, such as occur in multiple regression models and what Friedman and Schwartz called the prevailing fashion of econometrics. The analytical and empirical problems referred to are symbolized by what I call "the separation of effects problems" (Frazer 1994a, 29, 42–52, 134–135, 146; 1994b, 55–57, 120, 159–160 nn.2, 10, 184–185).

Although the indirect method as such is rooted in Friedman's early work, it was slow to evolve into the full blown system I offer. Wible asks why economists acted so slowly in learning about it; I raise other questions regarding the lag in understanding Friedman's work (text page 125).

9. The treatment of expectations as encountered in Keynes's, Friedman's, and George Katona's work comes forward in opposition to that found in the new classical school: This current treatment comes about in the Friedman system via several routes.

First, as indicated, for policy purposes Keynes treated expectations of the streams of income from additions to capital as constant. This was to hold in the short-run conduct of central bank policy, which was thought to be directed toward the prospect of stabilizing business conditions (say, for example, as in equation [3], text page 178). To place this in the Friedman-system concepts of time, this short-run approaches zero at a limit to yield static apparatus and makes a place for the long-bond rate as a surrogate for monetary policy denoted as accommodative disciplinary, or neutral. In it, a rise in the rate via inflationary prospects is in fact accommodative and so on (text pages 162–163). It is just the opposite of the interpretation found in the pre-Friedman approach. Along with this new and more factually based interpretation, Keynes's simple consumption function is in motion, including both the "helicopter money" and interest-rate/psychological time routes.

Next, as treated in the text, Friedman and Schwartz noted change in the structure underlying the formation of inflationary expectations and most significantly the changes in the lag between monetary acceleration (deceleration), income acceleration (deceleration), and rising (declining) interest rates. I recognize this and other problems regarding the conduct of monetary policy. I do so via a learning mechanism (personalistic probability) and the use of the long-bond rate as a surrogate for monetary policy.

Third, whereas Keynes saw volatility in the investment/capital-spending sector and Friedman saw it in terms of episodic impacts and monetary-policy impacts on both household and business sectors, Katona saw volatility in terms of greater credit availability and episodic impacts (Gestalt shocks) to household confidence and spending in the unspecified "short run." The connection Katona made between episodic impacts and households, on the one hand, and economic mechanics, on the other, was mainly just in reference to Marshallian supply and demand.

So—overall and by contrast to Keynes, Friedman and Katona—I retain major parts of the static economic apparatus (the liquidity preference curve, productivity curves, the simple consumption function, and Marshallian supply and demand schedules), as the change in time approaches zero at the limit, as I set it all in motion, and as I extend to the entire apparatus Katona's more limited notion of economic psychology. Here I retain the following and more: key features of Keynes's work the qay liquidity rules the roost, the definition of money introduced by Keynes and shared by Friedman; and the Friedman time frames where money matters enter (including Keynes/Cambridge quantity theory of money emphasis), where Friedman achieves his consumption function work with its celebrated permanent income hypothesis, and where Friedman introduces psychological time as first mentioned by Maurice Allais.

10. The empirical work: The empirical work is almost too vast to discuss in any one place, although results from the uses of statistical methods during the early part of the modern computer era appear in Frazer (1967; 1973) and in Hendry and Ericsson (1991). However, in addition to the liquidity structures work and of key importance to the evolution of the Friedman system are the following: (a) the empirical support for the liquidity hedging hypothesis (text, pages 84–91; Terrill and Frazer 1972) is of importance to the "bond trader" thesis regarding interest rates; (b) support for differences of opinion as an indicator of uncertainty permeates features of the Friedman system (Bomberger and Frazer 1981); (c) work on inflation rates, interest rates, and wage and productivity rates for the United States, the United Kingdom, and the Federal Republic of Germany, respectively, adds its support to the Friedman system. It appears in both Frazer (1994a) and Frazer (1994b).

11. The parts and the whole. In stating his Marshallian demand curve position, Friedman relates prices in Marshallian markets to the terms of a price index (w_1p_1, w_2p_2, . . . , w_np_n) and to the price level (P), which also appears in the simple quantity theoretic expression, $M = k (. . .) PQ$). Further, both groups constituting the markets and the economy as a whole may experience Gestalt-type shocks. Thus, in the Friedman system this sort of shared response may occur at so-called micro-group and macro levels. There is no sharp distinction between the behavior of the groups and that of the whole (Frazer 1994a, 53–90) in the general transitory context, although the bond-trader sector is the most sensitive of all the sectors in the anticipation of interest-rate changes, on the domestic side. This parallels the currency trades on the international side (Frazer 1994b, chap. 4). The theory of relative prices holds as to domestic prices, and these overall are extended internationally via movements in relative price levels and in exchange rates (Frazer 1994b, 119–161).

12. Hotelling's line and Rose Friedman's challenge. For the former and the labeling of the latter (Frazer 1994a, 82–85, 202–203), I am totally responsible.

13. The "U-Turn" hypothesis:

$H_{U\text{-}Turn}$ *The "U-Turn"*: The main non-Asian Western trading countries of the 1970s and 1980s were led for the most part by Keynesian ideas in the 1970s and—after crises in the United Kingdom, the United States, and to some extent elsewhere—by monetary/disciplinary and markets-oriented ideas in much of the 1980s.

For this and my work on the European Monetary System I am totally responsible (Frazer 1994b).

14. The open ended analytical system: It is a hallmark of the Friedman system and allows for the outside forces that weigh heavily on central bank in the performance of their stabilizing roles (Frazer 1994b).

"Autonomous," "exogenous," and "independent" are the terms commonly used to refer to the outside forces. These terms and their meanings are variously discussed and defined in Frazer (1994a, 222, 230; 1994b, 89-90, 103-104; and the present text, pages 163-164, 169-170, 114).

Chapter 14

An Analytical System with Emphasis on Behavior

Laband and Piette (LP) discuss the growth of economic journals during the 1970s and 1980s, pointing to the rise of field journals and specialization, as opposed to the general interest journals that once dominated:

> Their bad fortune in this regard apparently results from the increase in influence/importance of a number of specialty journals. The rapid entry by and success of field journals surely reflects the advantages of specialization. It has become virtually impossible to stay abreast of the scholarly literature in economics. (1994, 657)

So it is with considerable trepidation that I write this chapter about behavior as it may be broadly viewed along economic, political and social lines. To that end, I set out the negative and positive features of such an analytical system, note some additional characteristics, and review my personal experiences in coming to the Friedman system (Frazer 1994a, xix–x, and see index under "Friedman system").

THE NEGATIVE AND POSITIVE FEATURES

The Negative Side

First, on the negative side, the notion of a behavioral system for history, economics, and allied social sciences does not simply extend to a situation in which an economist of ordinary training joins in a research project with another ordinary social-science, noneconomist to produce an essay or research paper. Second, the notion of research herein does not extend to nonbehavioral work, such as found in the New Classical School's Rational Expectations

---

This chapter was presented first at meetings of the Atlantic Economic Society in Athens, Greece, in 1994 and later that year at meetings of the Southern Economic Association in Orlando, Florida.

(Frazer 1994b, 112–117, nn. 20–23) or to that by an economist who brings in a mathematician to extend further the logic of a traditionally mathematized economics (for example, Henderson and Quandt 1971; the NCS works; and R. G. D. Allen's 1938 book). Third, the notion does not encompass the extension of traditionally mathematized economics to include nontraditional areas of the discipline.

Although the highly original works by the Nobel laureates James Buchanan (Frazer 1988, 192–301) and Gary Becker (Frazer 1988, 772 n.50, 618 n.11) extended their respective areas of economic study to traditionally noneconomics areas, *The Friedman System* reaches for an even broader extension of economics to psychological and behavioral study with theoretic, empirical, and philosophical foundations. It does so even as it recognizes the predominance of episodic impacts (e.g., text pages 35–36 n.6, 116 n.2, 104 n.8, 190 n.4, and 229 n.3) and encompasses Friedman's uses of statistical methods.

The Positive Side

First, on the positive side, the attention to money and policy matters maintains a breadth and a tradition set on a course by European central banks of early vintage. It does so even as it provides key places for the monetary works of J. M. Keynes and Milton Friedman.

Second—with major paradigm shifts aside (Frazer 1988, 711–715)—the present notion of research and writing is that of a cumulative body of works with a shared philosophy of science and orientation toward a core of the mechanical apparatus found in economics. Once time and motion enter, key words here are "mutatis mutandis" as opposed to "ceteris paribus," and "modus tollens" as opposed to "modus ponens."

Third, science here means empirical science with *modus tollens* orientation and an underlying mechanical structure. The data emphasized in this *modus tollens* orientation—where predictive error gets passed backward—regard time series, relate as well to institutions (and, for example, facts surrounding operations, as in the conduct of policy), and include the cross section timeless state surveys. The sample surveys may be a part of the tracking of changes over time, and thus designed to detect structural shifts, agent learning, voter and ideological matters pertaining to the state of business conditions and political leadership, changes in the formation of inflationary expectations, and anticipatory matters generally.

Fourth, in all of this, the body of work should be cumulative, in the scientific sense, and not simply a collection of literature in peer review journals. Those journals where articles appear should and likely do provide some stability to subject matter, some cleaning up of shared logic, and some order for shared views by those who teach, research, and write. However, stability in this sense is not the scientific notion of stability in a statistical relation, the observed recurrence of a phenomenon over a long period, or consistency between logic and observations.

Fifth, the shared behavioral work in question attracts different talents that perform in a familiar vineyard where the purpose of the work is known, for example, the services of psychologists, where group behavior enters and where expectations are formed; the services of sociologists, where cultural homogeneity and even differences appear in data surveys and series; and the services of those engaged in the assessment and description of policy-connected operations and the relevance of the perceptions and attitudes of the different behavioral groups.

Sixth, this shared behavioral work involves mechanical structure, as stated, but the system of analysis must remain open ended to accommodate the impact of shocks and learning (as it regards the outlook, anticipations, and perceptions of economic and political agents). To be sure, a goals-oriented economic system of analysis entails political values and even differences in the goals of diverse political entities. Where monetary matters enter—along lines set on a course by Milton Friedman (Frazer 1994a)—money arrangements have a special role in dispersing political power and in providing infrastructure for real goods markets. They carry ideological baggage, so, to repeat, ideology enters through investigators as well as agents. Bringing this into the analytical systems at hand, I offer Hotelling's line (text pages 39, 150 n.15).

Seventh, all of the preceding considerations are philosophically based. Although there may be an indefinite regression as to its ultimate beginning, I take up the roots at the close of the nineteenth century in the United States. There are connections to the University of Chicago at that time, where we find the eccentric Thorstein Veblen, the philosopher John Dewey, and Wesley C. Mitchell (Frazer 1988, 143–160, 191–230, 281–283; Frazer 1992; Frazer and Boland 1983; Friedman 1950; Hirsche and deMarchi 1990). The founder of the National Bureau of Economic Research (NBER) of the Mitchell/Burns/Friedman era, Mitchell is particularly influenced by Veblen, Dewey the behaviorist and pragmatist, and an early interest in the very eclectic subjects called "money" and "business cycles." Through Arthur F. Burns—the protégé of Mitchell in the cycles and NBER work—and through Mitchell himself, you reach the Mitchell/Burns/Friedman era at the Bureau (Frazer 1988, pp. 143–160; 1994b xiv). Following this line of thought, I arrive at "a Friedman system" (Frazer 1994a, xix–xx, 6–9, 13, 15–17, 23–27, 29, 39, 47–50, 54, 60–68, 119–120, 144–146, 149, 161, 184, 203, 219–245, 238–239). To quote an aphorism that emerges: "There is no theory without facts, no facts without theory, and no policy without theory" (Frazer 1994a, xv, 25).

This economics at hand takes on policy, statistical, and monetary dimensions, as I state, via Friedman's research and writing. In doing so, it connects, respectively, to Keynes of the 1920s and 1930s (Keynes 1923, 1936) and to Friedman's distinctive contribution to the uses of statistical methods (Frazer 1988, chap. 18; Friedman and Schwartz 1991).

Further along in the philosophical vein comes a connection to Karl Popper, via the Mont Pelerin Society, where Friedman touches on the instrumentalism of Popper, which engendered what I call Friedman's variant of instrumentalism (Frazer 1984a). Along this line I see Friedman as moving toward theories as instruments for prediction (modus tollens, and so on) and arrive at his famous essay. In such backing away from "economic man" axioms, an important road block is removed for those who see economics in behavioral and cultural terms as opposed to the pre-Friedman emphasis in some quarters on the truth of the axioms of extreme value analyses (for example, as found in Robinson Crusoe economics [Frazer 1988, 457–458, 476]).

EXTENDED FEATURES OF THE SYSTEM

The single activity economists and those in allied social sciences share is analyses of cross sections, time series, and survey data (cross-sectional as a rule but also usable as time series where a consistency is maintained over time in the surveys and in the questions asked).[1] My main caveats are that economics is the only social science with a mechanical structure and that I propose a behavioral approach that does not at the same time reject entirely a main portion of the analytical structure of economics. Economics is vulnerable to this: (1) because of the strained methods (ceteris paribus, modus ponens, and all) by which the structure was initially obtained and (2) because of a connection between this approach and a separation of effects problem (Frazer 1994a, 49–52, 134–135, 148, 165, 210). This concerns the use of multivariate regression technique and the presumption of independence for the respective right-hand-side variables of an equation, sometimes called a "reduced form" (or a solution equation).

The Friedman system circumvents the barriers indicated to entry into behavioral research. It does so in a way that does not at the same time reject major parts of the mechanical structure of economics. It does this by following a path encapsulated as "the indirect method" (Frazer 1994a, 4, 11–12, 16, 48–51, 73).[2] In the one case, it takes a static relation—such as Marshall's demand curve, where no locus of points can be found to identify with it—and proceeds to relate the curve to something that is measurable in terms of a price index. As Roger Alford of the London School of Economics pointed out to me (Frazer 1994a, 13–16), Friedman rather than Marshall took the crucial step of bringing in the behavior of small groups, and it was Friedman, of course, who connected individual product demand to a price index for the economy as a whole. According to Friedman's view of the Marshallian demand curve, an external impact on time series for the economy overall could also impact on the behavior of small groups.[3] Although a tax change was offered as an example of this, I rather see it with hindsight as the prospect of a major restructuring of the way economic agents interpret their world in response to episodes.[4]

In the second case, I turn to the time series and ask, What is the information contained in a single time series? The answer is that some component may be transitory (as in business conditions), another component may be more permanent (as in the secular trend and permanent income views), some of the change may be episodic (as in a response to an episode or shock, as noted, for groups of households), and there are errors in the data series. In such a context there is ample room for the study of history, the time series, and the experiments by government that interact with the time series data. The approach is open to economists and allied social scientists with interests in group, social, and mass behavior. Also, as regards the data series, they are analyzed a few at a time—rather than proceeding directly to the use of multiple regression methods—and consideration is given to the Leamer problem (Frazer 1994a, 210, 218, n.6; 1994b, 69 figure 3-1, 73 figure 3-3, and 107 n.1).

The FS approach to a few variables at a time and independent evidence conflicts with the econometrics of the former large econometric models, in Hendry and Ericson (1991), and in much that is traditional in the writing and teaching of economics. Hallmarks of FS's use of simple methods and their search for what is going on are setting the bounds on the true regression coefficient, knowing the experiment that generates the data, and separating out the episodic impacts on the time series.

In summary, I am offering an analytical system that does not exclude the responses of time series to episodes by the artificial, nonmathematical means of locking them up in ceteris paribus and of assuming the independence of variables when that assumption is unwarranted in the light of observation. As an example of the latter, we may think of GNP or GDP as dependent on interest rates, exchange rates, money growth rates, relative price levels, and other variables, which in various ways have been viewed as being independent and subject to fairly direct control, when in fact statistical results and prior analyses indicate interdependence when the variables are free to move along market-oriented lines.[5]

SOME PERSONAL EXPERIENCES

To give some further indication of how I reached the present interdisciplinary view, I traverse a few personal experiences. First, my introduction to economics on a liberal arts campus attracted me to the use of reason as a means of resolving differences of opinion, which abounded among a coterie of students. The differences centered about charity, self-interest, world government, the Kinsey report on sexual behavior, religious concerns about the virgin birth of Jesus Christ, the measurement of intelligence, environmental prospects for conditioning behavior, religion as a possible opiate of the people, the usual political Left and Right, and other concerns. At the same time numerous science courses flourished where opinions remained tediously unanimous (for example, the litmus test for acids, the measurement of the speed of light, the structure of the atom, the life cycle of certain insects, the genetic properties of peas.

Next, but close in time, in my graduate study of economics, philosophy, and history, I encountered efforts to view economics in terms of behavior, which I considered to be the intent of my studies. Not surprisingly, then, I became familiar with the works of John Dewey, Thorstein Veblen, Clarence Ayres, Wesley Mitchell, and, via the latter route, the prospect of economics as empirical science. Friedman did an essay along such lines on Wesley Mitchell (Friedman 1950) and later used the title "empirical scientist" in reference to himself (Frazer 1988, chap. 4). Further, as I traced Friedman's National Bureau roots, Dewey connected to Friedman only via Wesley Mitchell's connection to Dewey. Although I welcomed the philosophical comparison of Friedman to Dewey by several authors, I viewed parts of Hirsch and de Marchi's work on the subject critically (Frazer 1992), from the perspective of my work on Friedman and his economics (Frazer 1988; 1994a; 1994b). Friedman was no neoclassical economist, as they and some institutionalists claimed he was, and he had no direct ties to Dewey.

By way of Mitchell, especially Keynes, and then the National Bureau and Friedman, I zealously pursued all I could find about money, business conditions, and group behavior. There was the psychological emphasis Keynes gave to the short-run volatility of long-term expectations, liquidity shifts, speculation, and the consumption function, as well as the psychological emphasis I found in the early work of George Katona (Morgan 1987a, 1987b).

Katona's work got my attention, but for me it proved inadequately linked to the mechanical structure of the most relevant economics. However, in hindsight, I did come away with what Morgan (1987b) offers as the essence of Katona's work. It is the part I relate to survey data, inflationary expectations, and Friedman's episodic changes. From a background in Gestalt psychology arose the prospect that agents could learn and adjust their outlooks and behavior to changes imposed from outside. The survey of consumer confidence started along this line as an aid to short-term prediction and to an understanding of group and even mass changes in consumer attitudes—confidence in the economy, its future, and so on. However, I think Morgan's position regarding Katona overstates the case:

Katona developed the theory and substance of psychological economics, with particular attention to the effects of national events on the confidence, expectations, plans and ultimately behavior of masses of individuals. From a background in Gestalt psychology, he noted that there can be major restructuring of the way people interpret their world and its future, leading to sometimes dramatic shifts in behavior. And he had a firm belief in people's capacity to learn and to adjust their goals, so that behavior was more than a simple response to stimuli. (Morgan 1987, 15)

Morgan also said:

Like most great ideas, they were at the same time simple and profound, obvious (that attitudes would affect behavior) but not accepted, particularly by economists who preferred to keep attitudes and expectations endogenous so they need not be measured or dealt with directly.

In Keynes's work money was pervasive in its impact (liquidity shifts, and so on). That work—though along a very different route than the Keynesian one—gained considerable impetus via Friedman. So, from reading Friedman's work I was well prepared for early meetings with Friedman and for his rather explicit integration of monetary matters with the consumption function, liquidity preference, and National Bureau data gathering and measurements.

My experiences with faculty fellowships in mathematics and statistics underscore this for me. In mathematics, as opposed to mathematical economics, I saw great flexibility, as Friedman pointed out on various occasions. In statistics, I got the first links to Bayesian (or what Savage and Friedman call "personalistic") probability and to J. M. Keynes's fellowship thesis at Cambridge.[6] In an extended fellowship period at the University of Pennsylvania, I became immersed in what Friedman and Schwartz later called "fashionable econometric methods."

Indeed, I attended the presentation of the first version of what later came to be called the Fed/Penn/MIT model. The presentation was given by the then Penn-connected Albert Ando. The place was the Federal Reserve Bank of Minneapolis in 1965.[7]

In the present Chapters 1 and 2, I reflect on the foregoing class of models from the perspective of Friedman's time frames, growth and time rates of change, and the monetary umbrella under which markets, firms, and households function (certainly in the context of a market economy, even a managed market economy). Friedman's breadth was the route for my arriving at "the Friedman system." There were the moves on the philosophy of science, personalistic probability, ideology, and the closely related uses of statistical methods, liquidity preference, consumption, and foreign exchange markets.

Relevant terms encountered in the text are "command economy," as well as "managed market economy." At an extreme, "command economy" includes, for example, the former U.S.S.R., but it also implies efforts to force the economy to fit the model, including along the lines of Tinbergen's rule (text pages 29–30) and reliance on reduced form equations of the sort I illustrate earlier (text pages 189–190 n.4) and in note 5. The term "managed market economy" simply recognizes that the laissez faire concept of an economy and the automatic workings of gold in the vaults of banks and in the strict gold-flow mechanism are relics of the past (Frazer 1994b, 82–87, 137–141). The managed economy is all about us.

The relevant question concerns the best approach to its management— whether by command and use of force to make the economy fit the model or whether by government provision of stable monetary arrangements within which a market economy may function. Monetary policy substitutes for fiscal policy to provide the umbrella under which markets function (Frazer 1994a, 94–102; 1994b, 84–97). The need for protecting the environment and containing population growth, where resources are limited, is fully recognized. The determination of growth rates (and hence actual saving-to-income ratios, Brown and Gleason 1996, Frazer 1994a, 144–149, 166–181) is a matter of public choice, culture, and the tax code. The functioning of a market economy and its growth depend on the accumulation of capital in the nongovernment sector.

AN OVERVIEW

So, I end up with this. The Friedman system opens up prospects for study along behavioral lines without rejecting some main components of the structure of economics. However, the interdisciplinary behavioral prospects are very much limited to behavior under market-oriented arrangements, as opposed to regulatory, forced-conformity, command-economy arrangements.

Behind the interdisciplinary prospects stand two important strands of thought which I find in Friedman's work. One is the Friedman criteria for a stable (or scientific) relation (Frazer 1994b, 168, 175), which, to repeat, is a search for a stable statistical relation that holds outside of the sample-data period (and hence including into the future) as well as for other similar economies (as, for example, the United States and the United Kingdom). The other strand of thought is represented by a question: What is the information contained in a single time series? Friedman's work and my own indicates that the series respond to episodes (extending to prospects for learning, structural changes, and psychological time) and contain transitory and permanent components. There is throughout the Friedman system an anticipatory orientation rooted in personalistic probability. Now combining the two strands of thought, we have a twofold statistical/social-science problem—namely, that of separating repetitive and nonrepetitive changes, and that of stating those phenomena that are in fact repetitive (and hence that hold outside of the sample period).

As an example where repetition may be found, I would point to Friedman's law (text page 142, at least in conjunction with my view of monetary and fiscal policy as substitutes (Frazer 1994a, 94–101; 1994b, 87–93). The prospects for work involving psychological time seem potentially fruitful.

Of some importance to Friedman's own reliance on statistical methods, I may point to Milton Friedman's belief (not shared by Rose Friedman or me) that use of statistical methods can resolve differences of opinion about policy matters.[8] By contrast, Rose Friedman contends that one can predict economists' political views from information about their factual or statistical-result views (Frazer 1994a, 195–202). This I see as elevating the need for political identification with regard to the uses of methods, the alternative arguments economists employ to support political action, and those bodies of economics that have purposes somewhat different from Friedman's view of "empirical science." As an example of the latter, I would point to areas where economists want to make the world conform to the model and/or shape it ideologically (text pages 27–33and 150 n.15).[9] I even find myself somewhat guilty of such advocacy in two special instances. One case occurs when I say the Bank of England is poorly suited for conducting policy along money and credit aggregates lines and then jump to suggesting a change (Frazer 1994b, 237 n.2). A second case arises when I appear to favor a specific sort of EuroFed bank in the event of any European Monetary System that has one money and one market (Frazer 1994b, 167–240).

NOTES

1. This use of cross-sectional information is common. It appears when the results from a given survey are compared over time with a picture at a given time and the sequence of pictures from the comparable surveys over time. Such information bears on both the impact of episodes on time series and Bayesian learning (Frazer 1994a, 73–74).

2. On this, one may note the Friedman criteria (Frazer 1994a, 46, 73, 240–241; 1994b, 26, 55, 168, 175).

3. Lists of episodes of this sort appear in Frazer (1994a, 88; 1994b, 239, n.12). To mention a few for the 1970s and 1980s only, as they may apply to some principal economic systems, we have periods of direct price controls, Richard Nixon's closing of the gold window, the European responses to the closing and to the subsequent partial floating of exchange rates, the privatization of British industry once Margaret Thatcher made the Big U-Turn in the economic affairs of the United Kingdom, the move to viewing money and credit aggregates in policy terms rather than simply in credit (or interest rate) condition terms, the change in the structure underlying the formation of inflationary expectations, the U.S. Treasury pronouncements under James Baker about trading off some monetary discipline for a decline in the foreign exchange value of the dollar, the breaching of the Berlin Wall, news about American efforts to reduce budget deficits, and major changes in tax structure in the United States and the United Kingdom with Margaret Thatcher and Ronald Reagan.

4. See note 1.

5. The equation may be written as follows:

$$\text{GNP and/or GDP} = a_0 + a_1 i + a_2 \, \$/DM + a_3 \, \$/Yen + a_4 \, P_{US}/P_{\text{rest of world}}$$
$$+ \, a_5 \text{ fiscal policy (with accommodation)}$$
$$+ \, a_6 \, \tilde{M}_{US} / \tilde{M}_{UK} + \cdots$$

I treat the equation as symbolic of a separation-of-effects problem regarding much that we encounter in economics.

I call attention to the separation of effects as a means of ruling out areas of economics that I do not expect other social science specialties to accept since doing so rules out the use of otherwise commonly accepted empirical approaches to the study of behavior (for example, use of survey results where episodic impacts appear in responses with great frequency).

6.   See Bayesian learning, note 1.

7.   My reactions to the Minneapolis session while an economist at the Federal Reserve Bank of Chicago led to several papers (Frazer 1968; 1973, 287–311). Also, see Frazer (1994a, 210–214).

By the time of the Carter presidency, Lawrence Klein had extended the big models considerably.   They were not serving as useful guides to policy, as was originally the claim for them (say à la a solution or reduced form equation, also see note 5).   However, they gained visibility and got the attention of political leaders.

Paul Volker and Toyoo Gyohten review the extension of the Klein model even to the prospect of fine-tuning exchange rates by way of it (Frazer 1994b, nn. 6, 10 chap. 4).

8.   Except by the special extension of what I call Hotelling's line (Frazer 1988; 1994a, 82–85; 1994b, 77–79, 105–106, 120, 156–157), where ideology and the use of force are explicit, the system proceeds apart from those aspects of economics where the purpose is a use of force to attain a fit to the economics.   For example, the work of Tinbergen advances the following "rule" about policy (Frazer and Yohe 1966, 616–620):   the number of nonredundant policy instruments (for example, instruments whereby two or more do not influence precisely the same target) available to the policymaker must be at least equal to the number of independent targets (or policy goals).   I have encountered some economists who say that if the government does not adhere to Tinbergen's rule, then economists should not be expected to offer solutions to the economic problems of instability, inflation, and so on.   Said differently, if the world we confront does not conform to the model, then one concludes that the world should fit the model instead of rejecting the model.   I see this as calling for classifications along ideological/political lines.   Behavioral work along even market-economy lines is most likely to thrive where purpose and ideology are overt.

9.   See note 8 also.

Bibliography

Alford, Roger. 1956. "Marshall's Demand Curve." *Economica* 23 (February): 23–48.

Allais, Maurice. 1966. "A Restatement of the Quantity Theory of Money." *American Economic Review* 56 (January): 1123–1157.

Allen, R.G.D. 1938. *Mathematical Analysis for Economists*. London: Macmillan & Co.

Arak, Marcella. 1977. "Rational Price Expectations: A Survey of the Evidence and Implications." *Research Paper No. 7716*, Federal Reserve Bank of New York, March.

Bagehot, Walter. 1873 (original date). *Lombard Street*, Fourteenth edition. London: Reprinted by John Murray.

Barro, Robert J. 1977. "Unanticipated Money Growth and Unemployment in the U.S." *American Economic Review* 67 (March): 101–115.

_____. 1981. *Money, Expectations, and Business Cycles: Essays in Macroeconomics*. New York: Academic Press.

_____. 1984. *Macroeconomics*. New York: John Wiley & Sons.

Barro, Robert J. and Grossman, Hershell. 1971. "A General Disequilibrium Model of Income and Employment." *American Economic Review* (March).

Baumol, William J. 1961. *Economic Theory and Operations Analysis*. Englewood Cliffs, New Jersey: Prentice–Hall.

_____. Blackman, Sue Anne Batey, and Wolff, Edward N. 1989. *Productivity and American Leadership: The Long View*. Cambridge: MIT Press.

Boland, Lawrence. 1979. "A Critique of Friedman's Critics." *Journal of Economic Literature* 17 (June): 503–522. Reprinted in Wood, John Cunningham, and Woods, Ronald N., eds. 1990. *Milton Friedman: Critical Assessment*, Vol. 3. London: Routledge.

_____. 1980. "Friedman's Methodology vs. Conventional Empiricism: A Reply to Rotwein." *Journal of Economic Literature* 18 (December): 1555–1557.

Reprinted in Wood, John Cunningham, and Woods, Ronald N., eds. 1990. *Milton Friedman: Critical Assessment*, Vol. III. London: Routledge.

_____. 1984. "Methodology: Reply." *American Economic Review* 78 (September): 795–797. Reprinted in Wood, John Cunningham, and Woods, Ronald N., eds. 1990. *Milton Friedman: Critical Assessment*, Vol. III. London: Routledge.

Bomberger, William, and Frazer, William. 1981. "Interest Rates, Uncertainty and the Livingston Data." *Journal of Finance* 36 (June): 661–675.

Bowman, Mary Jean, ed. 1958. *Expectations, Uncertainty, and Business Behavior*. New York: Social Science Research Council.

Braithwaite, R.B. 1975. "Keynes as a Philosopher." In Milo Keynes, ed. *Essays on John Maynard Keynes*. London: Cambridge University Press.

Browne, Lynn Elaine, and Gleason, Joshua. 1996. "The Saving Mystery, or Where Did the Money Go?" *New England Economic Review*, Federal Reserve Bank of Boston (Sept./Oct.): 15–27.

Brunner, Karl, and Meltzer, Alan. 1993. *Money and The Economic Issues of Monetary Analysis*. Cambridge: University Press.

Bundesbank. 1989. *The Deutsch Bundesbank: Its Monetary Policy Instruments and Functions*. Deutsche Bundesbank Special Series, no. 7, July 1989.

Cagan, Philip. 1965. *Determinants and Effects of Changes in the Stock of Money, 1875–1960*. New York: Columbia University Press for the National Bureau of Economic Research.

Caldwell, Bruce J. 1980. "Critique of Friedman's Methodological Instrumentalism." *Southern Economic Journal* 47 (October): 366–374. Reprinted in Wood, John Cunningham, and Woods, Ronald N., eds. 1990. *Milton Friedman: Critical Assessment*, Vol. III. London: Routledge.

_____. 1982. *Beyond Positivism: Economic Methodology in the Twentieth Century*. London: George Allen & Unwin.

Chamberlin, Edward H. 1948. *Theory of Monopolistic Competition*, 6th ed. London: Oxford University Press. The work was awarded Harvard's David A. Wells Prize for the year 1927–1928. The first edition appeared in 1933.

Christ, Carl F. 1966. *Econometric Models and Methods*. New York: John Wiley & Sons.

Christensen, Sandra. 1993. *Behavioral Assumptions for Estimating the Effects of Health Care Proposals*. Washington, D.C.: Congressional Budget Office, November.

Clinton, Bill. 1993. *Health Security*, The President's Report to the American People. Washington, D.C.: The White House Domestic Policy Council, October.

Committee. 1994. *The Role of the Bank of England*, Treasury and Civil Service Committee. London: Her Majesty's Stationery Office, December, Vols. I and II.

Congdon, Tim. 1978. *Monetarism*. London: Center for Policy Studies.

Courant, R. 1936. *Differential and Integral Calculus*, Vol. II. New York: Interscience Publishers.

Diewert, W.E. 1987. "Index Numbers." In John Eatwell, Murray Milgate, and Peter Newman, eds. *New Palgrave: A Dictionary of Economics*, Vol. 2. London: Macmillan Press.

Dorfman, Joseph. 1959. *The Economic Mind in American Civilization*, Vol. 4. New York: Viking Press.

Fand, David. 1970. "Monetarism and Fiscalism," *Banca Nazionale del Lavoro*, 94 (September, 3–34. Also published in *Kredit und Kapital*, Vol. 3, pp. 361–385.

Fisher, Irving. 1896. *Appreciation and Interest.* New York: Macmillan (reprinted by Augustus M. Kelley, New York, 1961).

Fisher, Stanley, ed. 1980. *Rational Expectations and Economic Policy.* Chicago: University of Chicago Press for the National Bureau of Economic Research.

Frazer, William. 1967. *The Demand for Money.* Cleveland: World Publishing Co.

_____. 1968. "Monetary Policy, Monetary Operations and National Economic Goals." *Schweizerische Zeitschrift fur Volkswirtschaft and Statistik* (March): 1–41.

_____. 1973. *Crisis in Economic Theory.* Gainesville: University of Florida Press.

_____. 1978. "Evolutionary Economics, Rational Expectations, and Monetary Policy." *Journal of Economic Issues* 12 (June): 343–372.

_____. 1980a. *Expectations, Forecasting and Control,* Vol. I. Lanham, Maryland: University Press of America.

_____. 1980b. *Expectations, Forecasting and Control,* Vol. II. Lanham, Maryland: University Press of America.

_____. 1982. "The Velocity–Rate Association: Inflation, Accelerated Inflation and Uncertainty." *Economic Notes* 12 (No. 1): 144–156.

_____. 1983. "Nicholas Kaldor: The Scourge of Monetarism." *Wall Street Review of Books* 11 (Fall): 261–284.

_____. 1984a. "Methodology: Reply." *American Economic Review.* 74 (September): 793–794. Reprinted in Wood, John Cunningham, and Woods, Ronald N., Eds. 1990. *Milton Friedman: Critical Assessments*, Vol. IV. London: Routledge.

_____. 1984b. *"The Economics of Supply and Demand* and Friedman." *Economic Notes* 13 (no. 3): 47–71.

_____. 1988. *Power and Ideas: Milton Friedman and the Big U–Turn,* 2 Vols., Gainesville, Florida: Gulf–Atlantic Publishing Company.

_____. 1992. "Review of *Milton Friedman: Economics in Theory and Practice.*" *History of Political Economy* 23 (4): 767–769.

_____. 1994a. *The Legacy of Keynes and Friedman: Economic Analysis, Money, and Ideology.* Westport, Connecticut: Praeger Publishers.

_____. 1994b. *The Central Banks: Analysis, and International and European Dimensions.* Westport, Connecticut: Praeger Publishers.

_____. 1995. "Review of *From Classical Economics to Development Economics.*" *Studies in Comparative International Development* 30 (Summer): 70–72.

_____. 1997. "The Monetarist School of Economics." In eds. Cate, Thomas, Harcourt, Geoff, and Colander, David C. *Encyclopedia of Keynesian Economics.* Brookfield, Vermont: Edward Elgar.

Frazer, William and Boland, Lawrence. 1983. "An Essay on the Foundations of Friedman's Methodology." *American Economic Review* 73 (March): 129–144. Re-printed in Wood, John Cunningham, and Wood, Ronald N., eds. 1990. *Milton Friedman: Critical Assessment,* Vol. III London: Routledge.

Frazer, William and Guthrie, John J. Jr. 1995. *The Florida Land Boom: Speculation, Money and the Banks.* Westport, Connecticut: Quorum Books.

Frazer, William and Sawyer, Kim, eds. 1984. *Taped Discussion on Uses of Statistical Methods with Milton Friedman,* June 25, 1984. Las Vegas, Nevada.

Frazer, William and Yohe, William P. 1966. *The Analytics and Institutions of Money and Banking.* Princeton, New Jersey: D. Van Nostrand Company.

Friedman, Milton. 1949. "The Marshallian Demand Curve." *Journal of Political Economy* 57 (December): 463–495. Also reprinted (Friedman 1953a, 47–99).

_____. 1950. "Wesley Clair Mitchell as an Economic Theorist." *Journal of Political Economy.* 58 (December): 463–495. Reprinted as "The Economic Theorist." In Arthur F. Burns, ed. 1962. *Wesley Clair Mitchell, the Economic Scientist.* New York: National Bureau of Economic Research.

_____. 1951. "Comment on 'A Test of an Econometric Model for the United States, 1921–1947.' " In *Conference on Business Cycles.* New York: National Bureau of Economic Research.

_____. 1952. "The Economic Theorist." In Arthur F. Burns, ed. *Wesley Clair Mitchell the Economic Scientist.* New York: National Bureau of Economic Research. The essay was originally published in the *Journal of Political Economy* 58 (December 1950), under the title "Wesley C. Mitchell as an Economic Theorist."

_____. 1953a. "The Methodology of Positive Economics." In Milton Friedman, *Essays in Positive Economics*, pp. 3–43. Chicago: University of Chicago Press.

_____. 1953b. *Essays in Positive Economics.* Chicago: University of Chicago Press.

_____. 1956. *Studies in the Quantity Theory of Money.* Chicago: University of Chicago Press.

_____. 1957. *A Theory of the Consumption Function.* Princeton, New Jersey: Princeton University Press.

_____. 1962a. *Capitalism and Freedom.* Chicago: University of Chicago Press.

_____. 1962b. *Price Theory: A Provisional Text*, revised edition. Chicago: Aldine Publishing Company.

_____. 1968. "Factors Affecting the Level at Interest Rates." In Donald P. Jacobs and Richard T. Pratt, eds., *Savings and Residential Financing: 1968 Conference Proceedings.* Chicago: U.S. Savings and Loan League, 11–27.

_____. 1976. *Price Theory.* Hawthone, New York: Aldine Publishing.

_____. 1981. "An Open Letter on Grants." *Newsweek* 97 (May 18): 99.

_____. 1992. "Communication: Do Old Fallacies Ever Die?" *Journal of Economics Literature* 30 (December): 2129–2132.

Friedman, Milton and Kuznets, Simon. 1945. *Income from Independent Professional Practice.* New York: National Bureau of Economic Research.

Friedman, Milton and Schwartz, Anna J. 1963. *A Monetary History of the United States, 1867–1960.* Princeton, New Jersey: Princeton University Press (for the National Bureau of Economic Research.

_____. 1982. *Monetary Trends in the United States and the United Kingdom: Their Relation to Income, Prices and Interest Rates, 1867–1975.* Chicago: University of Chicago Press for the National Bureau of Economic Research.

_____. 1991. "Alternative Approaches to Analyzing Economic Data." *American Economic Review* 81 (March): 39–49.

Galbraith, John Kenneth. 1958. *The Affluent Society.* Boston: Houghton Mifflin Company.

Goodhart, Charles E. A. 1982. "Monetary Trends in the United States and the United Kingdom: A British Review." *Journal of Economic Literature* 20 (December): 1540–1551.

Greenspan, Alan. 1993. "Statement Before the Committee on Banking, Housing, and Urban Affairs, U.S. Senate." *Federal Reserve Bulletin* 79 (April): 292–302.

Hansen, Alvin H. 1951. *Business Cycles and National Income.* New York: W.W. Norton & Company.

Harrod, Roy. 1971. Discussion Paper." In G. Clayton, J. C. Gilbert and R. Sedgewick, eds., *Monetary Theory and Monetary Policy in the 1970s.* Oxford: Oxford University Press.

Hass, Jane M., and Frazer, William. 1979. "The Political Business Cycles: Adjustments Through Persuasion Techniques." *Economic Notes* 8 (No. 2): 113–133.

Henderson, James M., and Quandt, Richard E. 1971. *Microeconomic Theory.* New York: McGraw-Hill.

Hendry, David F., and Ericsson, Neil R. 1983. "Assertion Without Empirical Basis: An Econometric Appraisal of *"Monetary Trends in . . . the United Kingdom* by Milton Friedman and Anna Schwartz." A paper presented to the Bank of England's Panel of Academic Consultants in October 1983, and revised December 1983, in the light of comments made at the October 1983 meeting.

_____. 1984. *Assertion Without Empirical Basis . . .,* paper presented at National Bureau of Economic Research Conference, Sonesta Hotel, Cambridge, July 12 and 13.

_____. 1985. *Assertion Without Empirical Basis . . .,* International Finance Discussion Papers, no. 270, Board of Governors of the Federal Reserve System, revised December 1985.

_____. 1991. "An Econometric Analysis of U.K. Money Demand in *Monetary Trends in the United States and in the United Kingdom* by Milton Friedman and Anna J. Schwartz." *American Economic Review* 81 (March): 8–38.

Hicks, Sir John. 1946. *Value and Capital: An Inquiry into Some Fundamental Principles of Economic Theory,* 2nd ed. Oxford: Clarendon Press.

_____. 1983. "The Keynes Centenary." *The Economist* 287 (June 18): 17–19.

Hirsch, Abraham, and deMarchi, Neil. 1984. "Methodology: A Comment on Frazer and Boland, I." *American Economic Review* 74 (September): 782–788. Reprinted in Wood, John Cunningham, and Woods, Ronald N., eds. 1990. *Milton Friedman: Critical Assessment,* Vol. 4. London: Routledge.

_____. 1990. *Milton Friedman: Economics in Theory and Practice.* Hertfordshire, England: Harvester Wheatsheaf.

Hodson, Geoff. 1991. "The Essential Kaldor," a book review. *Journal of Economic Issues* 25 (March): 241–243.

Hoover, Kevin, D. 1984a. "Two Types of Monetarism: *Journal of Economic Literature* 22 (March): 58–76.

_____. 1984b. "Methodology: A Comment on Frazer and Boland." *American Economic Review* 74 (September): 789–792. Reprinted in Wood, John Cunningham, and Woods, Ronald N., eds. 1990. *Milton Friedman: Critical Assessment,* Vol. IV. London: Routledge.

Hotelling, Harold. 1929. "Stability and Competition." *Economic Journal* 39 (Spring): 41–57.

_____. 1933. "Review of *The Triumph of Mediocrity in Business* by Horace Secrist." *Journal of the American Statistical Association* 28 (December): 463–465.

_____. 1934. "Letter to the Editor." *Journal of the American Statistical Association* 29 (June): 198–199.

Huhne, Christopher. 1983a. "Monetarism's guru 'distorts his evidence.'" *The Guardian* (December 15): 1.

_____. 1983b. "Why Milton's monetarism is bunk." *The Guardian* (December 15): 19.

Hume, David. 1963. *Essays, Moral and Political*. London: Oxford University Press. First published Volume I, 1741, and Volume II, 1742. The essays comprising "Part II" of the 1963 reprint appeared separately, with three additional essays, as *Political Discourses*, which was originally published in 1752.

Kaldor, Nicholas. 1970. "The New Monetarism." *Lloyds Bank Review* 97 (July): 1–17.

_____. 1982. *The Scourge of Monetarism*. Oxford: Oxford University Press.

Keynes, John Maynard. 1923. *A Tract of Monetary Reform*. London: Macmillan & Co.

_____. 1930. *A Treatise on Money: The Applied Theory of Money*, Vol. II. New York: Harcourt, Brace & Company.

_____. 1936. *The General Theory of Employment, Interest and Money*. New York: Harcourt, Brace & Company.

Keynes, John Neville. 1891. *The Scope and Method of Political Economy*. London: Macmillan & Co.

Klamer, Argo. 1984. *Conversations with Economists*. Totowa, New Jersey: Rowman & Allanheld.

Klein, Lawrence R. 1966. *The Keynesian Revolution*, second ed. New York: Macmillan.

_____. 1983. *The Economics of Supply and Demand*. Baltimore: Johns Hopkins University Press.

Klein, Philip A. 1978. "American Institutionalism." *Journal of Economic Issues* 12 (June): 251–276. This article was Klein's presidential address to the Annual Meeting of the Association for EVolutionary Economics," December 1977.

Knight, Frank H. 1921. *Risk, Uncertainty and Profit*. Boston: Houghton Mifflin Company.

Koopmans, Tjalling C. 1947. "Measurement Without Theory." *Review of Economics and Statistics* 29 (August): 161–172.

Kuznets, Simon. 1937. *National Income and Capital Formation, 1919-1935*. New York: National Bureau of Economic Research, Inc.

Laband, David N. and Piette, Michael J. 1994. "The Relative Impacts of Economic Journals, 1970-1990." *Journal of Economic Literature* 32 (June): 640–658.

Laidler, David E. W. 1977. *The Demand for Money—Theories and Evidence*, 2nd ed. New York: Harper & Row.

_____. 1982. *Monetarist Perspectives*. Cambridge: Harvard University Press.

_____. 1991. "Karl Brunner's Monetary Economics—an Appreciation." *Journal of Money, Credit, and Banking* 23 (November): 633–658.

_____. 1994. "Monetarism Circa 1970—a View from 1994," Paper presented at 25th Annual Konstanz Conference on Monetary Economics.

_____. 1995. "Why Do Agents Hold Money, and Why Does it Matter?" In Hoover, Kevin D. and Sheffrin, Steven M. eds., *Monetarism and the Methodology of Economics*, Essays in Honor of Thomas Mayer. Aldershot, England: Edward Elgar.

Leamer, Edward E. 1978. *Specifican Searches: Ad-Hoc Inference with Non-Experimental Data*. New York: John Wiley & Sons.

_____. 1983. "Let's Take the Con Out of Econometrics." *American Economic Review* 73 (March): 31–43.

_____. 1985. "Sensitivity Analysis Would Help." *American Economic Review* 76 (June): 308–313.

Leigh-Pemberton, Robin. 1987. "The Instruments of Monetary Policy." Mais Lecture given at City University Business School, 13 May.

Leijonhufvud, Axel. 1968. *On Keynesian Economics and the Economics of Keynes*. New York: Oxford University Press.

Lerner, Abba P. 1944. *The Economics of Control*. New York: Macmillan Co.

Liebhafsky, H. H., and Liebhafsky, E. E. 1985. "Comments on 'The Instrumentalisms of Dewey and Friedman.'" *Journal of Economic Issues* 19 (December 1985): 974–983. Reprinted in Wood, John Cunningham, and Woods, Ronald N., eds. 1990. *Milton Friedman: Critical Assessment*, Vol. 4., London: Routledge.

Lucas, Robert E., Jr. 1981. *Studies in Business-Cycle Theory*. Cambridge: MIT Press.

Lucas, Robert E., Jr. and Rapping, Leonard A. 1969. "Real Wages, Employment and Inflation." *Journal of Political Economy* 77 (September): 721–754.

Lucas, Robert E., Jr. and Sargent, Thomas J., eds. 1981. *Rational Expectations and Econometric Practice*, Vols. 1 and 2. Minneapolis: University of Minnesota Press.

Macesich, George. 1984. *The Politics of Monetarism*. Totowa, New Jersey: Rowman & Allanheld.

Markowitz, Harry M. 1959. *Efficient Diversification of Investments*, Monograph 16, Cowles Foundation for Research in Economics at Yale University. New York: John Wiley & Sons.

Mayer, Thomas. 1982. "*Monetary Trends in the United States and the United Kingdom:* A Review Article." *Journal of Economic Literature* 20 (December): 1528–1539.

Mayer, Thomas (with commentary by Martin Bronfenbrenner, Karl Brunner, Phillip Capan, Benjamin Friedman, Helmur Frisch, Harry G. Johnson, David Laidler, and Allan Meltzer). 1978. *The Structure Monetarism*. New York: W. W. Norton and Company.

Meier, Gerald M., ed. 1994. *From Classical Economics to Development Economics*. New York: St. Martin's Press.

Mitchell, Wesley C. 1903. *A History of Greenbacks*. Chicago: University of Chicago Press.

Morgan, James N. 1987a. *Katona, George (1901–1981)*. In Eatwell, John, Milgate, Murray, and Newman, Peter, eds. *The New Palgrave: A Dictionary of Economics*, Vol. 3. London: Macmillan Press.

_____. 1987b. "Survey Research." In John Eatwell, Murray Milgate, and Peter Newman, eds., *New Palgrave: A Dictionary of Economics*, Vol. 4. London Macmillan Press.

Morris, Dick. 1997. *Behind the Oval Office: Winning the Presidency in the Nineties*. New York: Random House.

Mullineauz, Donald J. 1977. "Inflation Expectations and Money Growth in the United States." *Research Papers, No. 28*, Federal Reserve Bank of Philadelphia, July.

Muth, John. 1961. "Rational Expectations and the Theory of Price Movements." *Econometrica* 29 (July): 315–335.

Niehans, Jung. 1987. "Transaction Costs." In Eatwell, John, Milgate, Murray, and Newman, Peter, eds., *The New Palgrave*, Vol. IV London: Macmillan Press.

Niggle, Christopher J. 1991. "The Endogenous Money Supply Theory: An Institutional Appraisal." *Journal of Economic Issues* 25 (March): 137–151.

Oliver, H. M. 1947. "Marginal Theory and Business Behavior." *American Economic Review* 37 (June): 375–383.

Patinkin, Dan. 1956. *Money, Interest, and Prices: An Integration of Money and Value Theory*. Evanston, Illinois: Row Peterson & Company. Second edition by Harper & Row Publishers, New York.

_____. 1969. "The Chicago Tradition, The Quantity Theory, and Friedman." *Journal of Money, Credit and Banking* 1 (February): 46–70.

Pesek, Boris P., and Saving, Thomas R. 1967. *Money, Wealth, and Economic Theory*. New York: Macmillan.

Popper, Karl R. 1965. *Conjectures and Refutations: The Growth of Scientific Knowledge*. New York: Harper & Row.

_____. 1966. *The Open Society and Its Enemies* (Vol. 1, *Plato* and Vol. 2, *Hagel and Marx*). Princeton, New Jersey: Princeton University Press.

Redman, Deborah A. 1994. "Karl Popper's Theory of Science and Econometrics: The Rise and Decline of Social Engineering." *Journal of Economic Issues* 28 (March): 67–99.

Reischauer, Robert D. 1994. "Entitlements and Tax Reform," Statement Before Bipartisan Commission on Entitlements and Tax Reford. Washington, D.C.: Congressional Budget Office.

Robinson, Joan. 1932. *The Theory of Imperfect Competition*. London: Macmillan. Second ed., 1969.

Rotwin, E. 1980. "Friedman's Critics: A Critic's Reply to Boland." *Journal of Economic Literature* 18 (December): 1553–1555. Reprinted in Wood, John Cunningham and Woods, Ronald N., eds. 1990. *Milton Friedman: Critical Assessment*, Vol. IV. London: Routledge.

Sargent, Thomas J. 1987. *Macroeconomic Theory*, 2nd ed. Orlando, Florida: Harcourt Brace Jovanovic, Publishers.

Sargent, Thomas J. and Wallace, Neil. 1976a. *Rational Expectations and the Theory of Economic Policy*. Studies in Monetary Economics 2, Federal Reserve Bank of Minneapolis.

_____. 1976b. *Rational Expectations and the Theory of Economic Policy*. Studies in Monetary Economics Part II, Federal Reserve Bank of Minneapolis.

Schultz, Henry, 1938. *The Theory and Measurement of Demand*. Chicago: University of Chicago Press.

Secrist, Horace. 1934. Letters to the Editor, *Journal of the American Statistical Association* 29 (June): 196–198, 200.

Selden, Richard, ed. 1975. *Capitalism and Freedom: Problems and Prospects*. Charlottesville: University of Virginia.

_____. 1976. "Monetarism." In Sidney Weintraub, ed., *Modern Economic Thought*. Philadelphia: University of Pennsylvania Press.

_____. 1997. "Friedman, Milton (1912–   )." In David Glasner, ed. *Business Cycles and Depression: An Encyclopedia*. New York: Garland Publishing, Inc.

Shackle, G.L.S. 1952. *Expectations in Economics*, 2nd ed. Cambridge: The University Press.

Skidelsky, Robert. 1992. *John Maynard Keynes: The Economist as Saviour, 1920–1937.* London: Macmillan.

Smith, Adam. 1937. *Wealth of Nations.* New York: Modern Library. Smith's famous book first appeared in 1776.

Sprinkle, Beryl Wayne. 1971. *Money and Markets: A Monetarist View.* Homewood, Illinois: Richard D. Irwin.

Staff. 1993. *President Clinton's Health Care Reform Proposal and Health Security Act,* as presented to Congress on October 27, 1993. Chicago: Commerce Clearing House.

Stein, Jerome, ed. 1976. *Monetarism.* Amsterdam: North Holland.

Stigler, George. 1952. *The Theory of Price*, revised edition. New York: Macmillan Company.

Stigler, Stephen M. 1994. "Some Correspondence on Methodology Between Milton Friedman and Edwin B. Welson." *Journal of Economic Literature* 32 (September): 1197–1203.

Terrell, William T., and Frazer, William. 1972. "Interest Rates, Portfolio Behavior, and Marketable Government Securities." *Journal of Finance* 27 (March): 1–35.

Tobin, James. 1958. "Liquidity Preference as Behavior Towards Risk." *Review of Economic Studies* 25 (February): 65–86.

Townsend, Robert M. 1978. "Market Anticipations, Rational Expectations, and Bayesian Analysis." *International Economic Review* (June).

Tugwell, Rexford Guy. 1978. "The Well-Ordered Economy: Remarks Upon Receipt of the Veblen-Commons Award." *Journal of Economic Issues* 12 (June): 243–249.

Veblen, Thorstein. 1898. "Why Is Economics Not an Evolutionary Science?" *Quarterly Journal of Economics* 12 (July): 373–397.

Vickrey, William S. 1964. *Microstatistics.* New York: Harcourt, Brace & World.

Volcker, Paul, and Gyohten, Toyoo. 1992. *Changing Fortunes.* New York: Random House.

Walras, Leon. 1954. *Elements of Pure Economics.* English translation of W. Jaffé. London: First ed., Lausanne, 1874, final def. ed., 1926.

Walters, Alan. 1987. "Friedman, Milton": In *The New Palgrave,* Vol. 2, pp. 422–427. London: Macmillan Press.

Webb, James. 1987. "Is Friedman's Methodological Instrumentalism a Special Case of Dewey's Instrumental Philosophy? A Comment on Wible." *Journal of Economic Issues* 21 (March): 393–429. Reprinted in Wood, John Cunningham, and Woods, Ronald N., eds. 1990. *Milton Friedman: Critical Assessment*, Vol. 4. London: Routledge.

Weber, Max. 1930. *The Protestant Ethic and the Spirit of Capitalism.* New York: Charles Scribner & Sons. Copyright dated 1911.

Wible, James R. 1982. "Friedman's Positive Economics and Philosophy of Science." *Southern Economic Journal* 49 (October): 350–360.

———. 1984. "The Instrumentalism of Dewey and Friedman." *Journal of Economic Issues* 18 (December): 1049–1070. Reprinted in Wood, John Cunningham, and Woods, Ronald N., eds. 1990. *Milton Friedman: Critical Assessment*, Vol. IV. London: Routledge.

_____. 1985. "Institutional Economics, Positive Economics, Pragmatism, and Recent Philosophy of Science: Reply to Liebhafsky and Liebhafsky." *Journal of Economic Issues* 19 (December): 984–995. Reprinted in Wood, John Cunningham, and Woods, Ronald N., eds. 1990. *Milton Friedman: Critical Assessment*, Vol. IV. London: Routledge.

_____. 1987. "Criticism and the Validity of the Special Case Interpretation of Friedman's Essay: Reply to Webb." *Journal of Economic Issues* 21 (March): 430–440. Reprinted in Wood, John Cunningham, and Woods, Ronald N., eds. 1990. *Milton Friedman: Critical Assessment*, Vol. IV. London: Routlege.

Williamson, Jeffrey G. 1991. "Productivity and American Leadership: A Review Article." *Journal of Economic Literature* 29 (March): 51–68.

Wood, John Cunningham, and Woods, Ronald N. eds. 1990. *Milton Friedman: Critical Assessments*, 4 Vols. London: Routledge.

Woodward, Robert. 1994. *The Agenda: Inside the Clinton White House*. New York: Simon & Schuster.

Yohe, William P. and Karnosky, Denis S. 1969. "Interest Rates and Price Level Changes. 1952–69." *Review*, Federal Reserve Bank of St. Louis, December.

Zarnowitz, Victor. 1985. "Recent Work on Business Cycles in Historical Perspective." *Journal of Economic Literature* 23 (No. 2): 523–580.

Index

About the Author

WILLIAM FRAZER is Professor of Economics at the University of Florida. Dr. Frazer has written widely, including *The Florida Land Boom: Speculation, Money, and the Banks* (Quorum, 1995), *The Central Banks: The International and European Directions* (Praeger, 1994), and *The Legacy of Keynes and Friedman: Economic Analysis, Money, and Ideology* (Praeger, 1994).

ISBN 0-275-95843-4

90000>

EAN

9 780275 958435

HARDCOVER BAR CODE